RISK AND FAILURE IN
ENGLISH BUSINESS 1700–1800

RISK AND FAILURE IN ENGLISH BUSINESS 1700–1800

JULIAN HOPPIT

University College London

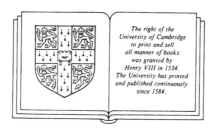

The right of the
University of Cambridge
to print and sell
all manner of books
was granted by
Henry VIII in 1534.
The University has printed
and published continuously
since 1584.

CAMBRIDGE UNIVERSITY PRESS

Cambridge
London   New York   New Rochelle
Melbourne   Sydney

Published by the Press Syndicate of the University of Cambridge
The Pitt Building, Trumpington Street, Cambridge CB2 1RP
32 East 57th Street, New York, NY 10022, USA
10 Stamford Road, Oakleigh, Melbourne 3166, Australia

First published 1987

Printed in Great Britain by the University Press, Cambridge

British Library cataloguing in publication data

Risk and failure in English business 1700–1800.
1. Business enterprises – England – History – 18th century
2. Bankruptcy – England – History – 18th century
I. Title
338.6′0942   HF5349.G7

Library of Congress cataloguing in publication data

Hoppit, Julian.
Risk and failure in British business, 1700–1800.
Bibliography.
Includes index.
1. Bankruptcy – England – History – 18th century.
2. Business enterprises – England – History – 18th century.
3. Business cycles – England – History – 18th century.
I. Title.
HG3769.G73E54   1987   332.7′5′0942   87-743

ISBN 0 521 32624 9

CONTENTS

FIGURES

TABLES

PREFACE

There is a certain perversity about the subject of this book. It examines business bankruptcy and risk-taking in eighteenth-century England, traditionally a period when businessmen are looked at in terms of success and achievement. The germs of this perspective were planted while I was an undergraduate at Selwyn College, Cambridge. They flourished there for some years before reaching maturity and fruition first at Pembroke College and then at Magdalene College, Cambridge. I am grateful for the support and friendship provided by these homes.

Like the subjects of this book I am a bankrupt. My debts outweigh my assets. I have been very lucky to come under the care of three great teachers. John Morrill taught me what commitment to and empathy with the past means – and still gives me refresher courses from time to time. Richard Overy awakened and helped sustain my enthusiasm for English social and economic history. Finally and most significantly, Donald Coleman supervised the thesis which this book rests on. Without his care and attention, his promptings and criticisms, this book would have been much poorer. Somewhere he found the stamina to read complete drafts of both the book and the thesis. What he had to say will never be forgotten.

Joanna Innes read a draft of this book with typical speed and thoroughness. More than that, since my first year of research she, more than anyone, has made me think carefully and precisely about 'the eighteenth century'. Andrew Hoppit, Robert Jones, Leslie Pressnell and David Souden all helped at important points. My final debt, to Karin Horowitz, will never be repaid. Indeed, it will grow and grow.

1

BUSINESS ENTERPRISE IN EIGHTEENTH-CENTURY ENGLAND

The spectre of the Industrial Revolution haunts our understanding of the English economy in the eighteenth century. In the fashion of Whig history, there has been a tendency to concentrate on those parts of the economy which were developing most quickly and making the most significant contribution to industrialisation and economic growth. Remembering the old cliché that history is written by the victors not the vanquished, this is largely to be expected. Consequently, we have been told about the growth of foreign trade, the expansion of home demand, the wave of gadgets, the surge of capital formation, the rise of population and urbanisation, the revolution in agriculture and of the achievements of entrepreneurs. In short, the eighteenth-century economy has often been seen as a success story and as a place in which to uncover the origins of the Industrial Revolution. Nowhere has this been more true than in studies of business enterprise and the role of businessmen in economic growth. That role is often enough described in terms of success and achievement, usually with reference to the great and the famous. Yet if we try to rid ourselves of hindsight, then the likes of Wedgwood and Arkwright become just a part of the story. Alongside such heroes stood more mortal businessmen. This book adopts a less optimistic perspective, arguing that enterprise can be properly understood only when due regard is paid to bankruptcy and that the undoubted success of business expansion over the century has to be placed in the context of the possibility and reality of such bankruptcy. It is worth bearing in mind Richard Cobb's belief: 'Failure is much commoner than success, at any period, though it has seldom been accorded even a small corner in the work of historians; it is also more endearing, and much more human.'[1] We shall see. But looking at failure should make us think about more than just the financial mortality of business in a period of general economic growth. For by studying the patterns of bankruptcy evidence is produced that adds detail and substance to the pictures of growth, decay and structural change which have been built up by historians since they began to describe the Industrial Revolution a century ago.

[1] *Death in Paris* (Oxford, 1978), p. 102.

BUSINESSES IN EIGHTEENTH-CENTURY ENGLAND

In the late nineteenth and early twentieth centuries historians commonly stressed the insignificance of economic change before 1760 and the cataclysmic importance of developments thereafter. In this view the Industrial Revolution happened suddenly and unexpectedly, striking a backward and almost medieval economy like a flash of lightning. By the 1940s, however, it was clear to historians that the English economy before 1760 had in many ways been well developed and relatively sophisticated by the standards of pre-industrial economies. The economic constraints of the guilds in industry and of feudal relations in agriculture had long since weakened. Moreover, slow growth and economic preparation before 1760 were seen as vital in providing a fertile seedbed for the substantive and dramatic changes ushered in by technical developments in cotton, iron and steam. Rostow's 'take-off stage', 'the great watershed in the life of modern societies', took place after the economy had served its agricultural, industrial, commercial, scientific and intellectual apprenticeships in the seventeenth and early eighteenth centuries.[2] In 1948 T. S. Ashton noted that 'capitalism had its origins long before 1760, and attained its full development long after 1830: there is a danger of overlooking the essential fact of continuity'.[3] Ashton and others did not deny the significance of change but merely stressed the perils of ignoring continuity. Unfortunately, many studies into the origins of the industrial transformation did. Images of the Industrial Revolution as the sum of spinning jennies, steam engines, factories, ironworks, of power and machines in short, have proved very resilient. So much so that the picture of continuity and slower growth has recently been rediscovered and reinterpreted by historians trying to pin down the eighteenth-century economy in quantitative terms.[4]

Although overall rates of growth may have been modest in the eighteenth century there were still significant changes in the structure of the economy. The early stirrings of the Industrial Revolution saw some regions and industries

---

[2] W. W. Rostow, *The stages of economic growth* (Cambridge, 1960), Chs. 1–4. C. H. Wilson, *England's apprenticeship, 1603–1760* (London, 1965).

[3] *The industrial revolution 1760–1830* (Oxford, 1977), p. 2. J. H. Clapham was the first major historian of the Industrial Revolution to stress the expansion of old forms of industry and the strength of continuity after 1760: *An economic history of modern Britain*, 3 vols. (Cambridge, 1926–38).

[4] N. F. R. Crafts, 'British economic growth 1700–1831: a review of the evidence', *Economic History Review*, XXXVI (1983), pp. 177–99 and his *British economic growth during the industrial revolution* (Oxford, 1985). C. K. Harley, 'British industrialization before 1841: evidence of slower growth during the industrial revolution', *Journal of Economic History*, XLII (1982), pp. 267–89. The historiography of the Industrial Revolution has been discussed recently by David Cannadine, 'The present and the past in the English industrial revolution 1880–1980', *Past and Present*, CIII (1984), pp. 131–72.

grow with unforeseen speed and vigour as others stagnated or decayed. In Lancashire and the West Riding the cotton and woollen industries expanded dramatically; overseas trade developed significantly; agriculture grew; and as the population increased so a higher proportion of people came to live in towns. But these areas of substantial change took place in the context of a national economy that was evolutionary rather than revolutionary, and where change was not always in the direction of 'progress'. Where there were no developments in techniques or organisations and where demand was inert then productivity advance was absent. Areas sometimes became less competitive and stagnated or decayed. If the textile industries of Lancashire and the West Riding were hugely successful, those in East Anglia, the West Country and the South West were not. England was still a green and pleasant land in 1800, but it was becoming distinctly mottled because some industrial areas were turning into Coketowns while others were reclaimed by the fields.

This book examines some of the ways businessmen contributed to points of continuity and change in the eighteenth-century economy and looks at those points from both a long- and short-term perspective. While concentrating on bankruptcy as broad a sweep as possible is taken so that enterprise is seen in its own terms rather than simply in relation to nineteenth-century industrial maturity. Bankruptcy helps to describe the restructuring of the economy in sectoral and geographical terms, the fluctuations and variability of economic activity and the contribution and place of businessmen in those moments of growth, stagnation and decay.

Businessmen have long been seen as focal points in any market economy. In an oft-quoted statement A. H. Cole argues that 'to study the entrepreneur is to study the central figure in modern economic development, and to my way of thinking, the central figure in economics'.[5] In Neil McKendrick's words, 'the entrepreneur is rightly seen as the most important human link between those non-economic variables and the production end of the economy'.[6] In a private enterprise economy the firm is the basic unit of production and distribution. And

The patterns of economic life, including the patterns of consumption as well as of production, are largely shaped by the multitude of individual decisions made by the businessmen who guide the actions of the business units we call firms. The very nature of the economy is to some extent defined in terms of the kind of firms that compose it, their size, the way in which they are established and grow, their methods of doing business, and the relationships between them.[7]

[5] *Business enterprise in its social setting* (Cambridge, Mass., 1959), p. 28.
[6] 'General introduction' to R. J. Overy, *William Morris Viscount Nuffield* (London, 1976), p. x.
[7] E. T. Penrose, *The theory of the growth of the firm* (Oxford, 1959), p. 9.

Some of these issues can be considered with reference to eighteenth-century England by looking at bankruptcy.

Studies of eighteenth-century business enterprise not only tend to ignore failure but have also concentrated on the spectacularly rich and successful. Inevitably our picture of the impact of enterprise is partial and distorted so that the patterns Penrose mentioned have been imperfectly described. This introductory chapter identifies where the gaps in our knowledge are and in what ways a study of bankruptcy can help fill some of them. In part this involves an historiographical examination of eighteenth-century enterprise, but in part it also glances at some issues economists stress when they look at businessmen. To do this it is important to begin with a descriptive outline of the different types of enterprise in the eighteenth century.

Then as now businessmen could be either producers or traders, or both. In the eighteenth century the interaction between these two functions was considerable and while those overlaps and conjunctions cannot be ignored a preliminary description will be clearer if they are separated. Unsurprisingly, because of the lure of explaining the Industrial Revolution the manufacturers and industrialists rather than the marketers or distributors have been given most attention hitherto. Tradesmen and marketing have been woefully neglected in studies of eighteenth-century business enterprise and their importance seriously underestimated. In 1760 Joseph Massie calculated that whereas nearly 19 per cent of all families were engaged in trade and distribution only 5.4 per cent were master manufacturers.[8] Numerically there is good reason to concentrate first on distribution and only secondly on production. Getting the goods from the manufacturer to the consumer was fundamentally important; as Adam Smith wrote, 'Consumption is the sole end and purpose of all production.'[9]

Contemporary observers never tired in their descriptions of distinguishing internal from external traders. And their faith in the efficacy of overseas trade, inherited from an earlier time and an admiration of Dutch commercial strength, perhaps made them exaggerate the importance of merchants relative to shopkeepers and domestic middlemen. Richard Campbell offered a typical eulogy: 'Some Tradesmen we have treated of employ several different Branches, some particular Crafts dependent on them; but the Merchant employs them all, sets the whole of Society at work, supplies them with Materials to fabricate their Goods, and vends their Manufactures in the most distant Corners of the

---

[8] If the definition of 'manufacturer' is stretched to include artisans and craftsmen then the proportion rises to nearly 21 per cent. But such 'manufacturers' were hardly businessmen. P. Mathias, 'The social structure in the eighteenth century: A calculation by Joseph Massie', in his *The transformation of England* (London, 1979), p. 189.

[9] *An inquiry into the nature and causes of the wealth of nations*, ed. E. Cannan (Chicago, 1976), Vol. II, p. 179.

Globe.'[10] Moreover, Gregory King (1688), Massie and Patrick Colquhoun (1803) all believed that merchants were the most prosperous group in the business community, earning as much as many gentlemen and much more than most of those in the professions. But if their wealth was considerable their numbers were not. There may have been 10,000 at the end of the seventeenth century and only 15,000 in the early nineteenth, despite the fact that the volume of overseas trade increased fivefold over the same period.[11] The merchants' financial wealth but their numerical insignificance immediately suggests that it was difficult to become one but rewarding if achieved.

If merchants stood apart as a distinct group among traders, elevated above the crowd, then it is less easy to isolate similarly differentiated concentrations in the home trades. A simple but unreliable division can be drawn between retailers and wholesalers, between shopkeepers and middlemen. Taken together, Gregory King believed there were 50,000 in 1688 while Joseph Massie put the figure at 162,500 seventy years later.[12] Massie believed that the majority of these earned only £40 per year. Yet although shops were often small businesses, generating modest profits, when they are aggregated together it is clear that they handled a good deal of the economic activity of the period. Obviously they were found in greatest numbers and variety where population was most concentrated. In the rural economy shopkeepers were usually general grocers or such like, but in towns their functions were often more closely defined. As the economy, transport, population and urbanisation all advanced in the eighteenth century the pattern and importance of retailing changed, as it did for the wholesalers. And if, as has been recently suggested, there was a consumer revolution in the eighteenth century, then shopkeepers were central lynchpins in articulating the new patterns of demand this involved.[13] By the end of the century, shops had spread from the cities and towns to the villages and hamlets.[14]

If merchants were few in number but rich, and shopkeepers numerous but poor, then middlemen stood between the two on both counts. The functions of

[10] *The London tradesman* (London, 1747; reprinted Newton Abbot, 1969), p. 284.
[11] Mathias, *The transformation of England*, pp. 186–7. H. J. Perkin, *The origins of modern English society, 1780–1880* (London, 1969), pp. 20–1. These are King and Colquhoun's estimates as given in W. E. Minchinton, 'The merchants of England in the eighteenth century', *Explorations in Entrepreneurial History*, x (1957), p. 62. P. Deane and W. A. Cole, *British economic growth 1688–1959* (2nd edn, Cambridge, 1969), p. 48.
[12] Mathias, *The transformation of England*, pp. 186–7.
[13] N. McKendrick, 'The consumer revolution of eighteenth-century England', in N. McKendrick, J. Brewer and J. H. Plumb, *The birth of a consumer society* (London, 1982), pp. 9–33. E. W. Gilboy, 'Demand as a factor in the industrial revolution', in R. M. Hartwell, ed., *The causes of the industrial revolution* (London, 1967), pp. 121–38.
[14] [Turner,] *The diary of Thomas Turner 1754–1765*, ed. D. Vaisey (Oxford, 1985) provides a striking picture of a small shopkeeper in Sussex.

middlemen were various. Some waited in their warehouses, or at alehouses, markets and fairs for the producers to come to them, so that middlemen and producers were only casually related. But other middlemen actively sought out manufacturers, sometimes trying to establish a dependent relationship where the producer put the bulk of his output into the hands of a single middleman. This second pattern was less likely when agricultural goods were involved, more likely with industrial goods. It was in industry, more particularly the dominant domestic system, where goods were made in the homes of the workers, that the division between producer and middleman is most difficult to maintain.[15]

In the domestic system of manufacture, a system which dominated English industry through the eighteenth century, despite the advances in factory production, workers were supplied with materials by a coordinating middleman to whom they usually returned the worked-up products. A middleman might sell the goods as a wholesaler himself or he might sell them off to other wholesalers. With so much interaction between production and distribution, it is unsurprising that middlemen were often known as merchant manufacturers. Of course, at a more specialised level, in craft production, they could be missed out altogether. Goods would be manufactured in a workshop at the back of the shop where they were sold. All in all then, there was no clearly defined position that retailers or middlemen occupied in the chain linking producer and consumer. It was the form of production and the structure of the market that fundamentally determined the role of the shopkeeper and wholesaler.

What this brief survey of distribution has shown is that merchants, middlemen and shopkeepers were numerous and played an important coordinating role in economic life in the eighteenth century. To ignore them by concentrating on manufacturers has happened too frequently for comfort. Distributors were not passive but active agents of change, striding alongside and falling over with producers. While it may be true that eighteenth-century marketing was consistently non-technological and that, therefore, inventions were of no direct importance, it is vital to remember the ways in which the marketing system could improve its productivity. Distributors could open up wider and wider markets allowing extensions of Adam Smith's division of labour through greater specialisation, more efficient organisations and more sophisticated techniques, such as advertising. Just as important, because production and distribution could be closely linked, manufacturers often found that they could expand their markets and productivity by paying more attention to marketing. The growth of Birmingham and Sheffield in the eighteenth century, for example, was

---

[15] It is a vivid testament to the lack of historical inquiry into the fate of middlemen that the best general study of wholesalers remains R. B. Westerfield, *Middlemen in English business particularly between 1660 and 1760* (New Haven, Conn., 1915; reprinted Newton Abbot, 1968).

explained by some contemporaries in terms of the way manufacturers successfully sought out markets on their own account and established closer ties with inland and overseas merchants.[16]

Several types of business firm existed on the production side of the economy. Manufacture might be either centralised or decentralised, rural or urban, mechanised or unmechanised, capital or labour intensive. There was no 'typical' manufacturing firm, employing average numbers of men who had average skills and used average tools or machines. The size, organisation and importance of a manufacturing firm was determined by an only partly predictable relationship between the size and structure of markets, available technologies and finance, the evaluation of scale economies and diseconomies by businessmen and the nature of competition and opportunities.[17]

Most commonly manufacturing was arranged in the rural domestic system, a system that allowed, but did not demand, some interaction of industrial and agricultural labour.[18] The central feature was the production of goods at the home of the workers. For centuries the woollen industry, the mainstay of the manufacturing economy, had largely been organised in this way. And so it remained in the eighteenth century. The benefits of the domestic system were clear enough: for if necessary skills were slight, tools few, underemployed labour plentiful, close supervision unnecessary and demand for the final good relatively weak then it produced acceptable goods at acceptable prices. Its manifest advantages ensured its survival in many areas and industries into the second half of the nineteenth century. Indeed, the system expanded as growth elsewhere encouraged the multiplication of existing processes, most famously in the growth of the handloom weaving industry between 1750 and 1800. Industrialisation involved the duplication of tried and tested methods just as much as the creation of new ones. The very flexibility of the domestic system, however, makes it impossible for it to be identified in a single form or for its businessmen to be characterised in a single way. In the woollen industry 'all the major centres varied in the ways in which they organised production, so did they in the marketing of their output'.[19] Businessmen might be large or small,

[16] J. Aikin, *A description of the country from thirty to forty miles round Manchester* (London, 1795; reprinted Newton Abbot, 1968), pp. 547–8. W. Hutton, *An history of Birmingham* (Birmingham,1781; reprinted East Ardsley, 1976), p. 70. J. Britton, J. N. Brewer, J. Hodgson and F. C. Laird, eds., *The beauties of England*, vol. xv (London, 1814), p. 291. See also S. D. Chapman, 'British marketing enterprise: the changing roles of merchants, manufacturers and financiers, 1700–1860', *Business History Review*, LIII (1979), pp. 205–34.

[17] E. A. G. Robinson, *The structure of competitive industry* (Welwyn and Cambridge, 1958), p. 12.

[18] D. C. Coleman, *The domestic system in industry* (London, 1960).

[19] R. G. Wilson, 'The supremacy of the Yorkshire cloth industry in the eighteenth century', in N. B. Harte and K. G. Ponting, eds., *Textile history and economic history* (Manchester, 1973), p. 239.

ranging from substantial merchant middlemen to less grandiose independent artisans.

In places the domestic system did break down or mutate during the eighteenth century. One impetus was that heightened demand for the final products led to the ever-increasing concentration of the worker's time on industrial production. For example, the metalworker in the West Midlands who kept a smallholding came under some pressure to give up the soil.[20] If he concentrated on industry he might then have moved to town and either continued to work in his home or in some type of workshop.[21] As an enterprise, workshop production was fundamentally different from domestic production. Under the dispersed domestic system, where labourers worked from home, merchant manufacturers operated from a warehouse. But when the labour began to be brought under one roof then the domestic system was changing into workshop or factory production and the businessman had to consider issues such as labour management and fixed capital formation which previously had been insignificant.

Some industries that were characterised by the domestic system in the early eighteenth century came under a serious challenge, however, because of technical developments. The low productivity inherent in the system could easily be exposed by successful mechanisation. This happened most dramatically in cotton spinning which was transformed from a small, non-mechanised industry, in 1750, to a large, machine- and factory-based one in 1800. Clearly, a mechanised, factory industry posed problems and provided opportunities for businessmen different from those of the unmechanised domestic system. In the last twenty years of the eighteenth century factories were rightly seen as one of the wonders of the age. The well-to-do flocked to see Wedgwood's Etruria, Boulton and Watt's Soho and Arkwright's Cromford. When they got there they knew they were looking at something unusual and novel – it was not typicality they were after. This is worth stressing; in 1800 factories were still very uncommon. Naturally, the bulk of business enterprises at the time was rather uninspiring in comparison, but it was no less important. Most businessmen ran firms that did things in time-honoured ways. Production outside the factory accounted for the major part of total enterprise, though growth was disproportionately connected to factories.

[20] M. B. Rowlands, *Masters and men in the West Midlands metalware trades before the industrial revolution* (Manchester, 1975).

[21] In 1808, however, one observer noted that although some iron was produced in Wolverhampton itself most of it came from 'the farmers for several miles round; for in this country every farmer has at least one forge, so that when farmers are not employed in the fields they work as smiths at their forges, and they bring all their work to market, where the Great tradesmen buy it up and send it to London'. *Holden's triennial directory* (4th edn, London, 1808), Vol. II, p. 291.

HISTORIANS AND ENTERPRISE

Business enterprise in eighteenth-century England was enormously varied and subject to a variety of influences. Some businessmen were producers, some distributors, some both. And there were many ways of doing business. Yet by and large that complexity has been avoided in general statements about eighteenth-century enterprise, largely because of the preoccupation with delineating the contribution of businessmen to growth. We know about the factory owners successfully pushing at the frontiers of enterprise but little about those who failed in the attempt or who operated in more representative ways.[22] This bias is worth uncovering in more detail.

In the early nineteenth century a long-lasting tradition was established which asserted that the Industrial Revolution was in large part caused by a dramatic expansion in the quantity and quality of business enterprise. Businessmen were viewed as the prime movers in the growth process. Their commitment, determination, courage and ability freed England from the shackles that bound the traditional pre-industrial economy. Samuel Smiles epitomised this view when he wrote that 'National progress is the sum of individual industry, energy and uprightness, as national decay is of individual idleness, selfishness and vice.'[23] By implication, Smiles believed that the nation had progressed because enough people had made the requisite effort. He was aware of course that it takes both privates and generals to win wars and that England's progress had been produced both by the ordinary and the extraordinary. But given his primary task, 'to re-inculcate those old-fashioned but wholesome lessons...that youth must work in order to enjoy, – that nothing creditable can be accomplished without application and diligence', he can hardly be blamed for having illustrated his themes with descriptions of generals; their medals and heavy epaulettes made for more brilliant and impressive examples.[24] The privates were forgotten, not least because the chroniclers forgot their faces and personalities. 'Great whose names are recorded in biography', he wrote.[25] Despite Smiles's belief in the importance and availability of self-improvement through all levels of society, the images that emerge from his collection of examples are unrepresentative and unrealistic. His examination of self-help in industry and trade called upon examples which reads like the *Who's Who* of the eighteenth-century business world: Wedgwood, Foley, Strutt, Boulton, Watt, Arkwright and Peel were the main names in the canon.

It was not simply that Smiles and his cohorts were over-impressed with great

---

[22] D. C. Coleman, 'Historians and businessmen', in D. C. Coleman and P. Mathias, eds., *Enterprise and history* (Cambridge, 1984), p. 41, pleads for a broader approach to business history.
[23] *Self-help* (London, 1859; reprinted London, 1910), p. 3.
[24] Ibid., p. vii. Perkin sees this as part of the early-nineteenth-century 'entrepreneurial ideal'. See his *Origins of modern English society*, p. 222.   [25] *Self-help*, p. 6.

men, but that they further limited their attention to the factory-owning industrialists and the great inventors, leaving the trader, salesman and ordinary
businessman out in the cold.[26] These traditions proved remarkably long lived.
As Professor Wilson pointed out, 'from Toynbee [1884] down to Usher [1929]
inventions took pride of place in the study of industrial history. Only with the
comparatively recent impact (in England) of sociology and economic theory on
historical method has the inventor's place in the process been re-assessed.'[27]
Although the significance of inventions has been reassessed, studies about the
role of enterprise still tend to concentrate on inventors and innovators, especially those operating in the rapidly developing parts of the economy. But
business enterprise in the eighteenth century encompassed a much broader
spectrum of activity. The importance of the inventor or the major industrialist
cannot be denied, but few businessmen were either.[28] Numerically, inventors
and innovators were swamped by derivative, modest imitators. Only part of the
business world has really been described with any degree of thoroughness. If
the brilliance of Wedgwood and the adventurousness of Boulton have been
expertly detailed, the ranks of businessmen filling the trade directories have
remained untouched and unsought by the historian. There are, however, two
good reasons to justify this exclusiveness, one theoretical, the other practical.

It was Joseph Schumpeter who constructed the most forceful and persuasive
arguments linking business enterprise with innovation. He believed that any
economy has a natural tendency towards equilibrium and stagnation and that
it grows because a few businessmen innovate – and innovation is closely related
to invention. He called innovators 'entrepreneurs'.[29] To his way of thinking all
entrepreneurs were businessmen but only some businessmen were entrepreneurs. And naturally enough, 'It is in most cases only one man or a few men
who see the new possibility and are able to cope with the resistances and
difficulties which action always meets with outside the ruts of established
practice.'[30] Innovators were those most worth studying, because they determined the new courses which economies occasionally followed, though Schumpeter never denied the collective importance of the ordinary businessmen. But
like sheep, ordinary imitative businessmen were led through the wilderness to
pastures new by shepherding entrepreneurs. In his scheme innovators were

---

[26] McKendrick, 'General introduction', pp. xx–xxi. R. H. Campbell and R. G. Wilson, 'Introduction' to Campbell and Wilson, eds., *Entrepreneurship in Britain 1750–1939* (London,
1975), p. 11.

[27] C. H. Wilson, 'The entrepreneur in the industrial revolution in Britain', *Explorations in Entrepreneurial History*, VII (1955), pp. 129–45.

[28] The most powerful restatement of the importance of the technologist is D. S. Landes, *The
unbound Prometheus* (Cambridge, 1969), Ch. 2.

[29] J. A. Schumpeter, *The theory of economic development* (Cambridge, Mass., 1934) and his 'The
creative response in economic history', *Journal of Economic History*, VII (1947), pp. 149–59.

[30] 'The creative response', p. 152.

heroic, dynamic, thrusting and often ambitious. But they were not necessarily successful. He was well aware that innovation involved risk-taking and that by definition some risk-takers are successful while others are not. Moreover, he was just as sure that the successful could only be properly judged by comparing them with the failures.[31] Here is one very important reason to study failure though, in the context of the English Industrial Revolution, it has never been given the importance Schumpeter demanded.[32]

Reinforcing the theoretical reasons for concentrating on innovators and inventors has been the availability of evidence. The little surviving raw material about eighteenth-century business tends to concern those firms that were highly successful, highly inventive or highly innovative. Moreover, for obvious reasons our understanding of businessmen has relied on a collection of biographies of the successful and distinctive. We have plenty of biographies of inventors and innovators but very few of imitators. Undoubtedly, the evidence that has survived has limited historians' room for manoeuvre here. But the biographical approach is not the only route into business history and it is important to be careful in generalising out from such a sample. After all, ephemeral firms have left few records, the long-lived rather more. And the biographical approach to business history, admittedly one of the most interesting ways into the subject, only yields effective generalisations when we have enough studies of a reasonably representative range of firms. But as yet we have not.[33] If the lives and work of Wedgwood, Strutt, Arkwright, Oldknow, Boulton, Watt and more have all been well written, 'What of the regiments of the anonymous; of those who made their major contribution to improving some process of invention, or who participated in short-lived partnerships, leaving perhaps only an entry in the docket books in the High Court of Justice in Bankruptcy?'[34] Given the lack of evidence of imitators, the biographical approach to a study of eighteenth-century enterprise has limitations which must always be kept in view. This is not to decry the biographies which have been written, but rather to emphasise that basing a general understanding of enterprise on such a selection can be misleading. The pioneering spirit would be exaggerated, the likelihood of successful risk-taking misunderstood, the foresight of businessmen too readily assumed, the availability of opportunities

[31] Ibid., p. 156.
[32] One of the few examples of a study of entrepreneurial failure is S. R. Cope, *Walter Boyd. A merchant banker in the age of Napoleon* (London, 1983).
[33] For a discussion of these issues see McKendrick, 'General introduction', pp. vii–ix and his 'George Packwood and the commercialization of shaving' in McKendrick, Brewer and Plumb, *The birth of a consumer society*, pp. 192–3. In a recent study F. Crouzet found that historians had produced reasonably coherent biographical information on only 200 businessmen in the Industrial Revolution: *The first industrialists* (Cambridge, 1985).
[34] P. L. Payne, *British entrepreneurship in the nineteenth century* (London, 1974), p. 24.

misrepresented, profit levels magnified, competition belittled, the achievements eulogised and the mistakes ignored.

Schumpeter did not set out to propose a methodology for the study of enterprise as a whole, quite the opposite. But the limitations of his scope have sometimes been ignored and the terms 'businessman' and 'entrepreneur' used interchangeably when it was his more limited innovator that was being thought of.[35] Consequently, definitions of 'entrepreneur' have multiplied with ever-diminishing returns.[36] Confusion has arisen because the dividing lines between inventive, innovative and imitative businessmen are hazy and unclear and because of the difficulties of reconciling biographical with non-biographical business history. Just as Smiles's obsession with inventors produced a distorted picture of enterprise, so Schumpeter's concentration on innovation could not hope to reflect the full reality of business enterprise. Most businessmen, whether viewed through the imperfect lens of economic theory or the mists of historical reality, are imitators, only tinkering with techniques and organisations.[37] Few businessmen in the eighteenth century were like the well-known technologists and industrialists. Twenty years ago Michael Flinn noted that the Industrial Revolution fundamentally depended on the multiplication of productive units by imitating businessmen. As he put it, 'for every Arkwright in the Industrial Revolution there were a hundred such anonymous, busy, tireless, profit-seeking employers'.[38] Equally, for every Arkwright and his hundred followers there were a hundred and one merchants, middlemen and retailers.

Two issues can be used both to sort invention, innovation and imitation from one another and to understand the relevance of a study of failure to each: first by examining the nature of economic opportunities available to each group and, second, by seeing how such opportunities mesh with the structure of competition to determine the size and structure of success and failure. Inventors, innovators and imitators all confront market opportunities from different angles and at different times and are, therefore, confronted with different problems, openings and pressures. Crudely, inventors create new opportunities (though not *all* new opportunities), innovators pioneer the utilisation of opportunities (which may have existed for some time), while imitators adapt and replicate the

---

[35] See B. W. E. Alford, 'Entrepreneurship, business performance and industrial development', *Business History*, XIX (1977), p. 116.

[36] 'The joys of defining "entrepreneurial" could fill a whole volume.' D. C. Coleman, 'Gentlemen and players', *Economic History Review*, XXVI (1973), pp. 111–12.

[37] Coleman, 'Gentlemen and players'. G. H. Evans, 'Business entrepreneurs, their major functions and related tenets', *Journal of Economic History*, XIX (1959), p. 253 and his 'A theory of entrepreneurship', *Journal of Economic History*, II Supplement 2 (1942), p. 144. F. H. Knight, 'Profit and entrepreneurial functions', *Journal of Economic History*, II Supplement 2 (1942), pp. 129–30. J. H. Dales, 'Approaches to entrepreneurial history', *Explorations in Entrepreneurial History*, I (1949), p. 11.

[38] M. W. Flinn, *Origins of the industrial revolution* (London, 1966), p. 80.

actions of the innovators. If a businessman seizes an opportunity earlier than other businessmen might have then he is more likely to be an inventor and/or an innovator; but if he seizes it later then he will more probably be an innovator and/or an imitator. Linked to this, a fundamental difference between inventors and innovators on the one hand and imitators on the other is in the realm of competitive market forces. A successfully developed invention or successfully introduced innovation, allied with ready markets, allows businessmen the potential to enjoy considerable profits until imitators rush in, following their example, intensifying competition and putting profit margins under pressure. Over the short term, inventors and innovators can reap the benefits of a quasi-oligopolistic position because of the temporary weakness of competition. Imitators enjoy no such protection from the chill winds of competition. Of course, it was no easy thing to be a profitable inventor or innovator, as Henry Cort, Lewis Paul and others found out to their cost. Because of novelty, ignorance and development charges, peculiar costs and risks are borne by inventors and innovators. Nevertheless, in the real world, therefore, supply and demand evolve out of step with one another because of the imperfections of the markets. Successful innovators can reap extraordinary gains because of the difficulties potential imitators face in entering the area. Those difficulties relate primarily to the threshold of entry into business and the diffusion of knowledge about opportunities. In eighteenth-century England although the threshold of entry is usually assumed to have been fairly low, at least in terms of the capital required, knowledge of opportunities was restricted by poor communications, ignorance of market size and structure, the secrecy of innovators – some early cotton mills, for example, were built without windows on the ground floor – and, finally, the patent system.[39] In short, the market had manifest imperfections. It was because Richard Arkwright, to take a famous example, had a new and a reasonably perfected technique with his water frame, protected by patents from 1769 to 1785, because he was fairly assiduous in the protection of those patents, and had a ready market, and hence because he side-stepped competition for so long that he amassed a vast fortune in so little time. As his opponents remarked in 1782, his patent gave 'Stability to a dangerous Monopoly'.[40] Equally, in building that fortune he did not have to obey all the rules of economic rationality. He ignored the principle of minimising costs when, for social and personal reasons, he sited his mills in Derbyshire, over seventy uneconomic miles away from Liverpool, the port of entry for his raw cotton. The hundreds of imitators who followed in his wake could not afford to act so

[39] In 1770 Arthur Young complained that in Birmingham 'I could not gain any intelligence even of the most common nature, through the excessive jealousy of the manufacturers.' *A six months tour through the north of England* (London, 1770), Vol. III, p. 342.

[40] *Journal of the House of Commons*, XXXVIII, p. 882.

casually.[41] Clearly, in this case, to have concentrated on the innovator alone in a study of enterprise in the early cotton industry would have seriously distorted an appreciation of the economic environment.

Inventive, innovative and imitative businessmen have, then, different relationships to both economic opportunities and the structure and intensity of competition and, through that, to risk. It is essential to recognise that opportunities were particularly and not generally available in the eighteenth century. Not everyone could be Watt or Wedgwood because, in spite of market imperfections, in time competition was sufficiently strong. To assume that during the eighteenth century the economic environment was generally favourable – that the expanding economy meant that anyone could succeed – is to perpetuate the myth of the self-made man popularised by Smiles. But in the eighteenth century it was never true that 'Anyone who devotes himself to money making, body and soul, can scarcely fail to become rich. Very little brains will do.'[42] Smiles's faith in self-help demanded such a posture; but the faith was misplaced and the posture absurd. Many people did devote themselves to business, but only a proportion of them would become rich. While the moral qualities and social background of businessmen are relevant to a study of enterprise they were of secondary importance in determining the degree of success or failure in any particular case.[43] What mattered most was traditional business skills and how quickly opportunities were created or seized.

Social explanations of enterprise can only be of decisive importance if social concentrations of business activity do not reflect the unequal distributions of the ability to create or seize opportunities. It is under this test that most social explanations of enterprise break down. Economic opportunities were not available to everyone in the eighteenth century: they were temporally, sectorally, geographically and financially limited. Available opportunities can only be seized if they are first seen. Many businessmen and many potential businessmen were simply in the wrong place at the wrong time, doing the wrong things and with inadequate resources or skills at their disposal to see and then seize the sorts of opportunities which were being created and made available. A corn merchant in Hemel Hempstead in Hertfordshire could hardly hope to know

[41] S. D. Chapman, *The early factory masters* (Newton Abbot, 1967), pp. 64–7.

[42] A. Smiles, *Samuel Smiles and his surroundings* (London, 1956), p. 107.

[43] The sociological explanations of enterprise in the Industrial Revolution have gradually been eroded by common sense and new evidence. The two main theories are in E. E. Hagen, *On the theory of social change* (Cambridge, Mass., 1962), especially Ch. 13. D. C. McClelland, *The achieving society* (Princeton, N.J., 1961). For a clear critique of these see M. W. Flinn, 'Social theory and the industrial revolution', in T. Burns and S. B. Saul, eds., *Social theory and economic change* (London, 1967), pp. 9–34. McKendrick, 'General introduction', pp. xiv–xv. Telling new information, albeit of variable quality, is in K. Honeyman, *Origins of enterprise* (Manchester, 1982); A. Howe, *The cotton masters, 1830–1860* (Oxford, 1984); Crouzet, *The first industrialists*.

enough about the market for cotton goods to pack up his bags and troop off to Bolton in the 1780s to set up as a cotton manufacturer. Unsurprisingly, businessmen during this century of transformation were of much the same socio-economic background as ever. 'Despite the transformation of the economy and of society *c.* 1750–*c.* 1830, there appears to have been little real change in the industrial leadership.'[44] Businessmen seizing new opportunities came from areas economically and geographically adjacent to those opportunities.

These factors help explain why there was an apparent surfeit of Quaker businessmen in the period but a relative shortage of Methodists. As Voltaire noticed, because Quakers were excluded from so many areas of advancement, such as the universities, government and the army, 'They are reduced to the necessity of earning money through commerce.'[45] And their meeting houses 'extended the ties of the family, and you lent and borrowed within your known community with a confidence hardly yet to be extended beyond such limits'.[46] Quakers tended to be in the right place and have the means of seizing opportunities. But the Methodists were not. Because they were concentrated among the lower echelons of society they lacked the funds to make a go of things, even if they had wanted to.[47] Thresholds of entry into business may have been low by modern standards, but they were high enough for the bulk of the population.

If a study of the patterns of opportunities takes us some way towards a better appreciation of the broad distinctions between inventors, innovators and imitators and the relevant economic and social contexts of enterprise then we still have to understand why some opportunities prove very profitable, some moderately so and others not at all. Here issues of risk and competition come to the fore. Economic opportunities are sometimes knowingly created by inventors, but more usually they emerge unwittingly or unknowingly in the interstices of business enterprise.[48] Once an opportunity exists it is the degree of risk and competition which determine its exploitation. One of the main worries of a businessman confronted by an opportunity is whether the good or service it relates to will be able to find a sufficiently large market at a sufficiently high price to be able to generate adequate profits. The risk and uncertainty involved in trying to assess market size and structure are intensified by difficulties of trying to gauge the character, extent and power of competition. It is these issues which interact to produce success *and* failure in a business community. Clearly the central problem for a business is one of the quality of available information, in other words of the degree of perfection and imperfection of the market. The

---

[44] Honeyman, *Origins of enterprise*, p. 166. Also Crouzet, *The first industrialists*.
[45] Voltaire, *Letters on England* (London, 1733; reprinted Harmondsworth, 1980), p. 35.
[46] Wilson, 'The entrepreneur in the industrial revolution', p. 131.
[47] Flinn, 'Social theory', pp. 25–8.   [48] Evans, 'A theory of entrepreneurship', p. 143.

imperfections of the market and the variability of competition are of central importance throughout the book, being a major factor structuring success and failure in the eighteenth century. The nature of those imperfections and variations determines the type of opportunities which businessmen seek to exploit.[49] The existence of opportunities and hence of enterprise can reasonably be viewed in terms of changing patterns and intensities of competition. Such changes result from variations in market size and the entry and exit of firms. By looking at bankruptcy in the eighteenth century and relating its geographical and sectoral distribution to known changes within the structure of the economy and by calculating changing rates of bankruptcy where possible then a start can be made towards outlining the nature of competition which allowed businessmen to invent, innovate and imitate. A series of relevant questions to be addressed in this book is: 'Was competition in growing areas of the economy more or less intense than in declining or stagnant ones?'; 'How did competition fluctuate over the short or medium term?'; 'How was competition assessed by businessmen at the time and what could they do to overcome it?'

Central to the limitations of general conclusions drawn from business biographies of the great and the famous is a tendency to misunderstand the structure of economic opportunities, the nature of risk and the role of competition in the eighteenth century. An examination of bankruptcy provides a useful corrective here. Because opportunities might work or they might not the pattern of bankruptcy helps chart the nature of opportunities. Risk-taking is part and parcel of enterprise and, as Schumpeter saw, those risks can only be properly appreciated if the unsuccessful are studied alongside the successful. The nature of risk, of attempts to combat risks as well as take them, were a major concern of all eighteenth-century businessmen. They tried to take some and avoid others; the security motive has been little appreciated. Our picture has been of risk-taking rather than risk avoidance. In fact, the security motive is one of the main aims weakening the urge to profit maximisation among businessmen. Economists have long argued that businessmen treasure both the survival of their firm and the accumulation of profits.[50] By looking at eighteenth-century reactions to the possibilities and realities of bankruptcy some broad assessment can be made of just how powerful the security motive was at the time. In fact, contemporary discussion of the risk of failure, the horror of failure and of ways of avoiding it demonstrate very clearly the strength of the

---

[49] I. M. Kirzner, 'Entrepreneurship and the market approach to development', in his *Perception, opportunity and profit: studies in the theory of entrepreneurship* (Chicago, 1979), pp. 107–19. It was F. H. Knight's *Risk, uncertainty and profit* (Cambridge, Mass., 1921), which paved the way for an examination of the absurdities of the neo-classical theory of the firm.

[50] K. W. Rothschild, 'Price theory and oligopoly', *Economic Journal*, LVII (1947), p. 308. Evans, 'Business entrepreneurs'. F. E. Hyde, 'Economic theory and business history', *Business History*, V (1962), pp. 1–10.

security motive in the eighteenth century, even in the early decades of the Industrial Revolution.

A study of bankruptcy in the eighteenth century should, in conclusion, help clear the route for a better understanding of both the economy in general and of business enterprise in particular in a number of ways. First, because bankruptcy hits inventors, innovators and imitators, whether producers or distributors, it avoids some of the pitfalls just described in generalizing out from the experience of individuals in some of these groups. Second, because bankruptcy is a measure of enterprise that has failed, studying its patterns – over time, regions and sectors – should reflect on changes in the distribution of enterprise in the century and help in descriptions of broad changes within the economy. Third, examining explanations of the pattern of bankruptcy should lead to a better appreciation of the nature of opportunity, competition, risk and uncertainty at the time. In particular, it should help with a more accurate assessment of the problems and opportunities of the economic environment over the short term. Finally, this should enable a better appreciation to be made of the contribution of enterprise to the eighteenth-century economy and, of course, early industrialisation. All in all, this book should go some way towards disproving Tawney's taunt that 'The economic life of an age is not to be judged by the proceedings of its bankruptcy courts.'[51]

Success usually outweighs failure in the scales of business enterprise and it would produce problems if bankruptcy were to be studied in isolation and its importance exaggerated. But the successful are only successful because they have not failed while others have. The connexion between success and failure cannot be ignored. Let us hope that the words of Shakespeare's Richard II will be borne out: 'O, but they say the tongues of dying men / Enforce attention like deep harmony.'

[51] R. H. Tawney, 'Introduction' to T. Wilson, *A discourse upon usury* (London, 1925), p. 29.

2

THE BANKRUPT: FRIEND OR FOE?

Firms can be killed by competitive forces in the marketplace or they can die solvent, peacefully in their beds. They come to the end of their lives for a number of reasons: because they have been transformed by a merger or takeover; because their guiding light goes elsewhere or retires; and because they are losing money. Only the last of these can definitely be thought of as failure, though on occasions the other two reasons involve it as well.[1] Failure is in fact very difficult to define. An inability to maximise profits is failure of sorts, just as is the non-achievement of goals specified by the businessmen themselves. But bankruptcy is a reasonable way of defining and quantifying business failure, for all firms try to avoid insolvency. Here, failure might best be thought of as a degree of indebtedness which either the creditor or debtor takes to be permanent. Unfortunately, in the eighteenth century bankruptcy does not precisely reflect such a state, largely because of the conditions attached to its legal definition. The eighteenth-century layman's definition of a bankrupt, which is similar to that which we use today, did not coincide with the law's specifications. Only some of those who were insolvent were dealt with as bankrupts; others were dealt with by alternative legal mechanisms; and some escaped the law altogether, though not necessarily their creditors. Only traders owing at least £100 who had committed an 'act of bankruptcy' could be dealt with by the law as bankrupts. Eighteenth-century bankruptcy, therefore, constitutes the tip of the iceberg of insolvency as failure. But quite what the relative proportions above and below the waterline were, it is impossible to judge. If the numbers and patterns of bankruptcy can be gauged other sorts of failure are largely lost from view.

Making sense of the bankruptcy statistics produced by the law lies at the heart of this book. Inevitably, this can only be done when the peculiarities of the eighteenth-century law of bankruptcy have been described and its context within the realm of credit, debt and insolvency has been detailed. The first step is to outline changing perceptions of bankruptcy and bankrupts from the time of the first relevant statute in 1543 through to the early nineteenth century.

[1] A useful outline of the typologies of failure is in P. L. Payne, *The early Scottish limited companies 1856–1895* (Edinburgh, 1980), p. 8.

ATTITUDES TOWARDS FAILURE

Eighteenth-century attitudes towards – rather than explanations of – bankruptcy were both new and inherited. Indeed, there was a constant struggle between an old, harsh and less friendly opinion of bankrupts and a new and more enlightened one that sprouted in the seventeenth century and flourished in the eighteenth. That struggle was fought on two fronts. First, it involved conflict over the legal terms of bankruptcy and other modes of debt collection. Second, a constant guerilla war was waged between general opinion, creditors, debtors, arbitrators, economic pamphleteers and moralists, where the issues contested were economic and moral. This complicated war, waged on two fronts and between a multiplicity of combatants, contested a surprisingly small number of well-defined positions. In brief, these can be viewed as a set of problems or questions. Were bankrupts honest or dishonest? Were they victims or criminals? Was bankruptcy accidental or avoidable, blameless or culpable? Should bankrupts be punished or consoled, deterred or encouraged? Should they be treated differently from other debtors? And were creditors innocent and virtuous, or cunning and usurious? By looking at these questions, as well as at the various answers offered, it should be possible to get some way towards an appreciation of eighteenth-century opinions of bankruptcy.

Bankruptcy entered the statute book in 1543 or, more precisely, dishonest bankruptcy did, for the act was directed only at preventing fraudulent practices, as its title, 'An act against such men as do make bankrupt', suggests.[2] The law ignored honest insolvents and counted as bankrupts only those who had made a conscious and premeditated decision to evade payment of just debts. The preamble muttered about men who

> craftily obtaining into their hands great substance of others men's goods, do suddenly flee to parts unknown, or keep their houses, not minding to pay or restore to any their creditors, their duties, but at their own wills and pleasures consume debts and the substance obtained by credit of other men, for their own pleasure and delicate living against all reason, equity, and good conscience.

As a legal category, bankruptcy was created because the dishonesty and immorality of some debtors could not be tackled by existing methods. For example, if a debtor kept his front door firmly shut he could easily defeat all writs out against him. All the early bankruptcy statutes rested on the assumption that honest debtors would keep their doors open and would not have to be dealt with as bankrupts, but that dishonest ones would lock their doors. Consequently, those laws counted bankrupts as immoral insolvents, and looked to drive them from the nation and commonwealth. A second act, in 1570, called for their

---

[2] 34 & 35 Hen. VIII, c. 4. The early history of bankruptcy law is recounted in W. J. Jones, 'The foundations of English bankruptcy: statutes and commissions in the early modern period', *Transactions of the American Philosophical Society*, LXIX (1979), Part iii.

'repression'; another in 1604 complained about those who 'wickedly and wilfully become bankrupts'.[3] Even the heart of the more generous eighteenth-century law, passed in 1706 and made permanent in 1732, went under the title of 'An act to prevent frauds frequently committed by bankrupts'.[4]

The implied continuity in the law's fundamental assumptions about bankrupts was only partly realised in the content of the statutes just mentioned. By 1706 the law made provisions for both honest and dishonest bankrupts, recognising the long-standing belief in their joint existence and in the value of one and the canker of the other. An early, colourful, description came in 1606 when Thomas Dekker argued that 'The infortunate Marchant, whose estate is swallowed up by the mercilesse Seas, and the provident Trades-man whom riotous Servants at home, or hard-headed debters abroad undermine and overthrow, blotting them with the name of *Bankrupts* deserve to be pitied and relieved.'[5] But he condemned at some length the 'politick bankrupt' who was

a *Harpy* that looks smoothly, a *Hyena* that enchants subtilly, a Mermaid that sings sweetly, and a *Cameleon*, that can put himselfe into all colours... for after he hath gotten into his hands so much of other mens goods or money, as will fill him to the upper deck, away he sayles with it, and politickly runnes himselfe on ground, to make the world believe he had suffered shipwreck. Then flyes he out like an Irish rebell, and keepes aloofe, hiding his head, when he cannot hide his shame.[6]

The politic bankrupt has haunted perceptions of the business world and failure from Dekker to the present day. The sight of a bankrupt with money in his pocket and a smile on his face inevitably causes outcry. What was more difficult, however, was distinguishing honest from dishonest bankrupts and deciding what their fate should be. Here issues of the culpability and the inevitability of bankruptcy in a trading nation were central concerns. It was easy enough to condemn and vilify the bankrupt who had contracted debts in the sure knowledge that they would never be repaid. He was a criminal who should be punished and coerced into repaying. But what of the poor soul who had borrowed money in good faith and began to shuffle only in the vain hope that his fortunes would revive? Questions such as this led, in the seventeenth century, to a more complex picture of bankruptcy than the early statutes allowed for, a picture that depicted varying shades and hues of honesty, dishonesty and culpability. Typifying this greater sophistication, William Petty distinguished the politic bankrupt from those bankrupts who 'have either spent their creditors money vainly and luxuriously, or have lost it by their unskilfulness in Trade and have been cheated, or else have lost it [in] inevitable accident or the hand

---

[3] 13 Eliz. I, c. 7. 1 Jac. I, c. 15.
[4] 4 & 5 Anne, c. 17. 5 Geo. II, c. 30.
[5] *The seven deadly sinnes of Londen* (London, 1606) in *The non-dramatic works of Thomas Dekker*, ed. A. G. Gosart, 4 vols. (London, 1885), Vol. II, pp. 26–7.   [6] Ibid., pp. 21–2.

of God'.[7] In 1734, one analysis separated bankrupts and insolvents according to whether they had collapsed because of criminal action, culpable action, negligence or, finally, misfortune.[8]

But it was one thing for commentators to divide debtors and bankrupts into 'the Honest, the hardly Honest, and the Down-right Knave', another thing to enshrine such distinctions into the body of the law.[9] It was frequently complained that the law was too soft or too vicious and too indiscriminate and blunt to be able to prise apart the various degrees of failure. At one extreme lay the creditors' advocates, who argued that honest debtors did not need a law of bankruptcy at all, because by behaving honourably and decently they were sure to win their creditors' indulgence. This argument held the upper hand with the statute makers until 1706. Creditors complained that the bankrupt laws simply encouraged honest men to turn knaves in the sure knowledge that 'A breaking is a making to some in this city, or they'd never do it so often.'[10] They also felt that they needed complete legal protection from debtors because the usury laws prevented them charging interest rates that sufficiently covered the risk of non-repayment. On the debtors' side, however, were retorts to the effect that only a tiny proportion of bankrupts behaved fraudulently and that the law should be directed towards the majority not the minority. Otherwise, everyone would be tarred with the same grubby brush.[11] Somewhat more forcefully, arguments were erected that, firstly, questioned the degree of power creditors should exert over debtors and, secondly, stressed the need for an enterprising economy to protect and cosset its risk-takers and men of action.

When a business failed it was never clear how much power creditors should have at their disposal to enforce repayment, because power could be used in a fit of pique or for unwarranted revenge. Through the century, many complained that creditors were cruel and capricious when dealing with debtors. One group of aggrieved debtors likened creditors to 'the Locusts that visited the Land of *Egypt* and eat up every green Thing'.[12] Bankrupts needed a law of bankruptcy to protect them from such greed, in particular to keep them from rotting away in jail. For creditors could easily, but mistakenly, believe that their debtors were recalcitrant rather than insolvent and use imprisonment, threatened or real, to coax repayment. And creditors could always use that threat or reality

---

[7] *The Petty papers, some unpublished writings of Sir William Petty*, ed. Marquis of Lansdowne, 2 vols. (London, 1927), Vol I, p. 249.

[8] *The case of bankrupts and insolvents considered* (London, 1734), p. 28.

[9] *Observations on the bankrupts bill: occasion'd by the many misrepresentations, and unjust reflections, of Mr Daniel De Foe, in his several discourses on that head* (London, 1706), p. 11.

[10] M. Draper, *The spendthrift* (London, 1731), p. 57. I am grateful to Professor W. A. Speck for this reference.

[11] *Observations on the state of bankrupts, under the present laws in a letter to a member of parliament* (London, 1760), p. 7.

[12] *The case of the insolvent debtors, now in prison* (London, 1725?), p. 1.

mischievously. Defoe, himself a bankrupt, wanted the 1706 statute to be retitled 'An act to prevent the Frauds, frequently committed both by Bankrupts and their Creditors'.[13] From the middle of the seventeenth century there was a steady barrage of concern about the jails being full of debtors unable to pay and unable to gain their liberty until parliament showed periodic mercy and set them free.[14] One reason behind the founding of the colony of Georgia in 1732 was the recognition that unhappy debtors were languishing in jail, rotting to death.[15] Until the early eighteenth century, bankrupts were still liable to be imprisoned and forgotten. One witness, perhaps self-pityingly, wept for such lost souls: 'For when any of them chance to be cast behind by Misfortunes, we seise withall Violence, and cast them into Prisons, where they lie like the *Damned*, without a *Moments Reprieve* or *End of their Torments*.'[16]

By 1700 it was felt that the law of bankruptcy ought to deal with both honest and dishonest bankrupts, not simply because the former were being hard done by at the hands of merciless creditors but, crucially, because it was also recognised that a certain volume of failure was not only inevitable but healthy. This position was pioneered as trade expanded in the seventeenth century. John Cary, for example, believed that 'Misfortunes may and often do befal industrious Men, whose *Trades* have been very beneficial to the Nation, and to such a due Regard ought to be had; but for those who design under the shelter of a Protection or Priviledge to spend all they have, and thereby cheat their Creditors, no Law can be too severe.'[17] It was sentiments like this, vigorously championed by Defoe, which constituted the decisive climate of opinion behind the legal reforms introduced in 1706. The new law threatened the politic, fraudulent and dishonest bankrupt with the prospect of the hangman's noose, but the honest, decent and god-fearing ones received protection from imprisonment, freedom from any obligation for the debts contracted before they failed and a proportion of their estate as a reward for good faith and to help them to make a new start.

[13] D. Defoe, *Defoe's review*, reprinted in 22 vols. (New York, 1939), 23 March 1706, p. 141.
[14] D. Veall, *The popular movement for law reform in England 1640–1660* (Oxford, 1970). P. J. Lineham, 'The campaign to abolish imprisonment for debt in England 1750–1840' (University of Canterbury, New Zealand, M.A. thesis, 1974).
[15] E. M. Coulter, *Georgia a short history* (Chapel Hill, N.C., 1947), pp. 14–16. James Oglethorpe headed a parliamentary commission in the late 1720s to investigate the state of the jails, which prompted him to take an active role in the establishment of Georgia. See his *A new and accurate account of the provinces of South-Carolina and Georgia* (London, 1732) reprinted in T. R. Reese, ed., *The most delightful country of the universe. Promotional literature of the colony of Georgia 1717–1734* (Savannah, Ga., 1972), pp. 130–43.
[16] *An humble proposal to cause bancrupts make better and more speedier payment of their debts to their creditors, than, by long experience hath been found, the statutes against bancrupts do effect* (London, 1679), p. 3.
[17] *An essay on the state of England, in relation to its trade, its poor, and its taxes, for carrying on the present war against France* (Bristol, 1695), p. 37.

The law was changed from one constructed solely for the benefit of creditors to one that conferred privileges on both creditors and bankrupts. With the certificate of discharge, freeing the bankrupt from his debts, the businessman was offered an escape from his unsuccessful spirit of adventure. Supposedly, the past would not hang round his neck like an albatross. It can be argued that this shift in opinion during the seventeenth century reflected the needs of an increasingly commercial society, particularly in relation to the growth of overseas trade after the Restoration.

Echoing Carey, one author had argued that

in a Trading Country, those who have become Insolvent, by pursuing Projects, or by any other Losses incident to Trade, ought to be gently dealt with; so even this of venturing another Man's Money upon a *reasonable* Project, or Scheme of Trade, ought not to be look'd on as a very gross Fault.[18]

This represented the standard contemporary interpretation and justification of the law. Blackstone, the great legal commentator, sanctified the spirit of the eighteenth-century law of bankruptcy by arguing that

at present the laws of bankruptcy are considered as laws calculated for the benefit of trade, and founded on the principles of humanity as well as justice; and to that end they confer some privileges, not only on the creditors, but also on the bankrupt or debtor himself. On the creditors; by compelling the bankrupt to give up all his effects to their use, without any fraudulent concealment: on the debtor; by exempting him from the rigor of the general law, whereby his person might be confined at the discretion of his creditor, though in reality he has nothing to satisfy the debt; whereas the law of bankrupts, taking into consideration the sudden and unavoidable accidents to which men in trade are liable, has given them the liberty of their persons, and some pecuniary emoluments, upon condition they surrender up their whole estate to be divided among their creditors.[19]

Clearly, in the eighteenth century contemporaries both inside and outside parliament took a realistic view of enterprise and risk-taking. Many people recognised the value of trade and industry and that growth and prosperity would only come if firms chanced their arms. 'Projects' and projectors were a mainstay of the philosophy of wealth and employment creation in the seventeenth century.[20] And, as with all chances, there was a possibility of failure as well as success. Such realism produced a law in 1706 which encouraged its use by creditors and insolvents; statistics of its utilisation are therefore a much more reliable indicator of business failure. Before then, the law was too unbalanced and too hostile to bankrupts to encourage much faith that those caught in its web were either numerous or representative. As Professor Supple

---

[18] *The case of bankrupts and insolvents considered*, p. 52.
[19] W. Blackstone, *Commentaries on the laws of England*, 4 vols. (Oxford, 1766), Vol. II, p. 472.
[20] J. Thirsk, *Economic policy and projects* (Oxford, 1978).

remarked, in the seventeenth century 'Bankruptcies could, of course, occur but they are perhaps not as good an index of crises in overseas trade as some historians have imagined.'[21] It would be wrong to think that the statistics of bankruptcy in the eighteenth century are perfect reflections of the volume of failure, however. In the first place, the legal system dealing with indebtedness and insolvency suffered severe fractures and, secondly, bankruptcy remained a major stigma. On the first point, it is essential to realise that the law of bankruptcy was just one of several ways in which debts could be chased or insolvency handled. (The alternative processes are outlined in the next chapter.) Moreover, only certain debtors fell within the jurisdiction of bankruptcy.

The law of bankruptcy was discriminatory because it applied only to 'traders' who had debts of at least £100 and who had committed an act of bankruptcy. An Elizabethan statute had introduced the 'trading' distinction in 1571, a distinction that survived until the middle of the nineteenth century.[22] Essentially, a trader was one who made his living by buying and selling. It was a simple enough distinction in theory, but in practice had complications that arose from its very intent. The main aim of the distinction was to keep the jurisdiction of bankruptcy away from the landowning and farming community. The law was meant to be limited to the business world, reflecting the sixteenth-century origins of the trading distinction when it had been assumed that only overseas traders were liable to the sorts of losses and used the sorts of credit which the law sought to deal with. But such distinctions were very hard to maintain and implement in a consistent manner, not least because of the way the economy changed and developed in the seventeenth century. Certainly, some occupations never fell within the scope of the law, such as farmers. But others were excluded or included on the basis of fine and misleading definitions. Much turned on the particular nature of buying and the particular purpose of selling. For example, one rule said that you could not be classified as a trader if you did not buy the materials you used. So a brickmaker who used raw materials from land he held freehold was not a trader, while one who used materials from land he rented was.[23] Clearly, these contradictions could weaken bankruptcy as a measure of failure and it is interesting to note that some American colonies that erected a law of bankruptcy in the eighteenth century did away with the trading distinction.[24] However, it seems that in most cases

---

[21] B. E. Supple, *Commercial crises and change in England 1600–1642* (Cambridge, 1959), p. 10.

[22] 13 Eliz. I, c. 17.

[23] Brickmaking provided a classic case which the law debated at great length until the reforms of the nineteenth century. See E. Chitty and F. Forster, *A digested index to the common law reports relating to conveyancing and bankruptcy commencing with the reign of Elizabeth, in 1558, to the present time* (London, 1841), pp. 65–8.

[24] P. J. Coleman, *Debtors and creditors in America. Insolvency, imprisonment for debt, and bankruptcy, 1607–1900* (Madison, Wis., 1974), p. 270.

a commonsense and realistic definition of trading was employed, such that the problems of what constituted trading did not cripple the system, though they did cause inconvenience. The real significance of the trading distinction, in fact, is evident in the light of the financial restriction that limited the applicability of bankruptcy.

In the early eighteenth century financial hurdles were erected to complement the trading distinction. By 1700 the earlier notion that bankruptcy should be limited to overseas traders had broadened out to include all those who traded on a reasonably substantial scale and were dependent on credit. In fact, the introduction of the financial restriction did not further limit the availability of bankruptcy but, rather, altered it to fit contemporary notions of credit. By 1700 it was widely recognised that credit was vital to many businessmen, for if in 1600 credit was mostly used by merchants, a hundred years later it was coming to be used extensively at home as well. Even so, the liberalisation of the scope of bankruptcy in 1706 was restricted, mostly because it seems to have been felt that credit should be used by wholesalers and manufacturers for the most part, and not really by retailers or artisans. There was an attempt to dovetail the financial and trading conditions with this perception, protecting credit within some areas of the business community but not in others. Blackstone believed that

If persons in other situations of life run in debt without the power of payment, they must take the consequences of their own indiscretion, even though they meet with sudden accidents that may reduce their fortunes: for the law holds it to be an unjustifiable practice, for any person but a trader to encumber himself with debts of any considerable value.[25]

As with the trading distinction, this attempt to separate reasonable from unreasonable credit was never likely to work in practice. Retailers who used credit were in fact common enough victims of bankruptcy in the eighteenth century (see Chapters 5 and 6). In the nineteenth century, in an attempt to clear up this point, it was suggested that bankruptcy be opened up to all those dependent upon bills of exchange, the main instrument of trade credit.[26]

Because of the trading and financial limitations that applied to the scope of bankruptcy we cannot hope that numbers of bankrupts give a full indication of failure. And the accuracy of such numbers may also be weakened by the horror with which businessmen viewed bankruptcy – assuming that insolvents tried to find other ways of clearing their position. One aspect of this derived from the tradition, inherited from the early statutes, that viewed bankruptcy as a crime.

---

[25] *Commentaries*, Vol. II, p. 473. See Defoe, *Defoe's review*, 18 January 1706, pp. 33–4. Also W. Cobbett, ed., *The Parliamentary history of England*, Vol. XXVII (London, 1816), p. 549.

[26] *Parliamentary papers*, 1818, Vol. VI, *Report from the select committee on the bankrupt laws*, p. 12.

Specifically, bankrupts had to commit an 'act' of bankruptcy for the laws to apply. It was all too easy to see such acts as criminal. An act of bankruptcy was an action which had sought to deny creditors the satisfaction of their just claims. Such acts were carefully defined: the main ones were flight, remaining indoors and refusing to see creditors, lying in jail under the insolvent debtor laws for more than two months, and fraudulent conveyance.[27] As such, they sought to point to moments when insolvency, be it permanent or temporary, had been recognised by the debtor. But this recognition could only be articulated in a legally acceptable form with the debtor committing a quasi-criminal act. Strikingly, debtors could not become voluntary bankrupts, declaring themselves insolvent in order to take advantage of the law. Clearly, this did not matter in the sixteenth century when bankrupts were assumed to be fraudulent, but in the eighteenth century, when they were not, it clashed a little with the sort of principles that Blackstone evinced. The eighteenth-century law of bankruptcy suffered from a touch of schizophrenia. As a commissioner giving evidence to the 1818 Select Committee put it, by the early nineteenth century

The supposition of the crime or offence of bankruptcy, is in general nothing more than a legal fiction, employed to lay a foundation for the absurdity of proceeding to convict a man of a crime behind his back, who from that moment is treated with every favour and indulgence, and is finally acquitted, consoled, and rewarded by a certificate of his innocence, and a discharge from all his debts.[28]

To Defoe, who had personal reasons to feel aggrieved, a commission of bankruptcy ruined a man's reputation:

Breaking is the death of a tradesman; he is mortally stabb'd...his shop is shut up, as it is when a man is buried; his credit, the life blood of his trade, is stagnated ... in a word, his fame, and even name as to trade is buried, and the commissioners that act upon him, and all their proceedings, are but like the executors of the defunct, dividing the ruins of his fortune, and at last, his certificate is a kind of performing the obsequies for the dead, and praying him out of purgatory.[29]

Elsewhere, Defoe complained that bankruptcy was likened by many to 'a Crime so Capital, that he ought to be cast out of Human Society'.[30]

The stigma attached to bankruptcy arose from two other main sources. Most simply, it was a personal failure. A businessman saw his hopes dashed, that his skills were inadequate, his knowledge faulty, and his judgement wayward. In

[27] See the longer list in E. Green, *The spirit of the bankrupt laws* (3rd edn, London, 1776), pp. 33–4.

[28] p. 103. See also, *Observations on the state of bankrupts, under the present laws in a letter to a member of parliament*.

[29] D. Defoe, *The complete English tradesman* (London, 1726), pp. 85–6. Sentiments duplicated by Steele in *The Spectator*, ed. D. F. Bond, 5 vols. (Oxford, 1965), Vol. IV, p. 108.

[30] *An essay upon projects* (London, 1697), p. 194.

this light, bankruptcy was a deep personal tragedy, as a man came to see his own shortcomings and mistakes. To Steele, it was the 'most dreadful of all Human Conditions ... Plenty, Credit, Cheerfulness, full Hopes, and easy Possessions, are in an Instant turned into Penury, faint Aspects, Diffidence, Sorrow, and Misery'.[31] Gibbon saw his father sink under a similar load: 'The pangs of shame, tenderness and self-reproach incessantly preyed on his vitals; his constitution was broken; he lost his strength.'[32] Although these sufferings and tortures rarely come to the surface through the records, they should never be forgotten. Businessmen made every effort to avoid them, though sometimes only to increase the agony of their decay.

If I were to run through the infinite Mazes of a Bankrupt, before he comes to the Crisis; what Shifts, what Turnings, and Windings in Trade, to support his Dying Credit; What Buying of one, to raise Money to Pay another; What Discounting of Bills, Pledgings and Pawnings; what Sellings to Loss for Present supply; What strange and Unaccountable Methods, to buoy up sinking Credit![33]

This leads to the second factor that significantly contributed to the stigma attached to bankruptcy, the use of credit. When a debtor fails to repay his creditors he inevitably breaks his word and wrecks their expectations of him on the rocks. In an instant, he becomes untrustworthy; he should not have been trusted in the past and must never be trusted in the future. The creditors have been fooled by the debtor, be it innocently or culpably. In short, from this angle, bankruptcy was always akin to dishonesty, even though it was recognised that 'losses which no human prudence could foresee, may happen to the most industrious and cautious trader. But such is the complexion of mankind that one mistake fixes a stigma perhaps for ever, the stain or tarnish may never be wiped off.'[34]

For some, death offered the only escape from the foul stench of bankruptcy. Because if 'Debt among the people of England, is too black a die ever to be forgiven', then a bankrupt had no place in society and could only live the life of an outcast in his own land.[35] Of course, this was the extreme case and life could go on for most. But the popular mythology of the desperate, disconsolate and depressed businessman throwing himself to his death or blowing his brains out has some validity in the eighteenth century. Mixing gravity with mirth, George Norton wrote from London to his brother in Virginia at the height of the financial crises in 1772, that 'not a day passes but we hear of suicides committed by those whose Cases are render'd desparate, Mr Bogle Junr. not

---

[31] *The Spectator*, Vol IV, p. 6.
[32] E. Gibbon, *Memoirs of my life*, ed. B. Radice (Harmondsworth, 1984), p. 153.
[33] *Defoe's review*, 19 February 1706, p. 85. See also Smith, *Wealth of nations*, Vol. I, p. 363.
[34] *The management and oeconomy of trade, or the young trader's guide* (London, 1783), p. 28.
[35] J. Dornford, *Seven letters to the Lords and Commons of Great Britain* (London 1786), p. 55.

being able to struggle with the Fire of adversity threw himself out of a window on the Second Story (in a phrenzy) he happily fell in such an attitude as only to bruise his latter end'.[36]

Responses towards bankruptcy in the eighteenth century were complex. Sympathy was mixed with rage, kindness with hostility. Yet this is hardly surprising, for bankruptcy is bound to elicit such extremes depending on whether the debtor behaved honourably and on whether comment came from general onlookers concerned with growth and risk-taking, or from creditors who had personally suffered from the failure of debtors. Fortunately, by the eighteenth century this dichotomy had been recognised in parliament and the value of adventurous businessmen to national prosperity appreciated, producing an attempt to accommodate legally the variety of positions which have been uncovered. Looking back over three centuries, some parliamentary commissioners in the nineteenth century saw that 'The Statutes relating to Bankrupts were originally enacted to meet cases of fraud for which the ordinary forms of the law did not offer effectual remedy, and were founded upon principles of extreme severity.' But after 'progressive alterations they have become more lenient'.[37] The eighteenth-century law did manage to strike some sort of balance that paid due respect to the opinions that bankrupts might be friends or foes. It sought to protect honest bankrupts whose commendable spirit of enterprise had been unsuccessful, and it sought to vilify and punish dishonest and fraudulent bankrupts. But the extent to which it succeeded in this depended on the actual letter of the law and the alternative processes to bankruptcy.

[36] *John Norton & Sons merchants of London and Virginia*, ed. F. N. Mason (Richmond, Va., 1937; reprinted Newton Abbot, 1968), p. 254.

[37] *Parliamentary papers*, 1840, Vol. XVI, *Report of the commissioners for inquiring into bankruptcy and insolvency*, p. 7. See also E. Cooke, *An inquiry into the state of the law of debtor and creditor in England* (London, 1829), p. 70.

3

*

FAILURE AND THE LAW

The variety of opinions about indebtedness and insolvency was matched in the eighteenth century by the variety of legal processes to deal with such situations. Bankruptcy was just one way in which a creditor could pursue his debt. Broadly, these processes can be thought of as either official or unofficial. Despite the alternatives, in the end bankruptcy is an effective way of judging patterns of business failure in the eighteenth century, for its limitations are easily outweighed by its strengths.

All businesses become indebted and can become insolvent. But insolvency is not an absolute state, largely because many more businesses become temporarily than permanently insolvent. Distinguishing short- from long-term insolvency was difficult enough for eighteenth-century businessmen, let alone the twentieth-century historian. It can be suggested, however, that failure as defined by insolvency comes either when the debtor recognises his inability to pay or when the creditor believes the debtor is unable to pay. It was the way these perceptions were handled which determined whether a failure was dealt with officially, by some legally constituted bureaucracy, or unofficially and informally.

INDEBTEDNESS AND INSOLVENCY OUTSIDE THE LAW

In the eighteenth century, business failure dealt with outside the law depended on the debtor recognising his insolvency and convincing *all* his creditors of it. That recognition might have come from an examination of his books or from the increasingly vociferous complaints of some of his creditors. Either way, indebtedness could be handled unofficially in two ways, depending on whether that indebtedness was felt to be temporary or permanent. Where a debtor was only temporarily insolvent it was usually in his creditors' interest to allow him to continue in business so that all of them would eventually be repaid in full. This might be formalised by an agreement known as a letter of licence. Further, creditors could choose, via a so-called deed of inspection, to keep a close eye on the debtor's affairs while allowing him to carry on – after all, there was always the chance that he might lose even more money.[1] In both cases, the creditors did not think that the debtor had actually failed. If they did, then it was in their interests to close down the debtor's business and realise his assets as quickly as possible. This was done by what were known as compositions, whereby the debtor's assets were assigned to one or more of the creditors acting as trustees for them all. They would collect the estate, sell it and distribute the proceeds among all the creditors in proportion to what they were owed. Compositions, like bankruptcy, attempted to equalise the position of all creditors, distributing both risks and rewards among them on a pro rata basis. 'It has been said in argument that compositions are private bankruptcies.'[2]

Plenty of commentators praised compositions, largely because they were relatively cheap and efficient: 'the vexations of arrest and imprisonment, and the costs of hostile proceedings, are avoided; and [the debtor's] estate and effects are not wasted by the expences attending a commission of bankruptcy'.[3] What distinguished compositions from bankruptcy and made them unofficial was that the administration of the debtor's affairs were not passed over to supposedly disinterested administrators, but remained in the hands of the creditors and/or debtor. Given the eighteenth-century feeling that the administration of bankruptcy could be wasteful and inefficient, this benefit was real enough. But the solid advantages of compositions were counterbalanced by the disadvantage that their success depended on the consent of all creditors, something that was not always forthcoming.[4] While compositions were undoubtedly popular, this weakness cautions us against exaggerating their importance. If a single creditor stood out against a composition, presumably because he felt he deserved to, and could, be paid in full, then the only way to get an equal distribution of the estate was by bankruptcy proceedings. In the early eighteenth century William Stout, the Lancaster grocer, described a case where a debtor persuaded two of his 'meanest creditters' not to comply with a composition. This obviously

put a stop to our proceeding by the assignment, to the great displeasure of most of the credditers. The principle of them were advised to sue out a commission of bankrupt against him, being there appeared no other way to keep effects together, or to get him at liberty to endeavour to retrieve. And upon which a comision was sued out, and such comisioners were named that we could confide in not to cause any more expense then

---

[1] W. Forsyth, *A treatise on the law relating to composition and arrangements with creditors* (3rd edn, London, 1854), pp. 1–4. See the example in J. A. S. L. Leighton-Boyce, *Smiths the bankers 1658–1958* (London, 1958), pp. 221–2.

[2] B. Montagu, *A summary of the law of compositions with creditors* (London, 1823), p. 39. Also see Defoe, *The complete English tradesman*, Letter XIII. See an example in K. H. Burley, 'An Essex clothier of the eighteenth century', *Economic History Review*, XI (1958–9), p. 290.

[3] J. Chitty, *A treatise on the laws of commerce and manufactures, and the contracts relating thereto*, 4 vols. (London, 1820–4), Vol. III, p. 688.

[4] See Historical Manuscripts Commission, *The manuscripts of the House of Lords*, Vol. II (New Series), *1695–1697* (London, 1903), p. 505. Forsyth, *A treatise on compositions*, p. 5.

was absolutly nessesary. And the same persons were appoynted assignees, to whom the effects were consigned by the aforesaid assignment.[5]

Even if compositions ran their course, it was still possible that fraud and deceit could take place, cheating creditors of what was rightfully theirs.[6]

Letters of licence, deeds of inspectorship and assignments were available to all and provided the mainstay of unofficial ways of dealing with insolvency and failure. However, their success depended fundamentally on the agreement of all a debtor's creditors which, because there were large grey areas making it impossible for businessmen to identify accurately the moments when a debtor became either temporarily or permanently insolvent (rather than when he was simply avoiding repayment), was often hard to achieve. It was often easier for creditors to move from haranguing their debtors for repayment to official forms of debt collection than for them to move from such cajoling to unofficial forms. Bankruptcy put all creditors upon an equal footing, allowed the bankrupt to be questioned closely about his estate and effects and had greater authority than any other form of debt collection available to private individuals.

There was a second significant, though limited, unofficial process for dealing with insolvency, constructed by the Quakers to deal with Friends who had failed. Like the law of bankruptcy, the Quakers believed that failure could result either from bad luck or from bad habits. But unlike the law, they took positive steps to root out fraud, questioning the morality with which the debts had been contracted. Under the dissenting discipline insolvency could be seen as breaking Paul's command to 'owe no man any thing'.[7] The Monthly Meetings of the Friends had to reply to the questions 'Are friends just in their dealings, and punctual in fulfilling their engagements? and are they advised carefully to inspect the state of their affairs once in the year?'[8] Where there was evidence of immorality and the good name of the Society was threatened, then the bankrupt Friend could be disowned. But expulsion was never automatic. So long as failure had resulted from mischance and so long as the insolvent showed due awareness of his folly, then membership of the Society continued.[9]

[5] [Stout,] *The autobiography of William Stout of Lancaster 1666–1752*, ed. J. D. Marshall (Manchester, 1967), pp. 156–7. On the breakdown of compositions see *Remarks on the late act of parliament to prevent frauds frequently committed by bankrupts* (London, 1707), p. 3. Also Public Record Office (hereafter P.R.O.), B3/2655, where attempts to deal with the failure of John Jackson, a merchant from Love Lane, London, by composition lasted two years before bankruptcy proceedings were taken out. Sheffield City Library Archives, TC 505-11.

[6] See for example *The diary of Thomas Turner*, p. 202.

[7] M. R. Watts, *The dissenters* (Oxford, 1978), Vol. I, p. 335.

[8] *Extracts from the minutes and advices of the yearly meeting of Friends held in London* (London, 1783), p. 196. See also E. D. Bebb, *Nonconformity and social and economic life 1660–1800* (London, 1935), pp. 65–6.

[9] I. Grubb, *Quakerism and industry before 1800* (London, 1930), p. 90. The records of the Society's Horselydown Monthly Meetings that I have examined at the London Friends Meeting

By and large then, while unofficial means of dealing with failure were superficially attractive they were of limited applicability. Official methods offered greater authority and more certainty. What though were the advantages and disadvantages of bankruptcy within the range of laws that existed to deal with indebtedness?

INDEBTEDNESS, INSOLVENCY AND THE LAW

During the eighteenth century, the law explicitly distinguished between degrees of indebtedness of businesses – small, medium and large – and implicitly distinguished between those businesses which had failed and were permanently insolvent and those who were just avoiding repayment. But those distinctions did not always mirror reality, so that a body of law was erected that was disunited, fractured and, in places, inconsistent. But although the law of bankruptcy did not deal with all those who failed and got caught up in the law it did deal with a significant and representative proportion of business failures.

Within the business world in eighteenth-century England, the law attempted to distinguish three sorts of debtor: the small debtor owing very little money; the insolvent debtor owing rather more; and finally, the bankrupt debtor who could never hope to pay off his fairly substantial debts in full. As well as representing a simple scale of indebtedness, this tripartite division also mirrored beliefs about the nature of credit arrangements. Legislation covering small debtors was applicable to the very base of society and economy, where debtor and creditor were everyday consumer and retailer respectively. The insolvent debtor laws – where, in fact, the debtor was assumed to be solvent – were meant to cover the debt–credit relations between retailers and small producers and distributors. Finally, bankruptcy was meant to apply to the top end of the debt hierarchy, to the shopkeepers, middlemen, merchants and manufacturers discussed in Chapter 1.

For small debts both the law and the creditor assumed that the debtor, far from having failed, was simply being bloody-minded and obstinate. The aim, therefore, was to give the creditor ready access to the property of the debtor, something that had to be quick and cheap to be worthwhile. Essentially, during the eighteenth century this increasingly came to be done in small debt courts known as Courts of Requests or Courts of Conscience. Between 1660 and 1846 around 400 such courts were created to hear pleas of debt, usually for sums of less than £5. These courts had geographically limited jurisdiction and were especially important in helping shopkeepers get payment. Naturally, they tended to spring up in the growing urban areas, where consumers were thick

House Library show both that failure among Quakers was not uncommon in the eighteenth century and that only a fraction of them were expelled.

on the ground. Dealing with individual debts they afforded a form of summary justice that was tailored to local conditions.[10]

The common feature of the procedure for recovery of small debts and those of insolvent debtors was that each creditor pursued his debt independently, without joining all the other creditors of the same debtor. Furthermore, the debtor was assumed to be recalcitrant rather than unable to pay and there was no discussion of failure. Statistics of its use would be of little help in charting the history of business collapses. So far as the law was concerned, all that was needed was more legal muscle behind the creditor to give an added twist to the arm of the debtor, already strained by threats and persuasion. For larger debts than those allowed for under the procedure for small debts the weight of the law was that much greater and took, broadly speaking, two forms. The creditor could proceed against the debtor's property. But the powers of the creditor were limited and easily avoided by cunning debtors. Secondly, a creditor could proceed against a debtor's body by moving to have him imprisoned. Once arrested, a debtor, or his friends and relations, could pay the amount demanded, put up bail or remain in prison on *mesne* process.[11] The law of insolvency assumed that the debtor could pay and that the way to ensure this was to menace him with the threat or the reality of imprisonment or to get legal judgement on his property. But if the debtor was obstinately strong willed, he could defeat all attempts to get at his property by keeping his front door firmly shut. Alternatively, he could lie in jail living off his property until it ran out, until he died (which would be sooner rather than later given the state of the prisons), until he yielded and gave it up, or, if his debts were large enough, until a creditor opened bankruptcy proceedings against him, or, finally, until parliament passed one of its periodic acts to empty the jails.

The law supposed that insolvent debtors had enough money to repay all their creditors. But this assumption was not always true, so that it was possible under the insolvent debtor laws for some creditors to be satisfied but not others. Those who began proceedings earliest would have the best chance of being

[10] W. H. D. Winder, 'The Courts of Requests', *Law Quarterly Review*, LII (1936), pp. 369–94. A. Harding, *A social history of English law* (Harmondsworth, 1966), p. 316. J. Hoppit, 'The use and abuse of credit in eighteenth-century England', in R. B. Outhwaite and N. McKendrick, eds., *Business life and public policy* (Cambridge, 1986), pp. 64–78. The Common Council of the Corporation of London, *The consideration by the court of the report from the committee appointed to enquire into the practice and fees of the Court of Requests* (London, 1774?).

[11] I. P. H. Duffy, 'Bankruptcy and insolvency in London in the late eighteenth and early nineteenth centuries' (University of Oxford D. Phil. thesis, 1973), Ch. 2. J. Innes, 'The Kings Bench prison in the later eighteenth century', in J. Brewer and J. Styles, eds., *An ungovernable people* (London, 1980), pp. 250–98, especially pp. 251–61. Lineham, Thesis. P. H. Haagen, 'Eighteenth-century English society and the debt law', in S. Cohen and A. Scull, eds., *Social control and the state* (Oxford, 1983), pp. 222–47. There is a large contemporary literature on the law of insolvency but perhaps the best is J. B. Burgess, *Considerations on the law of insolvency, with a proposal for reform* (London, 1783).

repaid. This, indeed, was one of the reasons why bankruptcy was initiated in the first place. As one sixteenth-century contemporary put it:

when any merchant or other, by loss of goods, by fortune of the sea, evil servants, evil debtors, by fire or otherwise, come to an afterdeal, and not able to pay his credit at due time, but by force of poverty is constrained to demand longer time – then you have a partial law in [the] making of attachments, first come, first served; so one or I shall be all paid, and the rest shall have nothing.[12]

This is one reason why the law of insolvency was unattractive to creditors when compared with bankruptcy, though there were others. Because creditors were allowed fairly easy means to imprison the debtor, the law was attacked on constitutional grounds – that creditors could be judges in their own cases – as well as practical ones – that the prisons were full of people rotting to death. Parliament dealt with these problems in the eighteenth century not by introducing comprehensive reforms, but by occasionally passing statutes to clear the jails. These clearances, however, failed to distinguish effectively the fraudulent from the honest debtor and so some felt 'That the Frequency of such Laws, tho' never so well design'd, tend to the Destruction of Credit and Trade' because they encouraged the rash or fraudulent contraction of debts.[13] On the other side, some imprisoned debtors rightly pointed out that 'A Prison can pay no Debts.'[14]

Compositions, the small debt courts and the law of insolvent debtors were the alternative processes to bankruptcy available to all creditors pursuing their debts.[15] Each had their positive sides just as each had their problems. What is clear is that bankruptcy was one of several ways in which creditors could try to enforce repayment. But bankruptcy was the only legally constituted method that put all creditors on an equal footing, forced the debtor to comply and acknowledged a permanent inability on his part to meet all his obligations. Clearly, it is not possible to believe that bankruptcy is a perfect indicator of business failure, but it is close enough. To judge the extent of its usefulness the virtues and vices of the law of bankruptcy itself have to be examined.

---

[12] Quoted in W. S. Holdsworth, *A history of English law*, 17 vols. (London, 1922–72), Vol. VIII, p. 232. Spelling modernised.

[13] *The case of the merchants and traders in and about the City of London*... (London, 1707?).

[14] *The case of the poor insolvent prisoners for debt, in the several gaols of this kingdom* (London, 1721?).

[15] The Crown and Crown debtors could use extents which offered considerable powers. But it seems that these became important on any scale only in the Napoleonic Wars. A good summary of the law of extents is E. West, *A treatise of the law and practice of extents in chief and in aid* (London, 1817). I discuss them a little more fully in 'Risk and failure in English industry, *c.* 1700–1800' (University of Cambridge Ph.D. thesis, 1984), pp. 15–16.

BANKRUPTCY AND THE LAW

For the bulk of the period under discussion the law of bankruptcy followed the lines established in 1706 during Anne's reign.[16] This new law was innovatory in several respects and reflected the significant changes of opinion about bankruptcy in the seventeenth century which were discussed in the last chapter.[17] But there were also short-term causes behind the new law: the warfare and consequent instability of overseas trade ushered in by the Glorious Revolution; the catastrophic winter of 1703 when the Thames froze over, shipping stopped and livestock was destroyed; the financial panic of 1701 associated with the Spanish succession and the battle between the old and the new East India Companies; and, finally, the massive fraudulent bankruptcy of Thomas Pitkin, a London linen draper.[18] This new law of 1706 was explained and altered a little in the next session of parliament as pleadings and petitions piled onto the table of the House of Commons. It was finally made permanent in 1732.[19] The original statute of 1706 was then the backbone of the eighteenth-century law of bankruptcy.[20]

In the eighteenth century, bankruptcy proceedings were always initiated by a creditor petitioning the Lord Chancellor. Debtors were meant to have no say in the matter and, indeed, it was not until the 1820s that voluntary bankruptcy was introduced. Clearly, the timing of events rested in the hands of creditors willing and able to make the effort and bear the immediate costs of opening a commission; and not all creditors reacted to similar circumstances in similar ways. Once the petition had been lodged, along with a bond of £200 to ensure

[16] 4 & 5 Anne, c. 17, An act to prevent frauds frequently committed by bankrupts.

[17] I. P. H. Duffy, 'English bankrupts, 1571–1861', *American Journal of Legal History*, XXIV (1980), pp. 285–6.

[18] W. R. Scott, *The constitution and finance of English, Scottish and Irish joint-stock companies to 1720*, 3 vols. (Cambridge, 1910–12), Vol. I, pp. 365–7. T. S. Ashton, *Economic fluctuations in England 1700–1800* (Oxford, 1959), p. 115. Pitkin raised £70,000 on credit which he conveyed to friends before he deliberately became bankrupt. On his case see *The case of the creditors of Thomas Pitkin* (London, 1706?). *The case of Mr Thomas Brerewood* (London, 1707?). *The case of the creditors of John Coggs, and John Dann, goldsmiths* (London, 1710?). Historical Manuscripts Commission, *The manuscripts of his grace the Duke of Portland*, 10 vols. (London, 1891–1931), Vol. IV, p. 167.

[19] The amendments came with 5 Anne, c. 2, An act to explain and amend an act of the last session of parliament for preventing of frauds frequently committed by bankrupts. The response to the earlier act can be gauged in the *Journal of the House of Commons* and a wide body of pamphlet literature. The law of 1732 was 5 Geo. II, c. 30, An act to prevent the committing of frauds by bankrupts.

[20] The following discussion is based on my reading of the statutes and contemporary literature dealing with bankruptcy. The eighteenth-century law is outlined in S. Marriner, 'English bankruptcy records and statistics before 1850', *Economic History Review*, XXXIII (1980), pp. 351–66. Duffy, 'English bankrupts'. Duffy, Thesis, Ch. 1. Holdsworth, *History of English law*. F. J. J. Cadwallader, 'In pursuit of the merchant debtor and bankrupt: 1066–1732' (University of London Ph.D. thesis, 1965).

against a malicious petition, the Lord Chancellor opened a Commission of Bankruptcy to see whether the debtor was indeed a bankrupt. It was the commissioners who decided whether and how to proceed and who provided the coordination and authority for each case. Petitions against a firm led to a commission against the collective trading of its partners. But a petition might be directed at one individual partner of a firm and not the others, so long as he traded on his own.

The Lord Chancellor directed each case to a group of five commissioners, although only three of them had to sit to be quorate. In London, which provided many bankrupts, there were permanent lists of commissioners (thirteen by 1800). But when both the debtor and his creditors came from outside the capital there were no lists and the commissioners would be nominated by the Lord Chancellor. Often these were barristers or solicitors coming from the same district as the bankrupt and his creditors. Once they had decided the debtor was a bankrupt, which was true in four out of five instances, then the substantive work of the commission could get under way. They had to satisfy themselves that the debtor under discussion met three requirements before they declared him a bankrupt. First, that he was a 'trader', one who made his living by buying and selling. Second, that he owed debts of at least £100 to one creditor, £150 to two or £200 to three or more. Finally, that he had committed an act of bankruptcy, which amounted to the unreasonable evasion of his creditors' just demands for repayment. An act of bankruptcy was, in fact, the law's attempt to identify failure. Only when these three conditions had been met and the commissioners had made their declaration can we properly speak of the debtor as a bankrupt in the eighteenth-century legal sense of the word. If they were not, then the creditor would have to pursue his debt using one of the alternative routes already mentioned. In the eighteenth century, therefore, bankruptcy was a process only applicable to some debtors, even if the word also had a more common meaning such as 'A man in debt beyond the power of payment'.[21] In commercial circles, however, there is no doubt that the legal definition was recognised and employed.[22]

When the commissioners made their declaration of bankruptcy they notified the bankrupt – who, incidentally, was not able to defend himself up to this point – by placing an advertisement in the *London Gazette*, ordering him to surrender himself and his property. His house would be searched and his immediate effects seized. A meeting of the creditors would then be arranged and assignees, the administrators and collectors of the bankrupt's property, would be elected, usually from among their own number.

[21] S. Johnson, *A dictionary of the English language* (London, 1755; reprinted London, 1979).
[22] See M. Postlethwayt, *The universal dictionary of trade and commerce*, 2 vols. (London, 1757), Vol. I, p. 202.

As creditors proved their debts before the commissioners so the assignees collected, valued and sold the bankrupt's estate. However, this could be a protracted business, especially where there were some intricate property rights to unravel or assets dispersed overseas to be drawn in. But once the money had been collected and the debts proved a division of the proceeds could be made among the creditors. Each would be paid at the same rate, so much in the pound on what they were owed. Usually, the collection of the estate would take some time and it was normal for there to be two or three dividends.

Finally, if the bankrupt had been forthcoming in the disclosure of his effects, he would be granted a certificate of conformity so long as this gained the approval of four-fifths of the creditors by number and value. This released him from any liability for any debts contracted up to the act of bankruptcy. And as long as the estate had realised 8 shillings in the pound then he also received 5 per cent of the realised estate, provided this did not exceed £200.[23] With that, the bankrupt was freed from his past and left to start life anew.

Such then is the bald and rather cold outline of bankruptcy in the eighteenth century – as an administrative mechanism implementing a set of rules and definitions. But it is the idealised picture its protagonists might have painted and ignores the problems that existed. These centred on the administration of the law.

PROBLEMS OF THE LAW OF BANKRUPTCY

The administration of the law depended on two groups, the commissioners and the assignees, and the way they did their job fundamentally determined the success of any commission. Both groups came under increasing fire in the early nineteenth century and investigations into the law at that time provide much of the evidence for the following discussion. It cannot be assumed, however, that the failings uncovered then were true for the whole of the eighteenth century as well.[24]

The commissioners, who apart from deciding on whether a debtor was a bankrupt also timetabled events and made decisions on points of law, were criticised on several fronts. First, there was a general charge of inefficiency because, it was argued, though they were meant to be barristers, they were not paid the professional rate for such men. So, they were either young, lively and inexperienced or old, pedestrian and experienced. Another criticism suggested that their low, piece-rate pay made them cut corners and fail to take due care

---

[23] The allowances were made more attractive still in 1732, 5 Geo. II, c. 30. If 12s 6d in the pound was realised then the bankrupt was allowed 7.5 per cent; if 15s in the pound then 10 per cent.

[24] E. Welbourne, 'Bankruptcy before the era of Victorian reform', *Cambridge Historical Journal*, IV (1932), pp. 51–62, provides an examination of some of the eccentricities of the law's administration.

and attention over each case. The more cases they heard per sitting the more they were paid.[25] Thirdly, it was said that because only three out of the five commissioners appointed to each case need sit at any one meeting, there was little continuity of personnel over the various sittings of any one case. In London, all these issues were compounded towards the end of the century because of alleged overcrowding at the Guildhall where the commissioners met.[26] As Edward Christian, himself a commissioner, put it in 1816,

This produces such confusion, that the crowds round the tables resemble more the rabble round the stalls at Smithfield, than an assemblage of persons interested in the decent and orderly administration of justice. Yet more property is probably disposed of in the course of a year by the commissioners of bankrupts, than in all the courts in Westminster Hall...[27]

Although this problem did not exist in the country there were others. In 1801 the Lord Chancellor thought that for country commissions at least, 'nothing is less thought of than the objects of the commission. As they are frequently conducted in the country, they are little more than stock in trade for the commissioners, the assignees and solicitor.'[28] Yet many of these problems concerning the commissioners, it should be stressed, became acute only towards the very end of the eighteenth century when the volume of bankruptcy began to put a terrible strain on the system. Nevertheless, such problems must have dampened enthusiasm for the law to some extent.

Much the same was true of the assignees. They were usually chosen at the first general meeting of the creditors and commissioners by those creditors who had proved their debts. Because that meeting took place within a fortnight or so of the declaration of bankruptcy some creditors remained ignorant of the very existence of the commission. Others would have been unable to attend that first meeting. Consequently, the assignees could be chosen by an unrepresentative selection of the creditors. This could be serious when the commission had been pre-arranged by the debtor to minimise his losses, as he could pack the

[25] *Observations and proposals most humbly offered to the parliament by several creditors, merchants and traders of London, relating to the bill now depending concerning bankrupts* (London, 1719?).

[26] A special building for bankruptcy was not set aside until 1821. 1 & 2 Geo. IV. c. 115, An act to repeal so much of an act...as requires the meeting under commissioners of bankrupt to be holden in the Guildhall... For some of these criticisms of the commissioners see B. Montagu, *Inquiries respecting the courts of commissioners of bankrupts, and Lord Chancellor's courts* (London, 1825), and *Parliamentary papers*, 1817, Vol. v, *Report from the select committee on the bankrupt laws* and *Parliamentary papers, Select committee* 1818.

[27] *Practical instructions for suing out and prosecuting a commission of bankrupt* (London, 1816), p. 171. See also the evidence of W. Stevens and H. Pages in *Parliamentary papers, Select committee* 1817 as well as the same committee's report the following year.

[28] Quoted in *Parliamentary papers, Select committee* 1818, pp. 8–9.

first meeting with fictitious creditors who would choose compliant assignees.[29] Beyond this, assuming that the assignees were honest, the job was far from easy. They undertook the hard work of the commission, attempting to recover property, realise assets and call in debts owed to the bankrupts. On occasions it could take years to unravel the mess, even if it was an intermittent responsibility. Clearly, the mess would tend to increase with the size of the failure. For example, the firm of John Abraham of Houndsditch, London, warehouseman, failed in November 1796 with debts totalling £65,000. His assignees were still trying to complete the collection of the sprawling estate ten years later.[30] Occasionally, assignees would give up the search after a while only to be pressed for renewed action by other creditors. Because of the time that could be involved in collecting the estate, large amounts of unclaimed dividends always rested with the Bank of England, awaiting claimants who had long since died or ceased to worry about repayment. Other mishaps could assault assignees, such as quarrelling with the creditors or failing themselves.[31] The price to be paid for such difficulties was that many creditors avoided becoming assignees. As one witness reported to the Select Committee in 1817, 'I would almost, myself, lose my debt rather than have the trouble of being an assignee.'[32]

It was equally the case that assignees could only be as good as the bankrupt's evidence, books and estate allowed. Some of the estate might have been deliberately concealed, though more usual and difficult was the unintentional concealment caused by the notoriously bad condition of most bankrupts' accounts. A wide body of opinion blamed a bankrupt's position on bad bookkeeping: 'generally speaking, bankruptcies originate in confusion of accounts'.[33] Defoe put it more colourfully when he wrote that

a sinking tradesman cares not to look into his books, because the prospect there is dark and melancholy; what signify the accounts to me? says he, I can see nothing in the books but debts, that I cannot pay, and debtors, that will never pay me.[34]

Even if commissioners and assignees were honest, conscientious and efficient, producing considerable income from the bankrupt's estate, the commission could still be expensive. In the first place, a bond for £200 had to be submitted to the Lord Chancellor when proceedings were initiated to ensure that it had

---

[29] See the example in P.R.O., Chancery Masters Exhibit, C110/153, case of John Merry, a bankrupt London merchant. He was bankrupt in 1734 but in the 1740s a case was brought against his assignees for fraud and negligence.

[30] P.R.O., B3/1.

[31] This happened in the case of a partnership of hosiers from Great St Helens, London: they were bankrupt in April 1778 and their assignees in January 1782. P.R.O., B3/812.

[32] *Parliamentary papers, Select committee* 1817, p. 90.

[33] Ibid., p. 116.   [34] Defoe, *The complete English tradesman*, pp. 342–3.

not been done maliciously. Then there were the petitioning creditor's legal fees to get a commission under way (though these would be repaid). Finally, the cost of administering a commission ate into the estate leaving less for the final dividend each time the commissioners met.[35] It is not surprising that there should have been periodic complaints that the cost of commissions cut the potential dividend by half.

The administration of the law of bankruptcy could sometimes be long drawn out and expensive; usually, though, it worked somewhat better than that. But all this helped to deter some creditors from using it. It might be expected that only where the estate was relatively large and complicated, where the authority of bankruptcy was necessary and where creditors saw that the debtor had failed, would a commission be called upon by creditors. Equally though, in smaller cases there would be fewer complications, fewer creditors and less to administer, making bankruptcy quite attractive. But the possibility exists that the problems of the law's administration added to the gap between the 'real' level of bankruptcy and that which was prosecuted under a commission.

Bankruptcy was a particular process within a broader body of laws that attempted to give creditors more power to collect their debts than any alternative. It particularity arose from its authority, from the three limitations that defined its scope and from the fact that it put all of a debtor's creditors on an equal footing. It made these creditors work in harmony with one another not, as was true of the small debt and insolvent debtor laws, in conflict. The rateable division of a bankrupt's estate was a critical characteristic which defined bankruptcy and distinguished it from all other official modes of debt collection.[36]

It was up to creditors to decide which process they would use and to determine to what extent bankruptcy met their needs. Before calling on any law creditors might attempt arbitrations and informal methods of debt collection. Using the law came at the end of attempts to enforce repayment by threats and arbitration.[37] Imprisonment for debt, for example, may have existed as something to worry a debtor with, but it was not always used willingly. As Thomas Turner, a Sussex shopkeeper, remarked in 1758,

[35] Some early-nineteenth-century estimates of the costs of a commission are made in the evidence of W. Spurrier, a Birmingham solicitor, in *Parliamentary papers, Select committee* 1817, p. 76. See also Christian, *Practical instructions*, pp. 166–9. And for the eighteenth century, *Considerations upon commissions of bankrupts* (London, 1727), p. 7, which put the costs at £60 over and above the initial fees.

[36] For a discussion of these principles, for both England and elsewhere, see L. E. Levinthal, 'The early history of bankruptcy law', *University of Pennsylvania Law Review*, LXVI (1918), pp. 223–50.

[37] See the example in *Joshua Johnson's letterbook, 1771–1774*, ed. J. M. Price, (London, 1979), pp. 90 and 93.

as soon I had breakfasted I set out for Lewes in order to commit the management of the debt due from Master Darby to me into the hands of Mr Rideout [a solicitor]... Oh, what a confusion and tumult there is in my breast about this affair! To think what a terrible thing it is to arrest a person, for by this means he may be entirely torn to pieces ...But then on the other hand...some of this debt hath been standing above 4 years...[38]

Such thoughts must have been commonplace, and further up the business ladder similar calculations had to be made. Every businessman had to weigh up the costs of the various alternative ways of getting repayment against rough estimates of the sort of return that might be expected. Debt collection was indeed akin to an investment. Moreover, like Turner, each creditor chasing his debt by using bankruptcy made a moral as well as a financial decision.

There were three main reasons why the business community might use bankruptcy against a failed debtor rather than any other means, once all the normal pressure and cajoling had been attempted. First, because it existed as a body of established procedures and administration that was widely understood and gave greater authority than any other process. Second, because compositions had been attempted but had broken down. Finally, because the insolvent debtor or small debt laws were being utilised by another creditor. This last reason was particularly acute when creditors were geographically dispersed and likely to act independently and against their mutual overall interest. If one of them imprisoned a debtor or took out an action against him, then another creditor might well have initiated bankruptcy proceedings to forestall any unequal distribution of the estate. Bankruptcy was used because it treated all creditors alike and gave full access to a debtor's estate. No other process, official or informal, was as certain on either point.

All in all, recourse to bankruptcy was not a simple decision. Other forms of action and inaction had to be considered. But the strength and fairness of bankruptcy recommended it to eighteenth-century businessmen. It was a tool tailored to their needs because of the three requirements that any debtor had to meet to be dealt with as a bankrupt. Consequently, bankruptcy would seem to offer a good chance of arriving at a fair sample of business failure in the eighteenth century. It may not have been the same as failure, but it was close enough.

[38] *The diary of Thomas Turner*, p. 149.

4
*

THE TREND OF
EIGHTEENTH-CENTURY BANKRUPTCY

During the eighteenth century some 33,000 businesses went bankrupt.[1] More than this number failed of course, but this many found themselves enmeshed in the law of bankruptcy just described. But what does this figure tell us about eighteenth-century enterprise and is it a large or a small total? This and the following four chapters look at changes in the numbers of bankrupts between periods, regions and occupations in an attempt to sketch the pattern of failure, to suggest some broad causes and to indicate its significance.

This chapter has two aims: to outline the ways in which data about bankruptcy were collected and adjusted and, secondly, to examine trend levels of bankruptcy in relation to trend developments within the economy as a whole. The second objective is in fact novel because earlier economic historians have invariably limited their use of bankruptcy to studies of short-term fluctuations rather than long-term developments. High levels of bankruptcy have usually been equated with depression, low levels with prosperity.[2] Over the short run, this equation is true, but over the long run, it is not. If anything, in the eighteenth century prosperity over the long term bred higher levels and rates of bankruptcy.

One of the main reasons why bankruptcy has been little used as an economic indicator by historians is because of the manifest problems in finding a reliable

---

[1] This figure is for England and Wales, though very few came from Wales. Scotland was dealt with by its own law and administration.

[2] G. Chalmers, *An estimate of the comparative strength of Great Britain* (London, 1794), pp. xlff. J. Sinclair, *The history of the public revenue of the British empire*, 3 vols. (London, 1803), Vol. II, Appendix VI. D. Macpherson, *Annals of commerce*, 4 vols. (London, 1805). N. J. Silberling, 'British prices and business cycles, 1779–1850', *Review of Economic Statistics*, V Supplement 2 (1923). T. S. Ashton, *An economic history of England: the eighteenth century* (London, 1955), Table XVI. Ashton, *Fluctuations*. A. D. Gayer, W. W. Rostow and A. J. Schwartz, *The growth and fluctuation of the British economy 1790–1850*, 2 vols. (Oxford, 1953). W. Beveridge, 'The trade cycle in Britain before 1850', *Oxford Economic Papers*, III (1940), pp. 74–109. W. G. Hoffman, *British industry 1700–1950* (Oxford, 1955).

data series. The various figures produced by the authors listed in footnote 2 are rarely consistent with one another. Mitchell and Deane ruefully drew attention to the fact that 'there are wide differences between the figures quoted... and random checks in the original source produced yet more different figures'.[3] The root of the problem has been an unwillingness to go to the commissioners' declarations of bankruptcy in the *London Gazette*, largely because the extraction of the relevant information is so time consuming.[4] Fortunately, a second source, the so-called Docket Books, include all the bankrupts listed in the *London Gazette*.[5] These two sources form the core of evidence used in much of this book.

To Chalmers, the *London Gazette* was 'that melancholy chronicle of our commercial failings'.[6] With characteristic verve E. P. Thompson wrote that 'the *London Gazettes* lie, like so many bi-weekly lobster traps, on the sea-bottom of Namier's England, catching many curious literary creatures which never, in normal circumstances, break the bland surface of the waters of eighteenth-century historiography'.[7] It was during the 1680s that it began regularly to list bankrupts, but these notifications offer only summary details, such as the names, occupations and addresses of the unfortunates. They give no hints as to the cause of failure. Using this source, therefore, it is possible to analyse information about the chronology, geography and occupation of eighteenth-century bankrupts but difficult to find the precise causes of failure. Indeed, among other sources direct evidence on the causes of bankruptcy is virtually non-existent. Bankrupts were never required to explain how they had fallen into the abyss of failure. However, by accurately describing the patterns of bankruptcy, by linking those patterns to our understanding of the eighteenth-century economy and by calling on contemporary perceptions it should be possible to identify indirectly the main causes involved.

Unfortunately, the *London Gazette* is not an easy source to use before about 1760, mainly because of the difficulties of avoiding double counting. Fortunately, before that date the Docket Books give a viable alternative, as they provide similar information to that in the *Gazette*. Beginning in 1710, they

---

[3] B. R. Mitchell and P. Deane, *Abstract of British historical statistics* (Cambridge, 1962), p. 245. See Marriner, 'English bankruptcy records', and Duffy, Thesis, Appendix II, on this point.

[4] Historians have often relied on the inaccurate second-hand listings in publications such as the *Gentleman's Magazine*; W. Bailey, *List of bankrupts 1772–1793* (London, 1794); W. Smith & Co., *A list of bankrupts...1786–1806* (London, 1806).

[5] The Docket Books are held at the P.R.O., B4. The Docket Books have occasionally been used by historians looking at particular areas of the eighteenth-century economy. J. M. Price, *Capital and credit in British overseas trade: the view from the Chesapeake, 1700–1776* (Cambridge, Mass., 1980), pp. 132–3. J. Feather, *The provincial book trade in eighteenth-century England* (Cambridge, 1985), pp. 30, 93–6.

[6] *An estimate*, p. xli.

[7] 'The crime of anonymity', in D. Hay *et al.*, *Albion's fatal tree* (London, 1975), p. 257.

continue, with a break of seventeen months in 1723–4, through to 1764 when their character changed significantly. The Docket Books not only provide information about the bankrupt; they also provide some details of petitioning creditors, additional information that is examined in Chapter 9. The *London Gazette* has been used for the two periods 1688–1710 and 1765–1800 and the Docket Books for the middle period.[8] But these sources, particularly the Docket Books, cannot be used uncritically. An entry was made in the Docket Books in response to a creditor's petition to have his debtor declared a bankrupt. But not all debtors were declared bankrupt by the commissioners. First, some of them failed to satisfy the three requirements outlined in the last chapter. Second, some dockets were struck as threats against debtors, to coax repayment rather than initiate a genuine attempt to get a declaration of bankruptcy. In 1776, for example, William Walton, a maltster from Hathersage in Derbyshire, must have felt his pulse race when he read this letter from Nathaniel Milnes of London:

I write this Letter to inform you that I have a Commission of Bankrupt in my Hands against you... This commission will be executed on Monday next at Chapel-en-le-Frith. Mr Marshall being desirous of giving you an opportunity of yet settling the matter if you or any of your ffriends pay him his demand with the costs of the commission et[c.] between [now] and Monday Noon, the execution of it will be stop'd, otherwise it will be proceeded in.[9]

Although such threats may have been made in response to real economic pressures, the fact is that some dockets did not lead to an advertisement in the *Gazette*, making the figures in the Docket Books too high.[10] For an occupational and geographical analysis, where proportions rather than totals are being used, this inflation hardly matters. However, it does matter for an analysis of total figures through the century and it is necessary to deflate the totals drawn from the Docket Books. Over the period 1771 to 1800, 73 per cent of dockets struck led to appearance in the *London Gazette*.[11] Using Ashton's data, it is also possible to compare the lists of bankrupts gazetted according to the *Gentleman's Magazine* with the dockets struck for the period 1732–64. Here the proportion was higher at 84 per cent. In what follows, I have used a compromise weighting of 79 per cent. This then allows the divides of 1710/11 and 1764/5 to be crossed, enabling us to make direct comparisons through the period.[12]

---

8 All discussion of numbers and proportions of bankrupts comes from these two sources and will not be cited hereafter.
9 Sheffield City Library Archives, Tibbitts Collection, TC 505-13.
10 There is no evidence that the inflation was geographically or occupationally specific.
11 After 1770 the Docket Books record total numbers of dockets struck but not geographical and occupational details.
12 A fuller discussion of the data can be found in my Thesis, pp. 43–8.

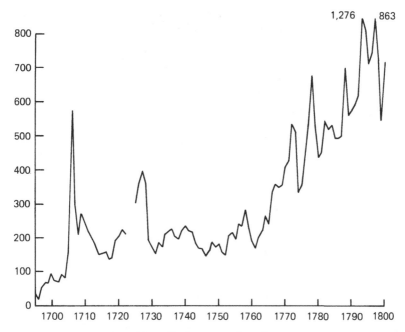

Fig. 1 Bankruptcy, 1695–1800
Note: No data available for 1723 III to 1724 IV.

THE TREND OF BANKRUPTCY

The adjusted data just described are presented in Figure 1, in summary form in Table 1 and in detail, alongside the raw data, in Appendix 1. Like any time series, the bankruptcy totals can be described in terms of trend movements and fluctuations about that trend. The trend of the annual totals charted in Figure 1 is clear enough, even allowing for the occasional marked peak and less noticeable trough. In Table 1, though, the trend is picked out by using annual decennial averages, though this is hardly more than a rough guide.

In the first place, it is clear that the change in the law in 1706 did see bankruptcy come of age as an economic indicator. Before then bankruptcy totals were too small to bear the weight of detailed interpretation. Equally clearly, short-run peaks in the bankruptcy totals can give a slightly misleading appearance to the broad trend movements presented in Table 1, as in the decades 1701–10 and 1721–30.[13] Nevertheless, superficially it appears as if eighteenth-century bankruptcy totals followed the course run by the rapid-growth model of the economy that was described at the start of Chapter 1.

[13] This warning has to be kept in mind whenever decennial averages are used.

Table 1. *Annual decennial averages of
bankruptcy, 1691–1800*

Decade	Average number of bankruptcies
1691–1700	44.9
1701–1710	207.1
1711–1720	174.2
1721–1730	278.1
1731–1740	204.2
1741–1750	181.0
1751–1760	210.2
1761–1770	291.9
1771–1780	478.0
1781–1790	539.4
1791–1800	762.7

Source: London Gazette; P.R.O., B4/1–20.

Numbers of bankrupts were relatively low and steady through the first half of the century, before rising very steeply and continuously thereafter. Arguably, 1750 marks the end of an old trend and the beginning of a new one – though 1761 also contests that honour. But this simple division into two trends is not quite as it seems.

One of the strengths of the bankruptcy totals is that after 1706 they were generated within an unchanged legal framework, a constancy that allows year-by-year comparisons through the period. Although this is a source of strength it is also a source of weakness, because inflation in the second half of the century would have meant that, in real terms, the financial specification attached to bankruptcy became easier for traders to meet.[14] After 1750 many prices rose, especially for food and housing, as population pressure mounted. Part of the rise in the number of bankrupts after 1750, therefore, may be attributable to the widening scope of bankruptcy caused by such inflation. Deflating the bankruptcy totals by employing the Schumpeter–Gilboy index suggests that, although in absolute terms the numbers of bankrupts rose by 268 per cent between the first and last decade of the century, in real terms the rise was about 168 per cent.[15] But this calculation is uncertain, not only because choosing the

[14] Debtors had to owe at least £100 to be classed as bankrupts.
[15] I have used an average of the consumers' goods and producers' goods indices. The data are conveniently accessible in Mitchell and Deane, *Abstract*, pp. 468–9.

right deflator is difficult but, also, because it is hard to prove or disprove the assumption that variations in the price level did have direct effects on the scope of bankruptcy among the business community. Arguably, bankrupt business-men were engaged in areas of activity where the prices of the commodities they dealt with lagged behind the rise in prices of food and rent. Given this, the suggested real increase of 168 per cent in the numbers of bankrupts across the century should probably be viewed as a low-bound estimate. In real terms, a tripling of the incidence of bankruptcy seems likely.

Here, a crucial distinction must be introduced between the frequency of bankruptcy and the rate of bankruptcy. Bankruptcy totals, rather like burial totals, can be useful in themselves, but they become much more persuasive when placed in the context of the available population at risk. It is much more interesting and significant to know that the rate of bankruptcy went up or down over the century than to know that its frequency roughly trebled. However, calculating the population of businesses at risk is fraught with difficulties. There were no industrial censuses in the eighteenth century; the national trade directories compiled during the last two decades of the century were inaccurate; and there is no taxation material that covers the whole business world. But some tentative suggestions of the rate of growth of the business community and its actual size can be squeezed from indirect evidence. In Chapters 5 and 6, more direct evidence about the size of the business community within particular areas is presented.

Among the indirect sources is population. Recently, our knowledge of the size of England's population has been vastly improved by the work of Wrigley, Schofield and the Cambridge Group. Assuming that the number of businesses grew at the same rate as population (a big 'if' that is discussed later) the business community grew by 58 per cent over the century, using annual decennial averages for the first and last decades.[16] This is well below the increase of 168 per cent in the numbers of bankrupts. Weighting the rise in the number of bankrupts by the population growth suggests that there was a real rise in the rate of bankruptcy of 77 per cent in the eighteenth century. Clearly, if popula-tion is accepted as a reasonable surrogate measure of the size of the business community at risk, then the rate of bankruptcy rose very significantly. Of course, it tells us nothing about what the rate of bankruptcy actually was and it improbably assumes that the business and non-business worlds grew at the same rate in eighteenth-century England. In fact, we know that England was more industrial and commercial in 1800 than it had been a hundred years before. Even so, the rise in the rate of bankruptcy seems large.

A second indirect route into the territory of rates of failure is via national

[16] E. A. Wrigley and R. S. Schofield, *The population history of England 1541–1871* (London, 1981), pp. 533–4.

income data. Here evidence is very scanty and fragile. Recently, however, considerable efforts have been made to improve on the pioneering efforts of Deane and Cole in this area. In particular, the social tables of King, Massie and Colquhoun have been adjusted, new output data have become available for some industries and, finally, there have been new estimates of sectoral shares within the whole economy.[17] What these improvements show is that the economy grew more slowly and more consistently through the eighteenth century than had previously been thought, not least because it started from a higher point. But, as Crafts points out, available 'estimates of economic growth prior to the mid-nineteenth century for Britain are bound to be in the nature of controlled conjectures rather than definitive evidence'.[18] Indeed, he resolutely refuses to provide his own figures for gross domestic product or national income. Presumably, however, he would broadly accept those produced by Lindert and Williamson. Using King's guesses for 1688 and Colquhoun's for 1801–3 and 1812, they estimated that in current prices national income rose from £54.44m to £198.58m. Translating this into constant prices is fraught with problems, but by employing the same indices used earlier to deflate the bankruptcy series, in late-seventeenth-century prices national income rose from £54.44m to £144.81m, an increase of 166 per cent. Remembering that this relates to a period of 113 years it is better to compare the annual growth rate with the bankruptcy material. National income grew by 0.87 per cent per annum, while numbers of bankrupts grew by 1.15 per cent per annum.[19] Once again, therefore, the rise in the number of bankrupts was well ahead of this surrogate measure of the development of the business community, pointing to an increasing rate of failure as the economy grew.

Yet it might, as with population, legitimately be complained that national income in the aggregate is a poor rough measure of the size of the business community and that it would be better to concentrate on the non-agrarian component of it. This has been done by Harley who, by dividing the economy between agriculture, industry and services, calculated that their respective annual growth rates between 1700 and 1815 were 0.6, 1.07 and 0.9 per cent per annum.[20] Crafts has further developed data on sectoral growth rates. These are presented in Table 2 alongside estimates of growth rates of bankruptcy. Before

---

[17] Deane and Cole, *British economic growth*. P. H. Lindert and J. G. Williamson, 'Revising England's social tables 1688–1812', *Explorations in Economic History*, XIX (1982), pp. 385–408. It is important to see their 'Errata' in *Explorations in Economic History*, XX (1983), pp. 329–30. Crafts, *British economic growth*, Ch. 2. Harley, 'British industrialization before 1841'.

[18] *British economic growth*, p. 9.

[19] I have calculated the growth rate of bankruptcy over a 90-year period by using annual decennial averages for 1701–10 and 1791–1800. If the rate is calculated over 100 years the rate drops to 1.03 per cent per annum.

[20] 'British industrialization before 1841', p. 286.

Table 2. *Rates of growth of industry, commerce and bankruptcy, 1700–1801*

	Industry	Commerce	Industry and commerce	Bankruptcy
1700–60	0.71	0.69	0.70	0.21
1760–80	1.51	0.70	1.05	3.55
1780–1801	2.11	1.32	1.81	1.08

Source: Crafts, *British economic growth*, p. 32; *London Gazette*; P.R.O., B4/1–20.

discussing the implications of this table it is worth emphasising the problems behind the bankruptcy figures. First, the annual growth rates given in the table must include a wide margin of error because of the difficulties of deflating the bankruptcy totals by realistic price weights. Second, the turning points of 1760, 1780 and 1801 are difficult to manage because they were war years, when we would expect bankruptcy totals to be high in any event. Still, Table 2, even allowing for errors, is very suggestive. There is an indication that over the first half of the eighteenth century rates of bankruptcy may well have fallen. This period was followed by one, coinciding with early industrialisation, when rates of bankruptcy rose very sharply. Finally, the rate of bankruptcy may have dropped slowly over the last twenty years of the century.

Given the particular difficulty that surrounds 1780 in calculating bankruptcy growth rates it is safer to split the eighteenth century once at 1760, rather than twice.[21] Crafts himself believed that 'In many ways I would have preferred to leave 1760–1801 as an undivided period.'[22] Using 1760 as a divide shows that the number of bankrupts rose in real terms at 0.21 per cent per annum, 1701–10 to 1756–65, but by 2.64 per cent per annum between 1756–65 and 1791–1800. All in all, using national income data, the weight of existing evidence strongly suggests that rates of bankruptcy fell slightly before the onset of the early Industrial Revolution, but rose significantly during it.

It might be wise to stop and consider the assumption that population and national income data provide a meaningful guide to changes in the size of the business population in the eighteenth century. Coming to a firm conclusion on this is not easy because historians have not considered, and have not been able to consider, whether businesses grew or shrank in size during the period – defining size to mean gross turnover. Working from first principles, however, it seems likely that the number of firms increased more slowly than either

[21] Because the American War of Independence had a greater impact than the Seven Years War.   [22] *British economic growth*, p. 46.

population or national income. After all, eighteenth-century England. experienced real growth, a growth that is of both output and productivity. Even if many areas of the economy did not enjoy large productivity advances in terms of the division of labour and scale economies, there were modernizing sectors like cotton, wool, iron and transport which did.[23] Productivity gains rested on more than new technology and the so-called 'wave of gadgets'. Growth of market size led to extensions of the division of labour and the creation of potential scale economies both within and without the firm. Consequently, some firms reorganised and grew in size, especially where there was technological development as well. In other words, at least a part of the growth of the economy over the eighteenth century came not from a proportionate increase in the number of firms but from a growth in the size of firms. Whether on average all firms became bigger is impossible to tell. But reinforcing this line of discussion would be a second point, stressing that the rising threshold of entry into business over the century made the business world more exclusive and the average firm larger, though these tendencies varied from industry to industry. It could well be that as some industries became more capital intensive and demanded more skills in terms of labour management, marketing and technological awareness, entry into those industries became progressively more difficult and restricted. Certainly, it cannot be assumed that thresholds of entry were static and in Chapter 6 some of the interesting distinctions which have to be made on this point are discussed. Although it is certainly true that in 1800 the cotton industry was far from being an exclusive sector, in which new entrants needed large amounts of money and brains, it would be wrong to think that there were no thresholds involved.[24] In all likelihood, the growth in the number of firms did lag behind the growth of population and national income. If this is right, it adds further credence to the earlier observations of a rising rate of bankruptcy during the early Industrial Revolution.[25]

So far, rates of bankruptcy in the eighteenth century have not been calculated. It has simply been shown when they may have been going up or down. But Colquhoun's social table provides some details which make a rough calculation of a bankruptcy rate in 1800 possible. Taking his commercial and industrial

---

[23] Crafts, *British economic growth*, pp. 81–7.

[24] R. Lloyd-Jones and A. A. Le Roux, 'The size of firms in the cotton industry: Manchester 1815–41', *Economic History Review*, XXXIII (1980), pp. 72–82.

[25] Little has been written about the size of firms in the eighteenth century and the discussion must remain theoretical and inconclusive. See, however, L. Hannah, *The rise of the corporate economy* (London, 1976), pp. 8–11. S. Pollard, *The genesis of modern management* (London, 1965), pp. 9–24. E. P. Duggan, 'Industrialization and the development of urban business communities: research problems, sources and techniques', *Local Historian*, XI (1975), pp. 457–65, especially p. 458, puts the opposite case to that which I have offered. R. G. Wilson, *Gentlemen merchants* (Manchester, 1971), p. 19, feels that firms did grow in size as the economy developed.

categories together and excluding those who seem unlikely to have been tradesmen within the scope of the bankruptcy laws, there were about 200,300 families
who might have gone bankrupt.[26] The annual average number of bankrupts
over the ten years 1791–1800 was 763, which means that about one out of every
263 businesses went bankrupt in any one year at the end of the century. A
similar calculation can be made for 1759 using Massie's work, though it is more
difficult because the categories he employed are less satisfactory for the task in
hand. However, by making some guesses it is possible that there were 135,000
businesses at risk in 1759. With the number of bankrupts averaging 224 over
the period 1756–65, the bankruptcy rate was about one in 605 per annum.[27]
Unfortunately, Gregory King's arithmetic is not at all amenable to these sorts
of attempts. And although much reliance cannot be put on the rates of bankruptcy just calculated, when they are taken in conjunction with the earlier
evidence of rising rates of failure after 1760 they help to confirm the picture
which has tentatively been drawn. It needs to be remembered, of course, that
the *failure* rates were higher than these *bankruptcy* rates because only a portion
of insolvents were dealt with as bankrupts. What is clear, however, is that failure
was not a rare phenomenon and that during the last third of the eighteenth
century, just when the early stirrings of industrialisation were being felt, rates
of bankruptcy increased significantly.

BANKRUPTCY AND LONG-TERM ECONOMIC DEVELOPMENT

Before the revisions of Crafts and other scholars, Figure 1 could have been held
to chart a course commonly used to characterise quantitatively the growth of
the economy as a whole. Now, however, it seems as if the growth in the number
of bankrupts after mid century outpaced developments in most other areas.
Before the middle of the century, the number of bankrupts stagnated and the
rate may have fallen. As the economy expanded and drifted into early industrialisation bankruptcy became not less of a threat, but more of one. This has
important implications for our understanding of the nature of business enterprise, risks and opportunities during the early Industrial Revolution. What
growth there was after 1760 – and the rate was undeniably high in some
areas – seems to have produced opportunities, but all within a competitive
environment that transformed those opportunities into risks, which meant that

---

[26] I have used Lindert and Williamson's reworkings and excluded the following groups from
categories B and C in their table: clerks and shopmen to merchants, hawkers, artisans etc.
and labouring people in mines etc. 'Revising England's social tables', p. 400.

[27] I have excluded from category B: tradesmen with an income of less than £40 (feeling that
many of them traded on too small a scale to get caught by bankruptcy), alesellers and cottagers. From category C I have only included those given as master manufacturers. Ibid.,
p. 396.

significant numbers failed. Heroic successes there were, but they were partnered by heroic and not so heroic failures.

There are two possible reasons why bankruptcy increased in quantity and in significance. It could have been because the business environment was becoming more competitive, or because businessmen were becoming increasingly rash and taking greater risks – or because of both possibilities. Risk and competition were, in fact, closely related to one another.

As was made clear in the first chapter, the issue of competition has rarely been addressed in any concerted way by historians examining enterprise during the Industrial Revolution. Implicit generalisations have ruled the roost. Smiles felt that competition was slight and that the economic environment was generally favourable. He believed that success would be produced more through diligence and application than business skills. Morality and industry rather than flair and ability would sort the wheat from the chaff. An alternative and more sophisticated version of this approach has been outlined as a suggestive hypothesis by Professor Payne. He thought that it was possible 'many industrial pioneers operated in what was in some ways a uniquely favourable economic environment. They faced a buoyant domestic market buttressed, particularly in cotton textiles, by a flourishing overseas demand in the exploitation of which they enjoyed monopolistic advantages.' Indeed, he went on to propose that 'It was the generally favourable demand situation which sometimes allowed the perpetration of the grossest errors to go unpunished by bankruptcy.'[28] From the evidence of bankruptcy we can see that there is some truth in this, but not much. Rising numbers and rates of bankruptcy indicate that imperfections in the competitive arena were lessening and uncertainties growing. Folly, ignorance and inability were not escaping punishment, bearing out Max Hartwell's belief that 'If industrialization enhanced the chance of gain, it also increased the chance, and the cost, of failure.'[29]

Innovators do manage temporarily to circumvent competition as Payne suggested. But such market security would only be long lived if imitators were slow to move in and spread available profits more thinly than before. This might happen either because of patents, imperfect information or a high threshold of entry. At first glance, the signs of a rising failure rate after 1760 suggest that imitators moved to exploit opportunities relatively quickly, sufficiently quickly, that is, to establish effective competition. Assuming constant firm size, then competition varies in relation to the number of firms that exist (relating in turn to entry and exit rates) and the size of the market. Both vary over the short and the long term. After 1760, the number of firms may have grown more quickly on trend than the expansion of the market or, alternatively,

[28] Payne, *British entrepreneurship*, pp. 31–2.
[29] R. M. Hartwell, *The industrial revolution and economic growth* (London, 1971), p. 307.

there may have been an intensification of short-run imbalances between the number of businesses and market size. To put it another way, higher rates of bankruptcy may have been caused by endemic or epidemic factors, or both. Distinguishing between them is not easy. In Chapters 7 and 8, when fluctuations in bankruptcy are analysed, there are some signs of increasingly virulent epidemics afflicting the business population after 1760.

Whether bankruptcies rose because of structural or short-run changes in the competitive balance, the issues that determined the entry of new firms into the business community still have to be discussed. In particular, why did entries apparently exceed the growth of demand and real market opportunities? Here the possibility arises of an increase in risk-taking and uncertainty during early industrialisation. For example, bankruptcy can be seen as an indicator of risk-taking that has failed. The volume of risk-taking is itself a function of opportunities, both real and perceived, and rewards. The rising rate of bankruptcy in the second half of the eighteenth century and the stagnant rate before then indicates that opportunities and rewards were stable down to *c*. 1760 but then grew. It is possible that the stagnant levels of bankruptcy down to *c*. 1760 arise from a shortage of opportunities because of what some historians see as a deceleration of economic development from 1725 to 1750.[30]

Higher rates of bankruptcy after 1760 do not in fact conflict with the slow-growth model of the economy because that model does allow for differential rates of growth between sectors. It is impossible, for example, not to believe that the cotton industry experienced a revolution. Over the century, economic opportunities opened up rapidly in overseas trade, in the cotton industry, in parts of the woollen industries and in transport. Contemporary enthusiasms for Coalbrookdale, the Potteries and Manchester cannot be dismissed lightly. And if other areas of the economy were scarcely revolutionised, then nevertheless opportunities emerged within them. After 1760, opportunities were unquestionably more numerous than before, which, when linked to low and then rising bankruptcy rates, shows that decisions involving an increasing degree of risk and uncertainty were encouraged by an expansive environment. A stable environment, on the other hand, seems to have been an unattractive environment for risk-taking and to have produced more certainty.

Eighteenth-century businessmen appear to have had a good sense of the availability of opportunities, but were rather less successful in their attempts to judge the degree of risk involved. This is not so surprising, for growth is inevitably associated with uncertainty as the economy expands into unknown and uncharted areas. But even so, guessing at the chances of success or failure does not seem to have been the strong point of businessmen at the time. This

[30] Summarised in A. J. Little, *Deceleration in the eighteenth-century British economy* (London, 1976).

phenomenon of the relatively successful perception of opportunities but their relatively unsuccessful exploitation can surely be explained by the quality of the information available. Most businessmen perceived opportunities in terms of examples set by innovators or other businessmen. Arkwright's success, for example, attracted the attention, admiration and imitative desire of many, as is clearly shown by his battles to protect his patent. Wedgwood was similarly beset by such emulation.[31] And well they deserved it. But while imitation may be the sincerest form of flattery, it will only lead to profits in the business world when done quickly and efficiently, before imitation turns to mass fashion. For businessmen trying to gauge the degree of risk involved in any opportunity that presented itself, one of the most difficult things they had to guess was the extent of the competition they would be faced with. But how could they hope to do this? They would have had to know about market size and structure, as well as the number and size of competitors they would face. Yet nothing like that sort of information existed. The commercial press was still in its earliest infancy. Outside London, trade directories were published only occasionally and were soon outdated, while market information was very variable in quantity and quality. At any one time some businessmen had good information, others average or poor information. Judging the quality of their information was not easy of course. In this situation increasing opportunities led to an increase in both successful and unsuccessful risk-taking. Moreover, as the population of firms grew so the average age of businesses fell, and young businesses, by definition, lacked the requisite experience to balance the thrills of risk-taking with the necessities of risk avoidance.

If bankruptcy does provide some testament to a flowering of risk-taking in the second half of the eighteenth century then this adds weight to long-standing arguments which have stressed the favourable social and economic climate within which enterprise operated.[32] If opportunities were emerging we cannot simply assume that they would be seized. Demand does not always evoke a supply response. In particular, social constraints cannot have been too great nor the threshold of entry too high, whether in terms of the capital or skill demanded. Opportunities were seized when they became available and risks were taken. But risks, by definition, involve some failure as well as success.

There is a distinction to be drawn between the absolute and the real level of bankruptcy because of the possible impact of inflation. But a more crucial distinction has to be drawn between the frequency and the rate of bankruptcy.

---

[31] Chapman, *The early factory masters*, pp. 72–100. Wedgwood's 'inventions were quickly copied and his quality easily reproduced'. N. McKendrick, 'Josiah Wedgwood and the commercialization of the Potteries', in McKendrick, Brewer and Plumb, *The birth of a consumer society*, p. 104.

[32] Summarised in Perkin, *Origins of modern English society*, Ch. 3. A. Thompson, *The dynamics of the industrial revolution* (London, 1973), pp. 104–13.

Attempts to relate the level of bankruptcy to the growth of the business community suggest slightly declining rates before 1760 and rising rates after 1760. The suggested explanation for this relates to an interaction between opportunities, competition, risk and uncertainty. Economic, technical and organisational developments after 1760 all prompted and promoted an increase in risk-taking which led to the entry of new businesses onto the scene and an intensification of competition. There was a growth in both risk-taking and risk. Whether the consequent rising failure rate was more the product of short- or long-term factors has yet to be discussed.

All this lends support to Schumpeter's plea that innovation and entre-preneurship be studied in terms of both success and failure. But it also lends support to the importance of imitation. More generally, it shows that the business world became not more, but less predictable through the eighteenth century. Uncertainty and risk grew, making it difficult to argue that business-men's control over either their fate or the economy's fortune increased. Peter Mathias rightly felt that 'The eighteenth century was a time of high risk and uncertainty in business, compared with later periods.'[33] But because so many of our images of enterprise during industrialisation have depended on atypical success stories this issue has, until now, been kept in a corner and out of the light. Examining the trend of eighteenth-century bankruptcy rescues it from obscurity.

[33] *The first industrial nation* (London, 1969), p. 161.

5

THE STRUCTURE OF EIGHTEENTH-CENTURY BANKRUPTCY

The conclusions in the last chapter were necessarily tentative. Explanations of the patterns of levels and rates of bankruptcy were more in the form of hypotheses than statements of fact. Such uncertainties can be partly dealt with by looking at trend movements in the sectoral composition of bankruptcy and at differential rates of bankruptcy between parts of the eighteenth-century business world. For if it is true that high trend levels and rates of bankruptcy are associated with opportunities and buoyancy and low levels and rates with certainty, stagnation and lack of enterprise, then the composition of bankruptcy should tie up with what historians know about the structural realignments taking place before and during early industrialisation. Prospering parts of the economy such as the Lancashire cotton industry, or declining areas like the Devon woollen trade, should be associated with high and low levels and rates of bankruptcy respectively. Moreover, it has become possible to appreciate better the extent of restructuring within eighteenth-century England following the new and vigorous impetus of the arguments of Crafts and others.[1] Answers to questions such as 'What share of the business community that went bankrupt was involved in overseas trade or textiles?' should help confirm perceptions of the relative weights to be attached to the various sectors of the economy at the time.

THE OCCUPATIONS OF BANKRUPTS

To help identify bankrupts both the *London Gazette* and the Docket Books gave occupational descriptions of everyone listed. Such evidence has to be handled cautiously for a number of reasons. Some descriptions were very broad, such as 'merchant', or had different meanings depending on the social and economic context of the individual. A clothier in Stroud, for example, was a businessman operating on a different scale and in different ways from a clothier from the West Riding; nor was a mercer in the country the same as a mercer in London. Dual occupations, so common at the time, present a further difficulty. A 'bookseller and carrier' or 'hosier and wine merchant' are not easily put into

[1] Crafts, *British economic growth*, p. 21. Harley, 'British industrialization before 1841'.

Table 3. *Sectoral composition of bankrupts, 1701–1800 (as percentage of all bankrupts for twenty-year periods)*

Sector	1701–20	1721–40	1741–60	1761–80	1781–1800
Agriculture	2.4	1.6	1.5	1.8	3.1
Fuel	0.2	0.4	0.8	1.0	1.3
Food	11.4	12.8	13.4	11.4	12.6
Drink	11.4	14.3	11.2	8.8	8.6
Construction	2.4	3.7	4.2	5.0	5.9
Textiles and clothes	27.7	26.2	25.6	23.9	23.9
Finance	1.6	1.1	1.3	2.1	3.7
Transport	3.0	4.1	4.1	5.1	5.8
Metal	3.3	3.4	4.0	5.6	5.6
Wood	1.0	1.4	2.0	2.8	2.0
Retail	9.8	10.1	9.1	8.7	7.6
Wholesale	19.0	14.1	15.7	16.6	13.1
Miscellaneous	6.8	7.0	7.1	7.2	7.2

Source: London Gazette; P.R.O., B4/1–20.

a single category.[2] Occupational analysis has sometimes to take a few liberties, therefore, and I have taken all occupational designations at face value for the time being.

As a first step, all eighteenth-century bankrupts can be assigned to one of thirteen broad sectors. Changing shares of these sectors for twenty-year periods through the century are presented in Table 3. Five sectors dominated eighteenth-century bankruptcy, accounting for over 70 per cent of the total: textiles and clothes, wholesale, food, drink and retail. These five sectors can be further aggregated into just three: food and drink (21.1 per cent), textiles and clothes (25.5 per cent) and distribution (24.8 per cent). The contribution of these areas declined a little over the course of the century, from 79.3 per cent of all bankrupts in 1701–20 to 65.8 per cent in 1781–1800. Bankruptcy became a little more evenly spread throughout all the sectors as the century wore on, with six small sectors slightly increasing their share of all bankruptcy. However, it would be easy to exaggerate the extent of change in the sectoral composition of bankruptcy, because the continued dominance of the five large sectors over the hundred years is much more striking. It is the sustained prominence of these sectors which needs to be explained.

[2] Some relevant points are made by P. H. Lindert, 'English occupations, 1670–1811'. *Journal of Economic History*, XL (1980), pp. 690–5. Crouzet, *The first industrialists*, pp. 62–3. Bankrupts with dual occupations have been assigned to their first mentioned occupation.

Historians have always emphasised the importance of the textile trades in eighteenth-century England. The woollen industry had been the basis of the nation's industrial strength for centuries and the cotton industry gradually took its place after 1760, becoming the keystone of Britain's economic supremacy by 1800. This is fully borne out in Table 3, where about one in every four bankrupts came from the textile and clothing trades.[3] What has been less certain has been the weights to be attached to wool, cotton, linen and silk within the sector. Especially interesting has been the relative significance of the wool and cotton industries. The second major area of bankruptcy was in distribution, bearing out an earlier complaint that historians have been too preoccupied with the production side of the economy. With nearly one in four bankrupts coming from wholesale and retail areas it is obviously true that substantial numbers of businessmen operated in this area and occasionally found themselves exposed to the full force of depression, stagnation and competition.[4] Finally, one in five bankrupts ran a business in the food and drink sectors of the economy. Again, historians have, with some notable exceptions, given little thought to describing and understanding the role of businesses that linked agricultural output with final consumers.[5]

People have three basic requirements: shelter, clothing and food. Businesses involved with satisfying two of these three were well represented among eighteenth-century bankrupts. But the construction industry was not, despite the fact that the population was rising rapidly by the end of the century, as was the proportion living in towns.[6] The reason for this is unclear, but probably relates to the nature of enterprise in the construction industry. Most firms there were small, with businessmen rising from the ranks of carpenters, masons and the like. Essentially, even as 'builders' such men traded on too small a scale to meet the financial specifications that limited the applicability of bankruptcy.[7]

The traditional dominance of manufacturing enterprise in studies of English business in the eighteenth century appears on the evidence of Table 3 to be somewhat misplaced. Neither the metal nor the wood industries produced

---

[3] Only a very small proportion were in clothing, the bulk being textile producers or distributors.

[4] In fact, the proportions involved must have been much higher because my 'retail' and 'wholesale' categories only include those who had no specific trade, for example 'shopkeeper' or 'merchant'. Retail occupations such as 'hat seller' and wholesale ones such as 'wine merchant' have been placed in their closest sector – in this case textiles and drink.

[5] But see P. Mathias, *The brewing industry in England, 1700–1830* (Cambridge, 1959). P. Clark, *The English alehouse: a social history 1200–1830* (London, 1983). Westerfield, *Middlemen in English business*, Chs. 2 and 3. J. A. Chartres, 'The marketing of agricultural produce', in J. Thirsk, ed., *The agrarian history of England and Wales*, Vol. ii, Part ii, *1640–1750* (Cambridge, 1985), pp. 406–502.

[6] Wrigley and Schofield, *The population history of England*, p. 211. P. J. Corfield, *The impact of English towns 1700–1800* (Oxford, 1982), Introduction.

[7] C. W. Chalklin, *The provincial towns of Georgian England* (London, 1974).

many bankrupts and the strength of the more service-orientated sectors among the figures is marked. Of course, this may reflect the greater vulnerability to bankruptcy of such occupations, but it seems more likely that it reflects the importance of such areas within the business community, a point made clear by examining the geography of bankruptcy.

THE GEOGRAPHY OF BANKRUPTCY

The easiest way of describing the geographical pattern of eighteenth-century bankruptcy is to look at those counties which had the most and the least numbers. Here, 'most' and 'least' have been defined as the top and bottom fifteen counties in a rank ordering of numbers of bankrupts by county over the century. Figures 2 and 3 present this approach graphically and more detailed proportions are given in Appendix 2.[8] This approach considers absolute levels of bankruptcy, not rates. The patterns shown in Figures 2 and 3 might have looked different if such rates could have been calculated, but the absence of evidence makes it impossible to do so.

A central feature of the geographical pattern of bankruptcy is the dominance of London. Over the long century, 1688–1800, some 46.0 per cent of all bankrupts came from the capital with Yorkshire, the second most important county of origin, accounting for just 4.4 per cent of the total. A fundamental distinction exists, therefore, between metropolitan and provincial bankruptcy. But if London was dominant, it is nevertheless worth stressing that every county produced some bankrupts. Even the smallest villages, tucked away in the corners of sleepy and remote counties, produced bankrupts every now and then. Knowledge of bankruptcy as a process to recover debts was obviously widespread, so if some areas of the country failed to produce bankrupts in any number it was presumably because such places had fewer traders who might fail and fall as bankrupts, or because debts were pursued there in other ways.

The pattern of bankruptcy shown in Figure 2 accords well with existing knowledge of the dynamics of eighteenth-century England's industrial and commercial spheres. The well-known significance of overseas trade and the metropolitan economy is witnessed by the prominence not only of London, but also of Middlesex, Surrey and Kent, most of whose bankrupts came from the riverside areas bordering the capital. In conjunction with the fact that so many wholesalers – mostly merchants – went bankrupt the significance of overseas trade to the pattern of bankruptcy is obvious. It is perhaps more than mere coincidence that only two out of the fifteen counties (13.3 per cent) in Figure 2 were inland ones, whereas for the nation as a whole 31.0 per cent of all counties

---

[8] The old county boundaries have been used and I have included London as a separate county, but excluded all the Welsh counties. Monmouth has been included, however.

Key: 1 Lancashire   9 Surrey
      2 Yorkshire   10 Hampshire
      3 Norfolk   11 Warwickshire
      4 Suffolk   12 Gloucestershire
      5 Essex   13 Wiltshire
      6 Middlesex   14 Somerset
      7 London   15 Devon
      8 Kent

Fig. 2 Fifteen counties with the most bankrupts, 1701–1800.

Key: 1 Cumberland   9 Cambridgeshire
      2 Westmorland   10 Bedfordshire
      3 Derbyshire   11 Buckinghamshire
      4 Nottinghamshire 12 Herefordshire
      5 Leicestershire   13 Monmouthshire
      6 Rutland   14 Dorset
      7 Northamptonshire 15 Cornwall
      8 Huntingdonshire

Fig. 3 Fifteen counties with the least bankrupts, 1701–1800.

were such. Direct links with coastal and international trade appear superficially to have had a profound impact on bankruptcy. This is reinforced by looking at the other side of the coin in Figure 3 where ten out of the fifteen counties producing the fewest bankrupts were landlocked. Others, such as Cornwall, Dorset, Monmouthshire, Cumberland and Westmorland, were on the periphery of the national economy, away from the main flows of internal and external trade.

The second major determinant of the patterns shown in Figures 2 and 3 was the localisation of the textile trades. Wool, the main textile industry, was primarily located in Devon, the West Country, the Essex–Suffolk border, Norfolk, the West Riding and Lancashire.[9] All of these areas show up in Figure 2 and there is no overlap between them and the counties with fewest bankrupts in Figure 3. Indeed, the significance of the textile industries is clearly demonstrated by the fact that Leicestershire and Nottinghamshire, two areas where domestic textile production developed over the century, increased their shares of all bankrupts over the eighteenth century (see Appendix 2).[10]

A corollary of the first two explanations of the regional dispersion of bankruptcy is, of course, the intensity of agriculture over the country. A distinctive block of nine inland counties in the East Midlands, all mainly agricultural areas, dominates the picture of the relative absence of bankruptcy drawn in Figure 3. Drawing up separate league tables for the incidence of bankruptcy for the decades 1701–10 and 1791–1800 shows that the three counties which made their way into the bottom fifteen over the century, Cambridgeshire, Hertfordshire and Cumberland, were all increasingly agricultural areas. Similarly, the increasingly industrial counties of Leicestershire, Nottinghamshire and Shropshire all left the bottom fifteen over the century. It was the development of the iron industry, especially in and around Coalbrookdale, which accounts for the exit of Shropshire.[11] Indeed, the developing metal trade produced more and more bankrupts, accounting for the presence of Warwickshire, Staffordshire and Worcestershire among the fifteen counties with the most bankrupts in the last decade of the century.

The occupational and regional pattern of eighteenth-century bankruptcy appears to reflect very closely what is known about the historical geography of trade and industry in that century. The centrality of textiles and trade is well attested. But the geography of bankruptcy throws up no real clues with which to explain the importance of the food and drink sectors within the occupational

---

[9] See H. C. Prince, 'England *circa* 1800', in H. C. Darby, ed., *A new historical geography of England after 1600* (Cambridge, 1976), pp. 139 and 145.

[10] J. D. Chambers, *Nottinghamshire in the eighteenth century* (London, 1932). D. Levine, *Family formation in an age of nascent capitalism* (London, 1977).

[11] B. Trinder, *The industrial revolution in Shropshire* (Chichester, 1973).

analysis. Perhaps that is not so surprising as both would have been highly dispersed sectors, evenly spread over the country, following patterns of population distribution.

As was discussed in the last chapter, high trend levels of bankruptcy as shown in the geographical and occupational patterns just described were associated with enterprise and growth, low levels with stagnation or the absence of business activity.[12] But the particular processes of articulation at work here have not yet been convincingly described. London, the home of nearly one half of all eighteenth-century bankrupts, provides a good starting point.

LONDON

In the first twenty years of the eighteenth century the capital provided 52.2 per cent of all bankrupts, but by the last twenty years the proportion had fallen to 37.3 per cent. Indeed, in the final three years of the century the proportion fell below a third. Obviously, the rate of growth of numbers of bankrupts from London failed to match that of the provinces, hardly surprising given the localisation of economic growth in the period.

It is possible that the dominance of London in the pattern of bankruptcy reflects administrative as well as economic facts of life. Because all bankruptcy proceedings began with a petition to the Lord Chancellor in London, it was arguably easier for metropolitan than for provincial creditors to initiate proceedings. It might be argued, on the other hand, that in the capital, with debtors and creditors living cheek by jowl with one another, it was easier to arrange compositions than in the country, so that bankruptcy was used less than would have been expected. On balance, the first possibility probably outweighs the second, so that London is somewhat over-represented.

In the main, the declining share of London in eighteenth-century bankruptcy mirrors the capital's declining share of total economic activity, be it in overseas trade, manufacturing, distribution or consumption. Even so, in 1800 London still served as a hub for the infant national economy. Eighteenth-century London was a vast concentration of people, about 11 per cent of the national total, who produced, marketed and consumed on a huge scale. The population of London rose from about 575,000 in 1700 to about 960,000 in 1801. People, food and goods gathered from the provinces were swallowed in ever-increasing amounts and in return London gave out services and finished products. It is the duality of London as a centre of both production and distribution, resting on

---

[12] The absence of evidence prevents calculations to be made of rates of bankruptcy in this general examination of the occupational and geographical pattern of bankruptcy. But where evidence exists for specific occupations and/or places such calculations have been attempted in what follows.

its population's own massive consumption, which accounts for its importance. Throughout the century, London remained the lynchpin of internal and external exchange and trade. But the pattern slowly changed. In 1699–1701 the capital's direct share of overseas trade had been about 75.8 per cent, but in 1790 it was down to 63.4 per cent.[13] As the century passed, not only did more overseas trade drift out of the direct orbit of the Thames, but manufacturing and exchange also grew much more rapidly in the Midlands and the North. London markets, finance and middlemen remained very important to provincial economic development, but in 1800 there were some signs of their being bypassed.

London's substantial contribution to bankruptcy was the product of its domination of overseas trade, the role it played in articulating flows of internal trade, its own manufacturing sector and, finally, servicing and supplying the needs of its own huge population. And although it seems legitimate to expect the capital's share of bankruptcy to decline over the century as it did, was its share really so large? Here the issue of rates of failure must be tackled once again.

One of the ways the size of local business communities in the eighteenth century can sometimes by gauged is by looking at trade directories. Considerable problems surround these sources, but they do at least provide a means of getting some sense of the rate of growth and composition of business communities in the main urban centres. Directories aimed to list the businesses of a town or city, so the main problems surrounding them relate to under- and over-enumeration and incorrect or ambiguous occupational specifications.[14] Obviously, directories can be error-ridden, but used cautiously they can be used to point to some broad trends.

The first directory published in England appeared in 1677 and listed merchants in and about the City of London. But the second directory, again covering London, did not come out until 1734 and improbably contained fewer names than its predecessor. A problem common to all eighteenth-century directories is that the first couple of editions covering any town were markedly unreliable. Directories for the capital become usable in the 1740s, but elsewhere

[13] Corfield, *The impact of English towns*, Ch. 5. E. A. Wrigley, 'A simple model of London's importance in changing English society and economy 1650–1750', *Past and Present*, XXXVII (1967), pp. 44–70. M. J. Daunton, 'Towns and economic growth in eighteenth-century England', in P. Abrams and E. A. Wrigley, eds., *Towns in societies* (Cambridge, 1978), pp. 245–77.

[14] See G. Shaw, 'The content and reliability of nineteenth-century trade directories', *Local Historian*, XIII (1978), pp. 205–9. G. Timmins, 'Measuring industrial growth from trade directories', *Local Historian*, XIII (1979), pp. 349–52. P. Wilde, 'The use of business directories in comparing the industrial structure of towns: an example from the south-west Pennines', *Local Historian*, XII (1976), pp. 152–6. P. J. Corfield and S. M. Kelly, '"Giving directions to the town": the early town directories', *Urban History Yearbook* (1984), pp. 22–35.

Table 4. *London's business population,*
1740–1800

Year	Number	Directory
1740	1,890	Osborn
1741	2,110	*Universal*
1744	2,180	Osborn
1749	2,520	Osborn
1752	3,180	Osborn
1754	3,520	Osborn
1755	3,850	Osborn
1757	3,740	Osborn
1760	3,920	Osborn
1763	4,210	Osborn
1765	4,220	Osborn
1768	5,860	Osborn
1770	6,470	Osborn
1771	5,730	*Kent*
1772	6,900	Osborn
1777	5,390	Osborn
1782	6,370	*Kent*
1783	7,180	Osborn
1799	9,480	*Kent*
1800	11,330	*New annual*

Source: Directories listed.

they did not even start to appear until the 1760s, 1770s and 1780s for the main towns.[15]

A common difficulty to be faced when using directories as a guide to the size of the business population at risk from bankruptcy is whether they included all 'traders' who were sufficiently indebted to fall within the scope of the bankruptcy law. Many of the other problems arise from the different methods and definitions used by their authors in research and compilation. These can partly be sidestepped by looking at directories that ran through a number of editions over a period of years and came from the same publisher. In such circumstances,

[15] C. W. F. Goss, *The London directories 1677–1855* (London, 1932); see especially pp. 16–30. J. E. Norton, *Guide to the national and provincial directories of England and Wales, excluding London, published before 1856* (London, 1950).

the compilers probably used a reasonably consistent methodology. For eighteenth-century London, Osborn's directory, first published in 1740, is available.[16] By 1783, when it ceased publication, it had run through sixteen editions. All these claimed to list 'The name and places of abode of the most eminent traders in *London*, alphabetically digested'. Table 4 shows the approximate number of names in each (excluding the first which was very incomplete) and, for comparison, includes evidence from other directories.[17]

These London directories usually claim to include only the 'eminent' or the 'principal' traders. It is not known how these terms were defined and put into practice, but they must go some way to excluding those who could never have become bankrupts because of the small-scale nature of their indebtedness. However, it may also mean that the directories exclude some small businesses which could have gone bankrupt. The occupational composition within the directories, when compared with the occupations of London bankrupts for the same periods, shows that the directories included some non-traders and excluded some traders. Strictly speaking, for example, attorneys and aldermen were not traders yet in Osborn's directories of 1768, 1772 and 1783 they account respectively for about 5.3, 3.8 and 3.3 per cent of all those listed. Conversely, two main groups of potential bankrupts did not usually appear in either Osborn's or Kent's directories: those in the building trades and those who were general retailers. It seems likely that the directories listed retailers more accurately than did the *London Gazette* or the Docket Books with the result that they can be found in different occupational categories. But the absence of carpenters, masons, painters and so on is a problem because in the 1760s, 1770s and 1780s they accounted for about 6 per cent of all London bankrupts. Apart from these more or less complete omissions, there are also some traders who appear to have been under-recorded in the directories. Primarily, these were retail traders in food, the small butchers and bakers for example. In some areas, therefore, the directories omitted 'traders' while in others they included some non-traders. The figures cannot be adjusted and it is likely that the estimates of the size of the business population at risk from bankruptcy produced in Table 4 are low-bound ones because of the missing shops from the food sector.

By making some estimates as to the annual decennial average of businesses in London on the basis of Table 4 it is possible to calculate rates of bankruptcy as given in Table 5. The bankruptcy totals have, as in the previous chapter, been

[16] J. Osborn, *A compleat guide to all persons who have any trade or concern with the City of London and parts adjacent* (London, 1740). In 1768 this directory became, with its eleventh edition, *Baldwin's new complete guide to all persons*.

[17] *Kent's directory* (London, 1771 and later edns) has the same coverage as Osborn's as does *The universal pocket companion* (London, 1741) and *The new annual directory* (London, 1800).

Table 5. *Annual rates of bankruptcy in London, 1740–83*

Period	Bankruptcies	Businesses	Rate
1740s	76.24	2,250	1 in 29.5
1750s	81.73	3,573	1 in 43.7
1760s	123.59	4,553	1 in 36.8
1770s	180.92	6,550	1 in 36.2
1780s (early)	158.35	6,775	1 in 42.8

Source: London Gazette; P.R.O., B4/1–20; directories listed in Table 4.

deflated by the Schumpeter–Gilboy price index. Nominally, the highest rate of bankruptcy came in the 1740s, but it seems likely that this is more the product of the imperfections of the directories in their early years than an indication of the extent to which businessmen went to the wall then. What is striking about the other rates of bankruptcy is, firstly, their broad similarity and, secondly, just how high they were. Rates of bankruptcy of one in 605 for 1759 and one in 263 for *c.* 1801 were calculated using Massie and Colquhoun as a basis (see above, p. 51). It is unlikely that the huge difference between the national and the metropolitan rates of bankruptcy can be accounted for solely by problems surrounding the directories. For example, in the 1750s there would have had to be 49,447 businesses in London to produce the same rate of bankruptcy as that based on Massie's figures. So although the rates of bankruptcy produced in Table 5 are likely to be an exaggeration it seems clear that the rate of bankruptcy in the capital can be thought of as both high and reasonably steady in comparison with the nation as a whole.

Adam Smith, writing between the commercial trauma of 1772–3 and the political crises of 1776, remarked that

After all our complaints of the frequency of bankruptcies, the unhappy men who fall into this misfortune make but a very small part of the whole number engaged in trade, and all other sorts of business; not much more perhaps than one in a thousand. Bankruptcy is perhaps the greatest and most humiliating calamity which can befal an innocent man. The greater part of men, therefore, are sufficiently careful to avoid it. Some, indeed, do not avoid it; as some do not avoid the gallows.[18]

In London at least and probably for the nation as a whole, Smith appears to have seriously underestimated the chances of failure, if the rates calculated in Table 5 are more than just windmills tilted at for the sake of mere quantifi-

---

[18] Smith, *Wealth of nations*, Vol. 1, p. 363. It is possible, but unlikely, that Smith included non-traders in his guesswork, given his reference to 'all other sorts of business'.

cation.[19] One possible reason for the very high rates in the capital which has already been pointed to is that it was easier to undertake bankruptcy proceedings in the capital than elsewhere because of the nature of the process and the administration. Again, though, could this have been sufficient to account for the differential rates of bankruptcy? It looks unlikely.

The second major explanation must lie with real economic factors such as competition, opportunity, risk and the degree of fluctuations. The differences in the nature of enterprise between London and the provinces were very important. At the most general level, it is vital to start by reemphasising the size, concentration and significance of London's economy. In terms of economic opportunities, the capital was the most attractive and invigorating arena in the country for the first three-quarters of the eighteenth century. Such an expansive and powerful environment may well have been conducive to a high level of risk-taking and adventurousness and concomitantly high rates of bankruptcy. Fortunes were often made in the capital; it could seem as if the streets were paved with gold. But the innocents soon found that ordinary reality was usually otherwise.

Such uncertainty was also partly a product of the considerable role overseas trade played in London's well-being. Somewhere between two-thirds and three-quarters of England's trade usually passed through the quays stretching from London Bridge to Limehouse.[20] And overseas trade was notoriously unstable, uncertain and precarious. Storms, war, piracy, tariffs, gluts and shortages could all hit and hinder imports and exports. This factor is given added weight by comparing the sectoral composition of bankruptcy between London and the provinces. For most sectors, that pattern was very similar between the two. For example, 23.5 per cent of London's bankrupts were in textiles and clothing, whereas for the provinces the proportion was only a little higher at 26.2 per cent. But there were two sectors where differences were more marked. In London, only 4.0 per cent of bankrupts were in retailing but elsewhere it was 12.2 per cent. Second, in London 21.0 per cent were wholesalers but elsewhere it was only 10.4 per cent. The first difference is probably explained by the closer occupational details attached to notifications of bankruptcy in London, though it presumably also relates to the greater degree of occupational specialisation in the capital, following Smith's maxim relating the extent of the division of

[19] Using Osborn's directories it is possible to calculate what proportion of entries in one directory failed to appear in the next edition of the directory, providing some indication of the exit rate of London businesses. Comparing the 1744, 1749, 1755, 1760, 1765 and 1770 directories produces a stable exit rate of one business in fifteen per annum. Using Kent's directories for 1755, 1761, 1765 and 1770 produces a similar figure. Clearly, the turnover of businesses in the capital was rapid.

[20] A detailed discussion of the overseas trade of the capital is in C. J. French, 'The trade and shipping of London, 1700–1776' (University of Exeter Ph.D. thesis, 1980).

labour to the size of the market. With a larger market businesses in the capital would often be able to specialise to a much greater degree than their provincial brethren.

Three-quarters of London's bankrupts from the wholesale sector were merchants. Many of the others were wharfingers or warehousemen, directly and actively involved in overseas trade. And outside the wholesale sector there were those who were intimately concerned with the export–import economy. Some 36 per cent of the bankrupts from the food sector were victuallers, probably provisioning the ships passing into and out of the capital. In the drink trades, 48.2 per cent of them were wine merchants, importing wines from Europe.[21] Other occupations from other sectors were also involved in overseas trade. London middlemen like the linen drapers or clothiers often played pivotal roles in linking England's domestic economy to the channels of international trade. In 1747, Richard Campbell argued that 'The Linen-Draper is... a very useful Member of Society; by his retailing of Linen Cloth of all sorts, he employs a vast Number of Hands both in *Scotland* and *Ireland*, and vends the Linens of *Germany*, *France*, and *Holland*.'[22] Problems of nomenclature arising from the ambiguities and imprecisions of occupational descriptions prevent a precise figure being put on the proportion of London bankrupts closely involved with overseas trade, but it cannot have been less than a third and may well have been a half.

Overseas trade was necessarily a high-risk area to the eighteenth-century business community. Markets, transport and finance were all prone to uncertainties that were more considerable than at home. Yet overseas trade was also more exclusive because a requirement for more money and skills, such as languages, raised the threshold of entry. It was an area, therefore, where it was easy to overstretch oneself in the very vulnerable early days of any firm. Essentially, all these reasons are linked by the central argument that a disproportionate number of businessmen tried to link relatively distant points of supply and demand. And long-distance decision-making was an unpredictable art. The more geographically dispersed a businessman's concerns, the less control he could exert over them. But this argument could be extended to businessmen who operated solely within the domestic economy as well. A high proportion of England's internal trade focused on the capital, and London middlemen were central to smooth connexions between producers and consumers. Even for the rapidly growing cotton industry in the late eighteenth century, which imported so much of its raw materials via Liverpool, Unwin felt

---

[21] H. E. S. Fisher, *The Portugal trade. A study of Anglo-Portuguese commerce 1700–1770* (London, 1971), pp. 79–80.

[22] *The London tradesman*, p. 282. N. B. Harte, 'The rise of protection and the English linen trade, 1690–1790', in Harte and Pointing, eds., *Textile history and economic history*, p. 88.

that at London 'a country manufacturer had more chance of finding there than anywhere else a middleman suited to his special circumstances'.[23] And Chapman has emphasised that 'Although the hosiery manufacture had all but deserted London by the middle of the eighteenth century, the hosiery market remained centred on the City of London until after the Napoleonic wars.'[24] London middlemen may well have traded over greater distances than their provincial counterparts, thereby taking on board a bigger share of both the risks and the rewards.

A related factor which set apart London businessmen from many of their colleagues in the country was finance. In particular, provincial eyes looked to the capital for the provision of credit to help solve the problems caused by the imperfections of the monetary system and the inevitable delays in business between purchase and sale. This was also true in overseas trade, where London merchants found that they had to extend considerable amounts of credit to overseas markets (see also Chapter 6).[25] Credit networks and flows of bills of exchange, centring on London, spun a vast and ever denser web over the national economy during the eighteenth century. Many distant parts of the trading and manufacturing economy were linked to London via bills. In effect, the London discount market served as the hub of the internal multilateral system of payments. In the Wiltshire woollen industry, for example, 'the bill on London was the characteristic form of payment'.[26] In retailing, 'it was reckoned that a provincial shopkeeper would probably in practice receive about twelve months' credit from London wholesalers'.[27] Even the great entrepreneurs of the age – Wedgwood, Boulton, Watt and the Lancashire cotton lords – found it most convenient to rely on the capital's financial intermediaries when searching for export orders.[28] The most rapidly growing parts of the economy felt no need to break the financial ties that bound the centre and the periphery to one another. Indeed, the growth of the economy elsewhere and the increased demand for bills on London saw the development of the London money market and the rise of specialist bill brokers in the 1770s.[29] Such

[23] G. Unwin, *Samuel Oldknow and the Arkwrights* (Manchester, 1924), p. 56. M. M. Edwards, *The growth of the British cotton trade 1780–1815* (Manchester, 1967), pp. 157–60. R. S. Fitton and A. P. Wadsworth, *The Strutts and the Arkwrights 1758–1830* (Manchester, 1958), p. 48. A. P. Wadsworth and J. de L. Mann, *The cotton trade and industrial Lancashire 1600–1780* (Manchester, 1931), pp. 236–7.

[24] Chapman, *The early factory masters*, p. 21.

[25] On the overseas aspect see Price, *Capital and credit*, Chs. 2 and 6.

[26] J. de L. Mann, ed., *Documents illustrating the Wiltshire textile trades in the eighteenth century* (Devizes, 1964), p. xxiv.

[27] S. I. Mitchell, 'Urban markets and retail distribution 1730–1815 with particular reference to Macclesfield, Stockport and Chester' (Univeristy of Oxford D. Phil. thesis, 1974), p. 310.

[28] Chapman, 'British marketing enterprise', pp. 208–11.

[29] K. F. Dixon, 'The development of the London money market 1780–1830' (University of London Ph.D. thesis, 1962), p. 24.

development is also suggested by the bankruptcy material. Without deflating the figures to take account of the possible impact of inflation it is worth noting that whereas the number of bankrupts from London as a whole rose by just over two and a half times between the 1750s and 1790s, in the capital's financial sector there was an elevenfold increase. This suggests that the financial sector grew more quickly than did London's economy as a whole and provides one reason why it was possible for London to remain so central to the nation's economic development.

If it is clear that London did play a vastly disproportionate role in the provision of credit for both internal and external trade why should that have contributed to higher rates of bankruptcy in the capital? A number of problems were associated with extensive involvement in credit. First, it could be over-indulged in, especially by younger men starting out in business, as an easy means of extending one's business. Generating returns at the right moments to meet repayments was never easy. Credit was also highly unstable because of its dependence on confidence and the interrelated nature of credit networks. Chains of credit bound producers, middlemen and retailers together but, like all chains, its strength was determined by its weakest rather than its strongest links. London businessmen often found themselves under financial pressures not directly of their own making. A typical jeremiad was that 'CREDIT...is a most destructive cancer.'[30]

If credit was one of the great lamentations of the eighteenth century, though others also proclaimed it as a source of great strength, then luxury was also condemned, and on both counts London can be seen to have been peculiarly involved and vulnerable. Neil McKendrick has stressed that 'London had long been regarded as the centre of conspicuous consumption but such was the qualitative change in the nature of commercial enterprise in the eighteenth century that London was now the centre of a new scale of commerce, the undisputed leader in the commercialization of fashion which had helped to bring about unprecedentedly high levels of spending.'[31] Complaints about the degree of luxury and the pervasive influence of fashion in London were a commonplace in the eighteenth century. Fielding complained that luxury had created a crime wave in the capital in the late 1740s and early 1750s.[32] Goldsmith, writing at much the same date, argued that

Of all the follies and absurdities which this great metropolis labour under, there is not one, I believe, at present, appears in a more glaring and ridiculous light than the pride

---

[30] *London Chronicle*, June 30–July 2, 1772, p. 4.

[31] 'The commercialization of fashion', in McKendrick, Brewer and Plumb, *The birth of a consumer society*, p. 86.

[32] H. Fielding, *An enquiry into the causes of the late increase of robbers* (London, 1751), in *The complete works of Henry Fielding*, 16 vols. (New York, 1967), Vol. XIII.

and luxury of the middling class of people, their eager desire of being seen in a sphere far above their capacities and circumstances, is daily, nay hourly instanced by the prodigious numbers of mechanics, who flock to the races, and gaming-tables, brothels, and all public diversions this fashionable town affords.[33]

It did not matter whether you argued like Mandeville that luxury and fashion were good, or like Brown and Bolingbroke that it was bad, or like Smith, Johnson and Hume that it could be both: everyone felt London was enjoying luxuries as never before and was more susceptible to fashion than ever.[34]

At the centre of fashion, London businessmen were open to a constantly changing range of opportunities making for success and a constantly changing pattern of uncertainty making for failure. Fashion heightened opportunities and risks – evidenced by the presence among the capital's bankrupts of some peculiarly urban and urbane occupations: two artificial-flower makers and one ostrich-feather manufacturer went bankrupt in the century.[35] If we accept Mandeville's claim that fashion was 'The very Wheel, that turn'd the Trade' then we ought also to bear in mind Steele's warning that 'The variableness of Fashion turns the Stream of Business, which flows from it now into one Channel, and anon into another; so that different Sets of People sink or flourish in their Turns by it.'[36] It would be wrong to imagine however that haute couture was restricted to the metropolis and the helpful and injurious effects of fashion similarly circumscribed. Increasingly, London fashions spread out to consumers and producers in the provinces. Shopkeepers from Chester travelled to London to see and supply themselves with the latest fads; cotton manufacturers in the north were kept in touch with fashion by their middlemen in the capital; and the Birmingham toy trades had well-established links with variations in the patterns of consumption in London.[37] William Hutton, looking at businesses in Birmingham, saw that 'Some of them, spring up with the expedition of a blade of grass, and like that, wither in a summer. If some are lasting, like the sun, others seem to change with the moon.'[38] But fashion

[33] O. Goldsmith, 'Of the pride and luxury of the middling class of people', in *The Bee*, *The collected works of Oliver Goldsmith*, ed. A. Friedman, 4 vols. (Oxford, 1966), Vol. I, pp. 486–7.
[34] S. M. Wade, 'The idea of luxury in eighteenth-century England' (University of Harvard Ph.D. thesis, 1968). J. Sekora, *Luxury. The concept in western thought, Eden to Smollett* (Baltimore, Md., 1977).
[35] M. D. George, *London life in the eighteenth century* (London, 1925; reprinted Harmondsworth, 1979), pp. 27, 162–6.
[36] B. Mandeville, *The fable of the bees*, ed. P. Harth (Harmondsworth, 1970), p. 68. *The Spectator*, Vol. IV, p. 193. Steele's sentiment was duplicated by Adam Smith, *Wealth of nations*, Vol. I, p. 128. W. Sombart, *Luxury and capitalism* (Ann Arbor, Mich., 1967).
[37] I. Mitchell, 'The development of urban retailing 1700–1815', in P. Clark, ed., *The transformation of English provincial towns 1600–1800* (London, 1984), p. 275. Unwin, *Samuel Oldknow*, p. 56. Edwards, *British cotton trade*, p. 157. E. Robinson, 'Eighteenth-century commerce and fashion: Matthew Boulton's marketing techniques', *Economic History Review*, XVI (1963–4), pp. 39–60.   [38] *An history of Birmingham*, p. 73.

undoubtedly held greatest sway and created the greatest sense of uncertainty in the capital for the bulk of the century.

The final explanation of London's higher rates of bankruptcy relates to the intensity of short-run depressions. Fluctuations were both more intense and more frequent in the capital than elsewhere. Severe fluctuations, defined as years when bankruptcy totals exceeded their fifteen-year moving average level by more or less than 30 per cent, occurred in London on eighteen occasions, nine high (depression) and nine low (boom). But for the provinces there were only ten years, six high and four low. It was not that fluctuations in the capital followed a radically different chronology from those in the provinces, but rather that severe fluctuations in London sometimes corresponded with only mild ones outside the capital. Naturally, there were occasions when there was a divergence. In 1715, for example, bankruptcy in London was 8 per cent above trend, but in the provinces nearly 40 per cent below. In 1739–40, levels in London were 33 and 43 per cent above the trend, while in the provinces there was little deviation at all. Finally, the depression of 1758 was much more marked in the provinces than in London. For the rest of the century, fluctuations between the two areas were in close accord, though a little more intense in London. The greater agreement in the second half of the century gives some credence to suggestions that the economy was becoming more efficiently interlocked and interdependent. It seems unlikely that the differences in fluctuations between the centre and the periphery are totally accounted for by the greater instability of demand in London. A second reason, which has already seen the light of day, relates to the greater financial interdependence of businessmen in the capital. Credit networks were larger, more powerful and more common there. Collapses sent out shock waves and rumours through the coffee houses and marts of the hive-like City. The author of a pamphlet suggesting remedies for the large numbers of bankruptcies in the capital concentrated his suggestions on ways in which credit might be stabilised there.[39]

The capital's greater involvement with long-distance trade, be it domestic or overseas, its role as a financial arbiter in those trades through the provision of credit and, finally, its commitment to the fashion trades all help explain why bankruptcy was such a problem in London. As the largest and, for most of the century, the most developed part of the nation's industrial and trading economy it provided a more sophisticated commercial environment for businessmen. It allowed countless opportunities for profit-making. But an inevitable concomitant of that was less predictability, and more uncertainty and instability. In London high rates of bankruptcy resulted not only from proportionately more risk-taking but also from more risk. But if this created failure, it also created great success. The wealth of the London business community, which

[39] *A proposal for rendering bankruptcies less frequent in and about London* (London, 1732).

became especially visible from the Commercial and Financial Revolutions of the late-seventeenth century, was well ahead of that of provincial businessmen.[40] Rewards compensated for risks, but the chance of failure was real enough.

London dominated eighteenth-century bankruptcy, but its domination was dwindling and by the close of the century only one in three bankrupts came from the capital. The composition of bankruptcy, in particular the importance of textiles, food and drink and distribution, has to be approached bearing this in mind. Uncovering the causes of a high rate of bankruptcy in the capital has suggested a series of areas which need to be discussed in relationship to bankruptcy as a whole, particularly to do with the distances involved in business enterprise, the significance of credit and the stability of demand.

[40] W. D. Rubinstein, *Men of property* (London, 1981), p. 37. L. D. Schwarz and L. J. Jones, 'Wealth, occupations, and insurance in the late eighteenth century: the policy registers of the Sun Fire Office', *Economic History Review*, XXXVI (1983), pp. 371–3.

6

---
*

TEXTILES, FOOD AND DRINK AND MERCHANTS

Seven out of ten bankrupts in the eighteenth century were involved in the textiles, food and drink and distribution sectors of the economy. Examining the patterns and causes of bankruptcy in those areas should shed some light on their wider fortunes as well as further fleshing out arguments which have been advanced about the interactions at work between risk and failure.

TEXTILES

Over the century as a whole, one in four bankrupts was involved in the production and distribution of textiles and clothes. But only a small proportion was involved in the clothing trades. If the contribution of clothes is taken out then textiles accounted for 26 per cent of all bankrupts 1701–20, 23 per cent 1741–60 and 20 per cent 1781–1800. If numbers of bankrupts there failed to grow as quickly as in other areas of the economy, it could be that this simply mirrors the declining importance of textiles within the English economy over the century. Alternatively, it may have been caused by the changing nature of bankruptcy within the various parts of the textile sector as they experienced variable rates of growth. What particularly needs to be examined is whether the rapidly expanding cotton industry suffered a different pattern of bankruptcy from the woollen industry, with its slower evolution.

In absolute terms, the number of bankrupts from the textile sector trebled between the first and last decades of the eighteenth century. Deflating this to take account of the possible impact of inflation produces a growth of 122.6 per cent, as against 185.0 per cent for non-textile bankrupts. London was easily the most common home of textile bankrupts: some 41 per cent of textile bankrupts came from the capital compared with 47 per cent for non-textile bankrupts. The other major sources of textile bankrupts come as no surprise: Lancashire, 7.8 per cent; Yorkshire, 6.1 per cent; Gloucestershire (which includes Bristol), 4.7 per cent; Norfolk, 3.9 per cent; Devon, 2.8 per cent; Somerset, 2.7 per cent; Wiltshire, 2.4 per cent; and Middlesex, 2.1 per cent. Yet these overall contributions mask three significant changes in the geography of textile bank-

Table 6. *Geography of textile bankrupts, 1701–1800 (as percentage of textile bankrupts in given periods)*

County	1701–20	1721–40	1741–60	1761–80	1781–1800
Devon	5.5	2.1	2.3	2.7	2.2
Glos.	4.3	4.9	7.5	5.2	3.9
London	47.4	41.0	37.7	44.5	36.1
Lancs.	1.4	2.3	4.2	7.1	15.0
Middx.	2.1	2.2	1.5	2.8	2.0
Norfolk	6.3	8.3	6.7	1.5	1.2
Som.	1.9	3.2	3.1	3.1	2.4
Wilts.	3.7	3.4	3.1	2.1	1.5
Yorks.	4.3	5.4	7.3	4.9	7.7

Source: London Gazette; P.R.O., B4/1–20.

ruptcy which took place over the century. (See Table 6.) London and Norfolk had shrinking shares, while Lancashire had a growing one. An increasing volume of bankruptcy bears witness to prospering areas of the textile industry, Lancashire cottons and West Riding woollens. Indeed, when the cotton industry's development got into full stride at the end of the century, Lancashire challenged London as the most important home of textile bankrupts. In 1798 numbers of textile bankrupts from Lancashire surpassed the capital's for the first time; and in absolute terms the number of textile bankrupts from Lancashire rose twenty times between the 1740s and 1790s.

Devon, London, Norfolk and Wiltshire all produced a more or less dwindling proportion of textile bankrupts. At the very least, this reflects the shortfall of dynamism and opportunity in these areas. More extremely, it may point to the real decline of the wool industry in some of these areas – the state of the woollen industry needs to be examined more carefully, especially its regional realignment. In fact, it was the relative and absolute decline in numbers of textile bankrupts coming from Norfolk that was the most notable counterpoise to the buoyancy of Lancashire in the second half of the century.

These concerns are enhanced by looking closely at the occupations of textile bankrupts. The original occupational descriptions given in the sources have been recategorised under twenty-seven headings (listed in Appendix 3). Table 7 shows the main occupations of textile bankrupts. Although this table must be handled cautiously because of the problems associated with the occupational definitions, some broad points can nonetheless be suggested. First, although the

Table 7. *Occupations of textile bankrupts, 1701–1800 (as percentage of textile bankrupts in given periods)*

Occupation	1701–20	1741–60	1781–1800	Century
Woollen manufacturer	17.6	12.4	7.5	12.2
Clothier	16.9	17.4	13.9	15.6
Linen dealer	12.0	18.4	21.5	17.5
Cotton manufacturer	0.8	0.8	11.2	4.7
Tailor	2.5	6.6	8.7	6.5
Hosier	3.4	6.1	5.3	5.6
Haberdasher	5.0	8.1	6.9	6.8
Mercer	25.0	15.6	9.6	15.0

Source: London Gazette; P.R.O., B4/1–20.

woollen industry – the woollen manufacturers and clothiers – was a very important source of bankrupts, the actual manufacturers – weavers, wool processors and so on – were a declining source. This may well result from the fact that manufacturing enterprise gradually slipped from the hands of the workmen into the laps of the merchant manufacturers. Consequently, the relatively independent producers, such as the weavers, became less significant as the industry centralised. Certainly, numbers of bankrupts from the heart of woollen production failed to increase with anything like the speed of the textile sector as a whole. This may also have something to do with the problems which beset some areas of woollen production, particularly the absence of prosperity and sustained growth outside the West Riding. But the low level of numbers of woollen bankrupts was not simply caused by the centralisation of the production and the stagnation of some region's industry; it also arose from the growth of the trade in alternative fabrics, most notably through the rise of the cotton industry and the growing market for linen wares, as evidenced by their rising shares of the sector's bankruptcies. The second point evident from Table 7 is that one-third of all textile bankrupts were more involved in distribution than production, because tailors, hosiers, haberdashers and mercers can all be thought of as retailers and wholesalers rather than manufacturers.

There is, therefore, some reason to believe that a closer examination of the bankruptcy material can help our understanding of four key areas of change within the textile industries of the eighteenth century: the prosperity of the West Riding; the fortunes of East Anglia; the rise of cotton; and the role of London and the distributive trades.

Over the eighteenth century the output of the woollen industry probably increased by about 150 per cent.[1] This growth was disproportionately concentrated in the West Riding woollen and worsted industries. 'By the end of the eighteenth century...the locus of domestic woollen production had shifted decisively northwards.'[2] It is difficult to gauge the extent of the success of the West Riding, despite the availability of returns giving the quantity of broad and narrow cloths fulled.[3] What is clear is that the number of textile bankrupts from Yorkshire rose markedly, from twenty-two in the first decade of the century to 128 in the last. It is even possible that this sixfold increase does not need deflating because Wilson argues that 'the price of the final product did not rise significantly over the long run before the 1790s'.[4] Once again, a period of general, though interrupted, prosperity experienced ever-increasing levels of bankruptcies. Unfortunately, the absence of reliable trade directories for sufficiently long time spans or of other material makes it impossible to calculate changing rates of bankruptcy. However, Wilson has suggested that the value of the West Riding's output was around £1m in 1700 and £8.4m in 1800.[5] If it is assumed that the number of firms increased proportionately, over the whole period rates of bankruptcy may have fallen a little. Wilson quotes approvingly Wolrich's estimate for the value of the Yorkshire cloth industry for 1772 as £3.3m. Yet in the 1760s there were just thirty-seven textile bankrupts in the county and in the 1770s only forty-three. So, between 1700 and 1770 the Yorkshire cloth industry appears to have grown threefold while bankruptcies only doubled. And between 1770 and 1800 the industry grew by two and a half times but bankruptcies trebled. The more gradual growth of the first three-quarters of a century appears to have produced a warm and sunny climate for the cultivation of enterprise. Rapid growth after 1770 appears to have given rise to an increase in the bankruptcy rate. General trend prosperity cannot then be casually equated with easy market conditions for businessmen, be they inventors, innovators or imitators (see Chapter 4). Evidence is slowly accumulating which demonstrates that rapid growth, while good for 'progress', necessarily exacted a heavy toll from businessmen.

Prosperity in the West Riding has sometimes been seen to have taken place at the expense of the woollen industries elsewhere, especially in Norfolk.[6]

[1] P. Deane, 'The output of the British woollen industry in the eighteenth century', *Journal of Economic History*, XVII (1957), pp. 207–23.

[2] D. Gregory, *Regional transformation and industrial revolution. A geography of the Yorkshire woollen industry* (London, 1982), p. 47. D. T. Jenkins and K. G. Ponting, *The British wool textile industry 1770–1914* (London, 1982), pp. 1–8.

[3] Conveniently presented in Mitchell and Deane, *Abstract*, p. 189. Serious problems surround these series. See Deane, 'Output of the British woollen industry'. Gregory, *Regional transformation*, pp. 44–6, 98–101.

[4] Wilson, 'Supremacy of Yorkshire', p. 231.   [5] Ibid., p. 230.   [6] Ibid., p. 232.

Jenkins and Ponting concluded that Norwich's 'relative importance in worsted manufacture was clearly declining in the face of the rapid rise of the Yorkshire industry'.[7] But they also confessed that 'Much has been written about the Norwich worsted trade and it is perhaps fair to say that there is still not total agreement about the fortunes and problems of that industry in the late eighteenth and early nineteenth centuries.'[8] The availability of statistics about bankruptcy in the industry may help settle muddy waters.

The particular bone of contention has been the rough date at which the Norwich trades can be said to have begun their decline. Long ago, Clapham plumped for *c.* 1815; Lloyd-Pritchard settled on *c.* 1760; and Edwards alighted on 1850 as the earliest possible date.[9] Numbers of bankrupts from the industry in fact show a decisive change in about 1760. Down to then Norfolk averaged thirty-five textile bankrupts per decade. After then the level dropped suddenly and dramatically to only thirteen. The history of bankruptcy in the Norwich cloth trades during the eighteenth century divides neatly into two sub-periods either side of 1760. Until that date, for example, some 55.6 per cent of all textile bankrupts from the county were 'woollen producers'; but after it there were very few, and in the 1790s none at all. Over 90 per cent of all woollen manufacturers who went bankrupt in the county in the century failed before 1760. Such evidence, given that we are unable to calculate rates of bankruptcy, does not allow irrefutable arguments to be erected, but broadly speaking only two can be possible: either, that after *c.* 1760 the low levels of bankruptcy resulted from some medium- to long-term shift in the prosperity and security of the Norfolk cloth industry; or alternatively, the evidence can be interpreted simply in terms of Lloyd-Pritchard's dating of the decline of the city's textile trades, with lower numbers of bankrupts after 1760 being used as evidence of stagnation and the lack of enterprise.

Reports of the prosperity of the Norfolk cloth trades were widespread in the first half of the eighteenth century, which coincides with the period at which bankruptcies were high on trend. But the industry may well have stopped growing by about the time of the outbreak of the American War of Independence in 1775, which meant that in relative terms it was giving more and more ground to the West Riding. Certainly, between 1700 and 1750 the population of the city rose by 24.7 per cent, but in the next half century the rise

---

[7] *British wool textile industry*, p. 4.   [8] Ibid.

[9] J. H. Clapham, 'The transference of the worsted industry from Norfolk to the West Riding', *Economic Journal*, XX (1910), pp. 195–210. M. F. Lloyd-Pritchard, 'The decline of Norwich', *Economic History Review*, III (1950–1), pp. 371–7. J. K. Edwards, 'The economic development of Norwich, 1750–1850, with special reference to the worsted industry' (University of Leeds Ph.D. thesis, 1963). J. K. Edwards, 'The decline of the Norwich textiles industry', *Yorkshire Bulletin of Economic and Social Research*, XVI (1964), pp. 31–41.

was only 1.9 per cent.[10] There is no good evidence to suggest that the industry did more than maintain output levels after *c*. 1770.[11] But it is known that the industry increasingly concentrated on finer worsteds, presumably to try to secure a healthy market position against the vibrant West Riding.[12] Such cloths, however, had a limited market. Moreover, Norwich cloth merchants did not pursue direct intervention in risky overseas markets in the way that their colleagues in Leeds did, preferring to leave it to London middlemen. In all likelihood, after 1760 or so the Norfolk industry became relatively unattractive and offered little inducement to risk-taking which led to a fall in the rate of bankruptcy. In a defensive situation it is natural to cut risks and costs. But low levels and rates of bankruptcy are not thereby to be adjudged indications of success in terms of the growth and prosperity of the wider industry. Also, by implication, entry into the cloth trades in the West Riding was easier and more attractive as the eighteenth century passed, giving rise to more risk-taking and, thereby, a higher absolute volume of success and a higher rate of bankruptcy. It may be that in Norwich a stagnant trade was being concentrated in a smaller number of firms which themselves were relatively profitable.

The woollen industry's declining share of all textile bankrupts through the eighteenth century was only partly produced by the stagnation or decline of the industry outside Yorkshire. It also resulted from the rapid rise in the number of bankrupts from cotton textiles in the last third of the century. Before 1760, the number of cotton manufacturers going bankrupt was very small, averaging just one every two years. In the 1770s there were twenty-four, in the 1780s eighty-three and in the 1790s 232. By 1800 the cotton industry was regularly as important a source of bankrupts as the woollen industry. Although the numbers of firms in the cotton industry cannot be measured directly to try to make some estimates of the rate of bankruptcy, it is possible to use levels of retained raw cotton imports as an indirect guide. In the decade 1771–80, retained imports totalled 51.3m lb, in 1781–90 179.2m lb and in 1791–1800 307.4m lb.[13] Between the 1770s and the 1790s levels rose sixfold. Deflating the cotton industry's bankruptcy figures, by calling on the price relatives produced

---

[10] Corfield, *The impact of English towns*, p. 111.

[11] Edwards uses evidence of the number of freemen enrolled from the textile trades: Thesis, Appendix 1. But the figures, which actually show a fall in numbers after 1771, are difficult to use because of the way enrolments were used politically by the Whigs early in the century. Similarly, Edwards's use of records of cloth exports via Yarmouth is unreliable both because of breaks in the series suggesting changing levels of administrative efficiency and because the proportion of total output that passed through the port is unknown. See also Wilson, 'Supremacy of Yorkshire', p. 232, on this point.

[12] On the vulnerability of Norwich products to cheap competition see P. J. Corfield, 'The social and economic history of Norwich, 1650–1850: a study in urban growth' (University of London Ph.D. thesis, 1976), p. 58. She summarises the debate on pp. 305–15.

[13] Mitchell and Deane, *Abstract*, pp. 177–8.

Table 8. *Manchester's business population,*
1772–1800

Year	Traders	Textile traders (%)
1772	1230	47.3
1773	1390	46.0
1781	1670	45.5
1788	2250	40.6
1794	4530	44.7
1797	4690	49.5
1800	5260	49.0

Source: Directories listed in n. 15.

by Crafts for the industry, indicates that bankruptcy there rose nearly eightfold over the same three decades.[14] As with all other surrogate measures of the size of business communities, raw cotton imports are an imprecise guide to changing numbers of firms in the industry. Nevertheless, there is a clear suggestion here linking revolutionary development and rapid growth in the cotton industry with rising rates of bankruptcy.

It is possible, by calling on trade directories for Manchester and Liverpool, to pursue this by looking at rates of bankruptcy at the heart of the cotton industry. These directories appear more reliable than those for London, with fewer obvious omissions. This is hardly surprising, as there was probably an inverse correlation between the quality of a directory and the size of the town it was trying to cover. Seven Manchester directories have been examined: 1772, 1773, 1781, 1788, 1794, 1797 and 1800.[15] These listed merchants, tradesmen, manufacturers and principal inhabitants, only clearly omitting some from the construction trades. A number of non-traders were also included and have been removed for the following calculations.[16] The results are summarised in Table 8.

There were seventeen bankrupts from the Lancashire cotton industry in the 1770s, sixty-nine in the 1780s and 180 in the 1790s, most of them coming from Manchester. Indeed, two-thirds of all the county's bankrupts came from Manchester and Liverpool. Deflating the figures for cotton bankrupts in the

[14] Crafts, *British economic growth*, p. 25.
[15] 1772 and 1773: E. Raffald, *The Manchester directory*. 1781: E. Raffald, *The Manchester and Salford directory*. 1788: E. Holme, *The Manchester and Salford directory*. 1794 and 1797: Scholer's *Manchester and Salford directory*. 1800: Bancks's *Manchester and Salford directory*.
[16] Two of these directories are discussed in Wadsworth and Mann, *The cotton trade and industrial Lancashire*, pp. 254–8.

Table 9. *Liverpool's business population,*
1767–1800

Decade	Traders	Bankrupts
1760s	1470	7.3
1770s	2300	11.5
1780s	3500	13.3
1790s	6090	17.3

Note: Figures are annual averages based on the directories which appeared in each decade.
Source: See n. 17.

1790s, there was a roughly sevenfold rise over these decades while the number of textile traders rose only between three and four times. Taking bankruptcy in Manchester as a whole, there were eighty bankrupts in the 1770s, 109 in the next decade and 319 in the 1790s. This represents a real rise of 3.22 times between the 1770s and 1790s, which is exactly the same as that for the number of traders in the directories. Generally the business environment in Manchester was steady enough, with a bankruptcy rate of around one in 200 per annum. But within the cotton industry the rate of bankruptcy worsened over the three decades and in the 1790s may have been about one in 120 per annum.

Similar exercises can be carried out for Liverpool, where eight editions of *Gore's Liverpool directory* have been examined (see Table 9).[17] Taking the 1770s and 1790s as our benchmarks again and deflating the bankruptcy totals for the 1790s in the same way as for Manchester, the number of bankrupts increased by just 21 per cent, while the number of businesses rose by 164.8 per cent. In the 1770s the rate of bankruptcy was one in 200 per annum, but in the 1790s it was down to one in 435 per annum.[18]

At the centre of cotton manufacturing, Manchester's experience of bankruptcy was different from that of Liverpool, its servicing port, and more terrible. Even if the actual rates of bankruptcy which have been produced are liable to error because of the problems associated with the directories there is little doubt that whereas in Liverpool bankruptcy became less of a problem as imports and exports mounted, in Manchester, as production increased, so bankruptcy in the cotton industry worsened. Manufacturing appears to have suffered more than distribution on this occasion. This can be explained by recourse to ideas about

[17] The first one in 1766 is patently unreliable. I have used the directories for 1767, 1769, 1774, 1777, 1781, 1790, 1796 and 1800.
[18] Without deflating the data the figure for the 1790s would be one in 352.

risk differentials between the two areas of enterprise. The most likely reason relates to the ease of entry into the respective areas of enterprise. In Liverpool, entry was relatively difficult, largely because of the substantial capitals involved in setting up a trading enterprise. Indeed, while the number of traders in Liverpool increased by 164.8 per cent between the 1770s and the 1790s and the tonnage of ships belonging to the port rose by 165.1 per cent over the same period, the tonnage of trade in and out of the port increased by at least 208.5 per cent.[19] The increase in trade was not being matched by the growth in the number of businesses, so that businesses must have grown in size, which may have been allied with weakening competition and, on the other side of the same coin, growing profitability. It may well be that so rapidly was Liverpool's trade growing, in large part because of the demands for raw materials and export markets from Manchester and its environs, that sources of imitative merchants and middlemen were exhausted and the size of the business community unable to expand quickly enough. For Manchester the reverse of this argument can be advanced. Businessmen flooded in to exploit opportunities more quickly than they were actually being created, heightening competition, insecurity and uncertainty. Presumably, this arose because of the attractiveness of what was happening in and around Manchester and the ease of finding the capacity to exploit opportunities. Crouzet has concluded that 'During the initial stages of the industrial revolution, the requirements of fixed investment were thus very modest and the threshold of entry into factory production quite low, especially in the textile industries.'[20]

Arguably, it was also easier to enter cotton manufacturing than the occupations directly involved in importing and exporting because contacts could be more readily accumulated. What is certain is that it was easier to be an imitator in the flourishing Manchester-based trades than in the Liverpool-based ones. But that is not to be confused with the ease with which one could be a successful imitator. Obviously, high levels and rates of bankruptcy in Manchester suggest that substantial problems confronted this leading sector of the Industrial Revolution. Not the least of these was the long period of war from 1793. Changes of fashion also took their toll. And too many small firms, imitating the role models of Arkwright or Peel, had a restricted range of contacts, making easy access to credit and markets difficult, although 'the granting of credit was

[19] R. Stewart-Brown, *Liverpool ships in the eighteenth century* (Liverpool, 1932), p. 18. R. Brooke, *Liverpool as it was during the last quarter of the eighteenth century* (Liverpool, 1853), p. 506. The data on trade for the 1790s is available only for 1791–3, so the suggested rise of 208.5 per cent must be low, given the continued growth of Liverpool's trade after the early setbacks with the declaration of war in 1793. Also see J. Langton, 'Liverpool and its hinterland in the late eighteenth century', in B. L. Anderson and P. J. M. Storey, eds., *Commerce, industry and transport. Studies in economic change on Merseyside* (Liverpool, 1983), p. 18.

[20] F. Crouzet, 'Editor's introduction' to Crouzet, ed., *Capital formation in the industrial revolution* (London, 1972), p. 38.

a risky business, even with the leading firms'.[21] All these potential sources of problems for the shock troops of the Industrial Revolution can be illustrated briefly by looking at the crisis which hit the cotton trades in 1788, in the middle of an era of exceptionally rapid growth.

In 1788 the total number of bankruptcies in England leapt by nearly 40 per cent from the average level for the previous three years. This crisis disproportionately involved the textile sector, with its share of bankruptcies rising from 22 to 29.7 per cent over the same period, and it was the rapidly growing cotton trade, centred on Manchester, Liverpool and London that was worst hit. In Lancashire the number of textile bankrupts rose by 255.8 per cent, mostly in Manchester rather than Liverpool. In Manchester there had been an annual average of only 6.2 bankrupts 1783–7, but in 1788 it was forty-one, a massive rise of 561.3 per cent. For Liverpool the figures were seventeen and thirty-seven, a rise of 117.6 per cent.[22]

Following the expiry of Arkwright's patent, the ending of the American War in 1783, the commercial treaty with France in 1786 and some dubious manoeuvres associated with the East India Company's monopoly, 'by 1787 production seems to have temporarily overtaken consumption' in cotton goods.[23] As the *Manchester Mercury* reported, 'The Spirit of Adventure overshot its Mark.'[24] Tensions were focused through the lens of credit to such an extent that substantial dislocation and collapse ensued. Credit, the lifeblood of the small firms in Manchester, disappeared as confidence turned to despair. Sanctimoniously, *The Times* felt the crisis was mainly caused by 'the reprehensible facility with which these desperate adventurers first obtained credit'.[25] Undoubtedly, the flood of imitators that poured into Manchester after 1783 was partly made possible by the easy and essential access to credit.[26] More generally, therefore, the heavy dependence on credit in Manchester may have both eased

[21] S. D. Chapman, *The cotton industry in the industrial revolution* (London, 1972), p. 40.

[22] Such figures go some way towards disproving the claim that 'the year 1788 was no crisis or depression year at all, but the early part of an expansion': P. E. Mirowski, 'The birth of the business cycle' (University of Michigan Ph.D. thesis, 1979), p. 545. I have discussed the crisis of 1788 more fully in 'The use and abuse of credit'.

[23] Edwards, *British cotton trade*, p. 11. *London Chronicle*, 1–3 May 1788, p. 426. Unwin, *Samuel Oldknow*, p. 96. P. Colquhoun, *An important crisis in the calico and muslin manufactory in Great Britain explained* (London, 1788), p. 11.

[24] 1 April 1788, p. 1.   [25] 23 May 1788, p. 2.

[26] A. Bailey, 'The impact of the Napoleonic Wars on the development of the cotton industry in Lancashire: a study of the structure and behaviour of firms during the industrial revolution' (University of Cambridge Ph.D. thesis, 1985), p. 187. In the early nineteenth century 'small firms died in large numbers'. R. Lloyd-Jones and A. A. Le Roux, 'Marshall and the birth and death of firms: the growth and size distribution of firms in the early nineteenth century cotton industry', *Business History*, XXIV (1982), p. 148. The impact of credit within Lancashire has been vividly outlined by B. L. Anderson, 'Provincial aspects of the financial revolution of the eighteenth century', *Business History*, XI (1969), pp. 11–22.

Table 10. *Bankrupt linen dealers and mercers, 1701–1800*

Decade	Linen dealers	Percentage from London	Mercers	Percentage from London
1700s	59	78.0	116	27.6
1710s	56	77.5	123	29.5
1720s	62	60.8	110	24.5
1730s	76	51.0	119	20.0
1740s	79	38.0	66	21.4
1750s	86	31.2	74	19.1
1760s	141	29.2	63	23.5
1770s	155	47.1	113	21.2
1780s	258	34.9	110	21.8
1790s	303	36.3	142	31.0

Source: London *Gazette*; P.R.O., B4/1–20.

entry into business and provided its own risks, perhaps explaining the heavier impact on Manchester than on Liverpool of the crisis of 1788 and the different long-term patterns and rates of bankruptcy uncovered during the growth of these cities from 1770 to 1800. Sidney Checkland may have been right to feel that 'From the outset Liverpool's trade...was highly speculative', but it was noticeably less risky speculation than that in Manchester.[27]

So far discussion of bankruptcy in the textile sector has tended to concentrate on the failure of producers rather than on that of distributors. Yet linen dealers and mercers were especially important in providing bankrupts, followed to a lesser degree by haberdashers, tailors and hosiers. Linen dealers, mostly linen drapers, accounted for 17.5 per cent of all textile bankrupts, and the mercers 15 per cent. The following discussion looks only at these two occupations.

Broadly speaking, the number of linen dealers going bankrupt increased about fivefold in absolute terms over the century, while the number of bankruptcies among mercers was halved between the 1710s and 1760s before springing back to earlier levels by the close of the century (see Table 10). If these figures are deflated using the Schumpeter–Gilboy index, then in real terms numbers of linen dealers rose by 274.9 per cent between the first and last decades and the number of mercers fell by 10.6 per cent. In 1700, mercers were a far more important source of bankruptcies in the textile sector than the linen dealers, but by 1800 the tables had been turned.

The rise in the number of bankrupt linen dealers took place mostly outside

[27] S. G. Checkland, 'Economic attitudes in Liverpool, 1793–1807', *Economic History Review*, V (1952–3), p. 59.

the capital, particularly in Yorkshire, Lancashire and Bristol. London's dominance until the 1740s almost certainly arises from the very heavy dependence on imported sources of linen until the middle of the century. After then Scottish and Irish supplies became increasingly significant. As Harte has warned, 'It is all too easy to overlook whole trades because they were not centred on London, and because they catered largely for a series of local and regional markets and only in part for a national and international one.'[28] But it was also true that linen drapers were extensively involved in the developing cotton industry and the meaning of the term 'linen draper' became increasingly imprecise and ambiguous. What is beyond dispute is that linen drapers sold cloth by wholesale and retail and that the volume of bankruptcy among their ranks points to the importance of distribution within textile enterprise. Unfortunately, the lack of suitable evidence makes it impossible to calculate rates of bankruptcy among them.

In stark contrast to the linen trades, the mercery trade had at best an indifferent time of it in the eighteenth century, if low trend levels of bankrupts mark stagnation or secular decline. Numbers at the start of the century were maintained at a steady level until a pronounced trough from 1740 to 1770, before a recovery. Relative to the textile sector as a whole, this amounted to a very poor showing, for whereas mercers had accounted for one-quarter of all textile bankrupts in the period 1701–20, by the final decade of the century their proportion was down to just one-tenth (see Table 7). Among all textile occupations this was easily the worst performance. Explaining this pattern is difficult, not least because of terminological problems. In the eighteenth century a mercer did not simply sell silk and silk goods. The *Oxford English Dictionary*, for example, gives a definition of 1696 in which a mercer is 'in the City one that deals only in Silks and Stuffs; In Country Towns, one that Trades in all sorts of Linen, Woollen, Silk, and Grocery Wares'. In other words, 'mercer' was used inexactly and it would be facile to erect an exact explanation of the pattern of bankrupt mercers.

Some suggestions can be made by way of an explanation however. In theory it ought to be possible to judge the scale of the silk production and demand in England by looking at silk imports. Yet though there is a close correspondence between imports and bankruptcy for the period 1720–50, from 1750 to 1780 there is not.[29] In the 1750s and 1760s, low levels of bankruptcies among mercers have to be set against rising silk imports, suggesting an expanding but less competitive industry. What may have happened is that an exceptional surge of

[28] Harte, 'The rise of protection', pp. 75–6. W. G. Rimmer, *Marshall's of Leeds: flax spinners, 1788–1886* (Cambridge, 1960), Ch. 1.

[29] The best source of the relevant data and a discussion of the eighteenth-century silk industry is D. C. Coleman, *Courtaulds. An economic and social history*, 3 vols. (Oxford, 1969–80), Vol. 1, Ch. 2.

silk exports from England in the 1750s and early 1760s arose from the successful capture of the French trade in silk manufactures, leading to a period when mercers found their market position significantly enhanced. From the middle 1760s, as the French re-entered the international trade in silk, and as levels of domestic trade and production in silk grew, encouraging new entrants, so competition may have returned to pre-1750 levels, leading to a rise in the number of mercers going bankrupt.

Examining bankruptcy in the textile sector has done more than confirm the argument of Chapter 4 that trend expansion is usually associated with increasing levels and, often, rates of bankruptcy and trend stagnation or contraction with the reverse. It has pointed to the care which needs to be paid to understanding the full complexity of the competitive situation businessmen faced. In Lancashire this related not only to the availability of markets but, crucially, to thresholds of entry and the role of credit. In the Norfolk worsted industry it related to the search for security and stability. And in the silk trades it may have been related, in the 1750s and early 1760s, to the collapse of French competition caused by their military failure in two long wars. Looking at rates of failure, either directly or indirectly, has shown the fundamental importance to be attached to the interaction between thresholds of entry and the perception of opportunities. This has helped clear some of the fog associated with the decline of Norwich. It has stressed the variety of experience in the development of the cotton industry and suggested that more attention ought to be paid to the interaction of production and distribution as evidenced by the examples of linen and silk.

FOOD AND DRINK

Together, the food and drink sectors provided nearly 23 per cent of all bankrupts in the century, though the two areas did not share identical histories. Numbers of drink trade bankrupts rose more slowly and at different times from those in the food trades. (See Table 11.) In absolute terms, the number of drink bankrupts increased by 2.4 times and the number of food bankrupts by 4.2 times between the first and last decades of the century. In real terms, the rises were 73.7 per cent and 203.6 per cent respectively. Compared with bankruptcy as a whole the food trades had a normal chronology, but the drink trades did not: whereas bankrupts from the food sector made a contribution to total bankruptcy that varied within narrow bounds right through the century, from 11.1 to 13.5 per cent using decennial totals, the drink trades' contribution sank as low as 8.3 per cent and rose as high as 16.1 per cent. The erratic contribution of the drink trades was concentrated in the period 1720–70. More specifically, outside the drink trades numbers of bankrupts fell by 15.5 per cent between the 1720s and 1730s, but in the drink trades there was a rise of 14.3 per cent. Then

Table 11. *Bankrupts in drink and food,*
1701–1800

Decade	Drink	Food
1700s	266	245
1710s	174	193
1720s	288	293
1730s	329	265
1740s	228	241
1750s	207	284
1760s	239	322
1770s	448	559
1780s	481	638
1790s	633	1019

Source: London Gazette; P.R.O., B4/1–20.

from 1740 to 1770 numbers of bankrupts from the drink trades stagnated while elsewhere they rose from a slump in numbers in the 1740s. For the drink trades, therefore, the particular problem to be addressed over its individual chronology is the relatively high numbers in the 1730s and the fall back in the sector's prominence in the following two decades. Doing this is made easier by first looking at the occupational composition of bankruptcy in the sector.

Six occupations dominated bankruptcy in the drink sector, of which four were especially important. Wine dealers were the most significant, accounting for 29.1 per cent of the sector's bankruptcies. These were followed by inn-keepers, 21.4 per cent; brewers, 16.0 per cent; those involved in malting, 14.0 per cent; distillers, 6.5 per cent; and spirit dealers, 4.5 per cent. Fluctuations and changes in the fortunes of this small group structured the pattern of bankruptcy in the sector as a whole. Figure 4 charts the numbers of bankrupts from these occupations by decades. From this it is clear that the rise in numbers in the 1730s took place mostly among the maltsters and, to a lesser extent, the brewers and distillers.

As ever, two alternative explanations of this pattern are possible: either that the rise in the number of bankrupt maltsters, brewers and distillers represents an increase in the rate of failure rather than an increase of the population at risk; or that the rate of failure hardly changed and that higher levels of bankruptcy indicate growth and buoyancy which led to firm formation and a consequent rise in the absolute level of bankruptcies. Glancing at Figure 4, the broad similarity of movements in numbers of bankruptcies among maltsters and brewers through the century – and of distillers too until the 1750s –

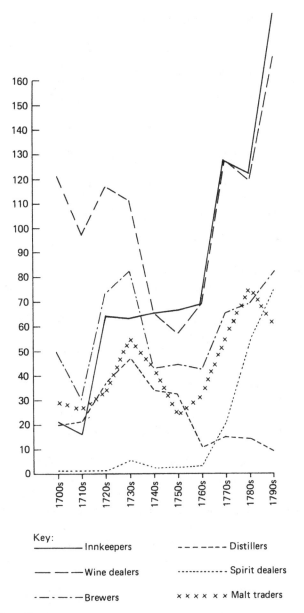

Fig. 4 Bankruptcy in the drink sector, 1701–1800 (decennial totals).

Table 12. *Annual decennial averages of*
bankruptcy in brewing, 1720–60

Decade	Bankrupt brewers	Common brewers	Rate of bankruptcy
1720s	6.9	832	1 in 120.6
1730s	6.5	934	1 in 143.7
1740s	3.4	958	1 in 281.8
1750s	3.5	1047	1 in 299.1

Note: Numbers of bankrupts for the 1720s have been
adjusted to take account of the absence of data in
1723–4.
Source: London Gazette; P.R.O., B4/1–20; Mathias,
Brewing industry in England, pp. 539–45.

suggests the strong possibility of common influences acting on each. What united them all was their dependence upon agriculture for raw materials, in particular for barley and hops. As is well known, the 1730s and 1740s were a period when a large number of harvests were good. Wheat, malt and hop prices all fell and demand for beer and spirits was strong.[30] With lower raw material costs and strong markets, conditions in the malting, brewing and distilling trades must have been very attractive. Probably, more bankrupts appeared among them in the 1730s because they were attracting more businessmen. But this does not explain why numbers of bankrupts should then have fallen in the 1740s. By implication rates of failure must have changed, with widening profit margins and weakened competition in the 1740s leading to lower rates of failure.

This proposition can be tested, albeit in a rough and ready fashion, because available excise records allow estimates to be made of the well-being of a large part of the drink sector at the time. The brewers can be taken as an example here.[31] If the data used in Table 12 are reasonably reliable then there is clear evidence of falling bankruptcy rates through the period. But this runs counter to the findings that growing sectors and trades, with significant numbers of entrants, tend to have rising bankruptcy rates because of the expansion of the fund of risk-taking and inexperience.

Given the massive restructuring that was taking place within the industry,

---

[30] Discussed most recently in P. J. Bowden, 'Agricultural prices, wages, farm profits, and rent', in Thirsk, ed., *The agrarian history of England and Wales*, Vol. v, Part ii, pp. 1–118.

[31] See Mathias, *The brewing industry in England*, pp. 369–83, for a discussion of the statistics, and pp. 539–45 for their presentation.

associated with the rise of porter brewing and legislative control, it is difficult to relate changes in the numbers of bankrupts to prices, output and the number of firms with any confidence. Professor Mathias conceded that 'It will never be possible to establish the cause of these trends scientifically: there are too many variables and so many unknowns.'[32] Although it is difficult to account for the apparent paradox of rising trend numbers of brewers alongside falling trend rates of bankruptcy, it is possible that the explanation relates to widening profit margins between 1720 and 1760 as the Assize of Ale held up the price of beer at a time when raw material costs were generally low owing to good harvests, advances in agricultural productivity and low levels of population growth. The increasing scale of production in brewing may also have lowered costs.[33] This was of course just the era when the early Whitbread and Truman fortunes were being amassed. Why then were there not more entrants into brewing to take advantage of this happy conjuncture and emulate the clear success stories? Presumably because the greatest opportunities were occurring in areas where thresholds of entry were high. It may well be that it was the more capital-intensive areas of brewing, as in London, that were the most attractive but that there 'Brewing was not an area to be entered lightly.'[34] Campbell believed that 'The Business of a Brewer requires a large Stock of Ready Money to set up with, and the Profits returned are proportionately considerable.'[35]

Given the substitutability that existed in the drink market, competitive conditions in brewing were partly affected by the productivity of producing other drinks. In particular, the four decades 1720–60 was a period of considerable change in the amount of spirits produced and drunk. After all, this was the age of Hogarth's Gin Lane, when babies fell from their drunken mothers' arms. In the 1720s the output of spirits from England and Wales averaged 3.9m gallons per annum. But the industry soon expanded and a century-high peak was reached in 1743 with 8.2m gallons being produced, before rapid contraction after 1751 following legislative control. In the 1750s output averaged 3.8m gallons per annum and in the 1760s just 2.4m gallons per annum.[36] Interestingly, a peak in the number of maltsters and distillers going bankrupt was recorded in the 1730s, very close to the timing of the peak of output. In distilling, where thresholds of entry were usually modest, rising output was produced by new entrants rather than dramatic scale economies being reaped by increasingly larger firms. The close correlation between levels of output and bankruptcy suggests that trend growth in these industries, unlike that in brewing, was not associated with lowering rates of failure.

So far, the drink sector has been looked at in terms of its highly individual chronology. But this has diverted attention away from the two groups which

[32] Ibid., p. 12.   [33] Ibid., p. 111.   [34] Ibid., p. 258.
[35] Campbell, *The London tradesman*, p. 264.   [36] Mitchell and Deane, *Abstract*, pp. 254–6.

determined the overall size of the sector for bankruptcy: the wine dealers and the innkeepers. Together they provided over half of all bankrupts from the sector. Particularly worth stressing is the importance of the wine dealers. Wine was a luxury commodity in the eighteenth century, wholly dependent upon imports, and the number of wine merchants going bankrupt seems unusually large given the size of the trade, implying a high bankruptcy rate. This is likely because as an imported luxury the trade was notoriously unstable and insecure, subject to Francophobia, changing tastes for fortified wines and the impact of wars and treaties. Perhaps it is not surprising therefore that broad changes in the levels of wine imports were followed in an exaggerated fashion by broad changes in levels of bankruptcy in the trade. For example, in the 1720s and 1730s, wine imports averaged over £540,000 per annum. But in the next three decades, they were down to just under £400,000 per annum.[37] Between these two periods wine imports fell by about 26 per cent but bankruptcies among wine dealers fell by 44 per cent. Later in the century, when wine imports grew, so numbers of bankrupt wine dealers grew even more quickly.[38] Given the notorious prominence of smuggling in wines it would be unwise to put much weight on these patterns. But perhaps there was some symmetry of risk attached to both the legal and illegal sides of the wine trade, because Adam Smith felt that 'Bankruptcies are most frequent in the most hazardous trades. The most hazardous of all trades, that of a smuggler...is the infallible road to bankruptcy.'[39]

The geography of failure in the drink sector divides into three broad groups. There were the wine dealers and the distillers, heavily concentrated in and around the metropolis. Then there were the brewers and the dealers in spirits who had what might be called a more 'normal' concentration in the capital – 38.7 and 33.7 per cent respectively. Finally, there were the innkeepers and maltsters who showed little sign of concentration at all. Only 11.6 per cent of innkeepers came from London and only two out of the hundreds of bankrupt maltsters came from there. The distribution of the malt trade has been explained by Professor Mathias and does not need repeating here, though it is worth remarking that the pattern of bankruptcy replicates his description.[40] It is the lack of concentration, but numerical importance, of the innkeeper that needs to be taken further.

Innkeepers were concerned with more than just the retailing of drink and the provision of accommodation for travellers. Dual occupations among innkeepers

[37] Ibid., pp. 285–6.
[38] For a discussion of the wine trade see R. Davis, 'The English wine trade in the eighteenth and nineteenth centuries', *Annales Cisalpines d'Histoire Sociale*, III (1972), pp. 87–106. A. D. Francis, *The wine trade* (London, 1972). Fisher, *The Portugal trade*, pp. 24–7.
[39] *Wealth of nations*, Vol. I, p. 124.   [40] *The Brewing industry in England*, pp. 393–4.

were especially common and help point to the central place inns had in the internal trade of the country: 'in the carriage of goods overland, from the smallest feeder service to the long-distance carrier, the inn was the basic and essential unit of organisation'.[41] The dispersion of bankrupt innkeepers gives weight to this conclusion. Every county produced some, and no county's total was significantly large. So, the long- and short-term fortunes of internal trade were perhaps the most important determinant of the fortunes of the innkeepers. According to Massie, there were 5,000 innkeepers and alesellers in 1759, ignoring his group 'ale-sellers and cottagers' because they were too small to get caught by the law of bankruptcy.[42] With an average of 5.3 and 6.3 bankrupt innkeepers per annum in the 1750s and 1760s the bankruptcy rate was of the order of one in 800–900. This is low compared with other occupations for which we have been able to calculate rates of bankruptcy. At the end of the century the rate was up to one in 546 on the basis of Colquhoun's data.[43] As this makes no allowance for the extension of bankruptcy because of inflation, this rate must be on the high side when compared with that for 1759. The validity of these calculations, however, is undermined by the fact that the law was uncertain as to whether innkeepers were traders or not. Consequently, some innkeepers were adjudged not to fall within the jurisdiction of the law and the figures of bankrupt innkeepers may fall short of offering representative coverage of failure among the occupation.[44]

Moving on, because the food trades escaped the excise's consuming grip and only a fraction was imported or exported it is impossible to detail the sector's fortunes in the same ways as those that have been attempted for the textile and drink trades. But the broad patterns can be briefly sketched. Two occupations were especially important: the grocers who provided 34.1 per cent of the total in this sector and the victuallers, who provided 23.0 per cent. These were followed by the butchers, 11.0 per cent, the bakers, 8.8 per cent and those from the cheese trade, 8.0 per cent. Together, these five groups account for nearly 85 per cent of all bankrupts in the food sector during the century. Figure 5 shows numbers of failures from among their ranks over the period and demon-

---

[41] J. A. Chartres, 'The place of inns in the commercial life of London and western England 1660–1760' (University of Oxford D.Phil. thesis, 1973), p. 253. On dual occupations the most famous case is examined by T. S. Ashton, *An eighteenth century industrialist. Peter Stubs of Warrington 1756–1806* (Manchester, 1939). Thomas Alcock, a Manchester 'innkeeper, carrier and chapman' was made bankrupt in 1783 but he also bought and sold 'Corn Beans Hops Horses' among other things. P.R.O., B3/5451. On the role of inns see George, *London life*, pp. 290–1. Clark, *The English alehouse*. A. Everitt, 'The English urban inn, 1560–1760', in Everitt, ed., *Perspectives in English urban history* (London, 1973), pp. 91–137.

[42] Lindert and Williamson, 'Revising England's social tables', p. 396. Mathias, *The brewing industry in England*, p. 220.

[43] I have assumed that the proportions ineligible for bankruptcy in 1759 and 1800 were similar.

[44] Chitty and Forster, *A digested index*, p. 67.

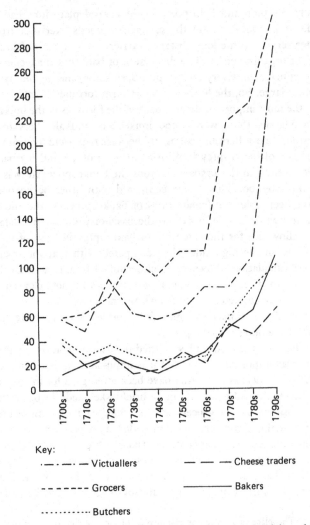

Fig. 5 Bankruptcy in the food sector, 1701–1800 (decennial totals).

strates that the pattern of bankruptcy among butchers, bakers and cheese traders
was remarkably similar. As a proportion of all bankrupts in the sector the graph
of their contribution describes a very shallow 'U', highest at the start and end
of the century and only a little lower during the middle. This suggests that the
buoyant output of agriculture during the 1730s and 1740s, with lower prices,
benefited those most closely involved in the retailing of food, just as it had the

brewers. The second feature of bankruptcy in these areas is the stability of their contribution to the sector as a whole – in other words, the shallowness of the 'U' just described. But this was far from being the case for the grocers and victuallers – numbers of bankrupt victuallers were especially erratic. In particular, relatively high levels in the 1720s and 1790s seem unusual and worth explaining.

Victuallers must not be confused with licensed victuallers in the eighteenth century. Primarily, they were provision merchants, to be found on the quaysides supplying ships with stores. Nearly eight out of every ten bankrupt victuallers came from London or the adjacent riverside areas of Kent, Middlesex and Surrey and the growth of their numbers follows the growth of overseas trade, though with the exception of the 1720s.

Over the ten years 1713–22 five victuallers on average went bankrupt each year. But for 1725–9 the average was seventeen. One possible explanation of this surge relates to the preparations which were being made for war against Spain. Another relates to the bad harvests of 1725 and 1727–8. In fact, both probably worked upon one another because, with the threat of war, the victuallers may have bought up substantial supplies which were costly both because of the growth in demand and the fall in supply associated with the bad harvests. And when war failed to materialise the victuallers would have been left with large debts and expensive provisions. Their indebtedness would have increased and bankruptcy spread. In essence, high levels of bankruptcy were caused by unsuccessful speculation as to future market trends.

Once the 1720s are taken into account, the changes in bankruptcy levels among the victuallers make more sense. From the 1730s until the 1790s they follow changes in the volume of trade (net imports plus domestic exports).[45] But the surge of numbers in the 1790s was much greater than the expansion of trade would have suggested. It is possible that war and very expensive provisions once again created a speculative movement that was, in the end, only partly warranted. War also created a more competitive business environment in the food trades since government contractors jostled for supplies which were normally destined for the domestic market. James Jenkins, who carried on a trade in bacon between Ireland and England, recalled how in 1780

our bacon-trade suddenly vanished as the morning dew – in consequence of war being declared against Spain, by our government, it made some Very large provision-contracts in Ireland...this caused such a great advance in price, that we could not obtain a single flitch at a price sufficiently low, to enable us to obtain any profit. – This lucrative trade we were therefore obliged to abandon...[46]

[45] Deane and Cole, *British economic growth*, p. 48.
[46] London Friends Meeting House Library, James Jenkins, Records and recollections, 1761 to 1821, MS, fo. 183.

Explaining bankruptcy among the food and drink trades has pointed to more than just secular developments within these sectors, either in their own right, or in relation to the wider economy. It has shown patterns of trading, particularly in relation to their geography, which point to essential differences between them. The susceptibility of these trades to trend changes in prices has also been exposed. Many of them appear to have flourished in the 1730s and 1740s when low prices helped protect them against the chill wind of competition. In the 1790s, on the other hand, with rampant inflation, these sectors suffered badly. Higher prices, over which they had minimal control, seem to have hit hardest those concerned with the satisfaction of basic needs. Prosperity in the food and drink trades was largely a matter of disposable incomes which in turn was heavily dependent upon the balance between population and agricultural and industrial productivity. With only slow change in the modes of business practice in these sectors (brewing excepted), the number of firms operating in them was a function of alterations in population, living standards and taste. The latter factor played a minor role in the food trades but was more significant in the drink sector. Finally, high levels and, probably, rates of bankruptcy among the wine merchants and the victuallers show the natural insecurity of those occupations involved in overseas trade.

MERCHANTS

Bankruptcies among merchants were more common than among any other single occupation in the eighteenth century, accounting for 11.9 per cent of the total. To some extent, this may arise from the legal history of bankruptcy and the origin of the trading distinction discussed in Chapter 3. It may also have something to do with the fact that 'merchant' was an indiscriminate catch-all term for overseas traders. But in large part it demonstrates the importance of overseas trade to the eighteenth-century economy, the merchants' role in that trade, the natural riskiness of their occupation and, finally, the place of credit in the import–export economy. 'The merchant...invests his capital in remote and comparatively hazardous concerns; he gives long credit, and on single security; he depends sometimes on the conduct of persons resident in distant countries; is liable to the rise and fall of markets, which are often very great; and is, more or less, at the mercy of seas and tempests...'[47]

The broad facts of numbers and geography of bankrupt merchants are clear enough from Table 13. In absolute terms, the number of bankrupt merchants doubled over the century, but in real terms the rise was just 44.7 per cent. Clearly this was a much slower rate of growth than for bankruptcy as a whole

[47] T. Gisborne, *An enquiry into the duties of man in the higher and middle classes of society in Great Britain* (London, 1794), p. 502.

Table 13. *Bankrupt merchants, 1701–1800 (as percentage of all merchants from given counties)*

Decade	Number	Devon	Glos.	London	Lancs.	Middx.	Norfolk	Yorks.
1700s	325	6.2	3.1	68.0	0.9	2.8	1.9	4.0
1710s	292	4.1	2.4	67.2	5.7	1.4	4.3	4.6
1720s	257	3.1	3.1	60.0	2.8	2.8	5.2	4.6
1730s	209	6.1	5.7	52.3	3.8	4.2	4.6	4.2
1740s	231	4.4	7.9	58.7	3.4	2.4	5.1	4.4
1750s	294	3.5	7.5	49.7	9.1	0.8	3.8	7.5
1760s	462	3.4	6.0	62.3	7.1	3.0	1.4	4.2
1770s	521	3.1	3.8	54.1	10.8	2.7	3.7	6.3
1780s	622	2.4	4.0	55.0	12.2	3.5	0.3	6.9
1790s	644	3.9	5.8	48.5	20.3	1.2	1.4	6.4

Source: London Gazette; P.R.O., B4/1–20.

and it was also much slower than the rate of growth of trade. In official values both imports and exports increased fourfold, and McCusker has estimated an increase in current values of over sixfold for exports.[48] From this it is likely that trade became more secure over the century, something that can be tested in a crude way by again calling on those three wise men, King, Massie and Colquhoun. They respectively guessed the number of merchants to be 10,000 at the end of the seventeenth century, 13,000 in 1759 and 15,000 in *c.* 1800. The rate of bankruptcy works out to be one in 308, one in 386 and one in 233 per annum at these three dates.[49] So, in the first sixty years of the century, when the number of bankrupt merchants stagnated and trade doubled, the environment may have become healthier. Over the last forty years however, as trade and the number of merchant bankrupts rapidly expanded, the air became less pure. What was distinctive about this second era was that the number of merchants in trade failed to keep pace with the actual growth of trade whereas numbers of bankrupts did.

One part of a possible explanation for this would be to repeat the argument about high thresholds of entry into trade that was used when looking at

[48] Deane and Cole, *British economic growth*, p. 48. J. J. McCusker, 'The current value of English exports, 1697 to 1800', *William and Mary Quarterly*, 3rd series, XXVIII (1971), pp. 620–2. McCusker's calculations involve a certain margin of error because the price index he uses is not entirely appropriate. See R. Davis, *The industrial revolution and British overseas trade* (Leicester, 1979), pp. 79–86.

[49] Lindert and Williamson, 'Revising England's social tables', pp. 393, 396, 400. I have used annual decennial averages of merchant bankruptcies for 1701–10, 1755–64 and 1791–1800 in these calculations.

bankruptcy in Liverpool (see p. 82). Yet there is no reason to expect that this would lead to a worsening of the rates of bankruptcy, quite the reverse in fact. It is possible that as trade grew it was riskier and more uncertain in terms of both commodities and markets. For example, the quick growth of the cotton trade involved merchants with a product of which they had little previous experience. And the period 1756 to 1800 saw three major and highly disruptive wars which led to particularly serious setbacks to the trend expansion of trade in the late 1770s and early 1790s.[50] Essentially, bankruptcy among merchants can best be understood in terms of a distinctive mix of uncertainty and speculation.

Overseas trade was inevitably risky and clearly more unpredictable than internal trade. Most obviously, 'the lottery of the sea' in the form of storms was a major problem.[51] But increasingly insurance should have offset the risks there. Then there were the risks of war and piracy. In wartime insurance rates often went so high that many could not afford them. And war also closed markets and sources of supply, either partially or completely. Finally, new or expanding overseas markets or sources of supply were of much more uncertain size, significance and potential than domestic ones. The interactions between uncertainty and speculation that were distinctive to overseas trade rested on the last two issues raised here: war and market size.

Any war can be conveniently split into three phases: the threat of war, the period of conflict and the making of peace. All three invited merchants to guess and speculate on what was going to happen to supply, demand and finance. Significantly, bankruptcies among them peaked not in the first year of war but two or three years into the conflict (1742, 1758–9, 1778 and 1796) *and* just at the end (1712–13, 1748–9, 1763–4 and 1783). Equally, the share of merchants as a proportion of all bankruptcies usually rose from a low point at the outbreak of a war to a peak at or just beyond its end. Although merchants appear to have been fairly successful with the early problems created by the threat and immediate outbreak of wars they tended to find themselves undone after a while. In particular, the prospect or advent of peace seems to have led to a surge of unsuccessful risk-taking among them, largely because they consistently misjudged the extent of post-war booms. Such miscalculations arose from the simple fact that although in wartime insurance rates rocketed, privateering grew and uncertainty increased, the official value of exports in the final year of any one of these wars was greater than in that war's opening year.[52] So if merchants rightly distinguished wartime conditions they failed to appreciate the consistent success with which trade adjusted to wars. In consequence, the

[50] Deane and Cole, *British economic growth*, p. 49.
[51] Smith, *Wealth of nations*, Vol. I, p. 122.
[52] Deane and Cole, *British economic growth*, p. 46.

onset of peace usually resulted in unwitting speculation on their part and the formation of wayward expectations.[53] Moreover, as wars progressed so the government tended to borrow more and more, pushing up interest rates and tightening monetary conditions, making it even more difficult for the merchants to generate the requisite profits as they found themselves competing for funds from their usual backers.[54]

Merchantry was susceptible to speculation beyond that arising from wars. In the late 1760s, for example, a dramatic expansion of trade, especially to the Thirteen Colonies, took place. But the boom rested on an imperfect understanding of the capacity of the colonies to soak up British exports, and expectations ran ahead of reality. Exports peaked in 1771 as the market became overstocked, before falling back for two years. As in all speculative booms, when the bubble burst, victims were claimed and, interestingly, merchant bankruptcy was much higher at that point than later in the decade when, after the outbreak of the American War of Independence in 1775, trade levels reached a thirty-year low. A similar speculative expansion took place with the return of peace in 1783, presumably accounting for the failure of James Dunlop of London in November 1785 who had exported 'Cloaths Silks Irish Linens Muslin Hosiery Haberdashery and Millinery Goods...to Maryland and Virginia in North America and to the Islands of Jamaica and Antigua receiving in return for such Goods divers quantities of Tobacco Sugars Rum Coffee and Cotton'.[55] While there may have been no overall export-based inventory cycle in the eighteenth century, some of the root causes of such cycles existed: the erratic flows of information that heightened risks, expanding markets and the inability of merchants to anticipate the extent of their competitors' response to market stimuli that usually took the form of price movements.[56]

Going into business as a merchant was expensive. For example, Price has estimated that before 1775 British merchants trading to Chesapeake needed

[53] B. Thomas, 'The rhythm of growth in the Atlantic economy of the eighteenth century', *Research in Economic History*, III (1978), p. 24. A. H. John, 'War and the English economy, 1700–1763', *Economic History Review*, VII (1954–5), pp. 335–8. In the Anglo-Dutch trade, for example, 'a high proportion of booms and slumps coincide with periods of war': D. J. Ormrod, 'Anglo-Dutch commerce 1700–1760' (University of Cambridge Ph.D. thesis, 1973), p. 399.

[54] L. S. Pressnell, 'The rate of interest in the eighteenth century', in Pressnell, ed., *Studies in the industrial revolution* (London, 1960), pp. 178–214. Price, *Capital and credit*, Chs. 4 and 5. A. H. John, 'Insurance investment and the London money market of the eighteenth century', *Economica*, XX (1953), p. 150.

[55] P.R.O., B3/1258. See also the example of Abraham Wilkinson and George Cook in my 'The use and abuse of credit', pp. 69–70.

[56] Fisher, *The Portugal trade*, pp. 115–17, argues for the existence of an inventory cycle. See also K. N. Chaudhuri, *The trading world of Asia and the English East India Company 1660–1760* (Cambridge, 1978), pp. 87–90, 480–1. For some good points on the problems of eighteenth-century overseas trade see J. F. Shepherd and G. M. Walton, *Shipping, maritime trade, and the economic development of colonial North America* (Cambridge, 1972), pp. 54–5.

between £5,000 and £10,000 to start out. European markets could be exploited with smaller capitals, but the amounts were still considerable.[57] This money was not tied up in ships or other fixed capital assets, but in stocks and credit. 'Most shipowners were merchants, most merchants were at some time shipowners, but shipowning claimed only a small proportion of each man's capital, and received a correspondingly small share of his time and attention.'[58] The real financial burden was in funding trade and exchange through the provision of credit. Adam Smith categorically declared that 'The capital of a merchant...is altogether a circulating capital.'[59] With the relatively slow movement of goods in the international arena, merchants found themselves having to keep up long and tenuous ties to link producers and consumers. The extension of credit by English merchants was intimately connected to the growth of overseas trade. Merchants were well aware that future profits depended on the way in which they advanced credit now and, on the whole therefore, the incentive was clearly to give more and more of it. It was this, for example, which underlay the rapid growth of trade to America. 'After 1730 the financial relationship between England and her American colonies began to change. The independent merchants...began to offer a large volume of credit on more liberal terms.'[60] At Leeds, 'To capture trade newcomers extended credit facilities and allowed abatements on their invoices. These features became especially prevalent in the American market.'[61] Such credit arrangements also appear to have been typical of some of the European trades too, not to mention the West Indies and Africa. In the Levant trade, merchants had to finance the gap between initial purchase and final sale that might be up to three years.[62] Closer to home, the Anglo-Irish trade was directed and financed by English merchants.[63]

Extending such large amounts of credit over such long distances, often on the basis of nothing more than personal security, meant that bad debts were endemic and balancing income with expenditure consistently difficult. If credit was given too generously, it often proved impossible for merchants to get the

---

[57] Price, *Capital and credit*, p. 38.

[58] R. Davis, *The rise of the English shipping industry* (Newton Abbot, 1962) p. 81.

[59] *Wealth of nations*, Vol. I, p. 295.

[60] R. C. Nash, 'English transatlantic trade, 1660–1730: a quantitative study' (University of Cambridge Ph.D. thesis, 1982), pp. 43–4. Price, *Capital and credit*. S. M. Rosenblatt, 'The significance of credit in the tobacco consignment trade: a study of John Norton & Sons, 1768–1775', *William and Mary Quarterly*, 3rd series, XIX (1962), pp. 383–99. B. L. Anderson, 'The Lancashire bill system and its Liverpool practitioners', in W. H. Chaloner and B. M. Ratcliffe, eds., *Trade and transport* (Manchester, 1977), pp. 59–97. W. I. Roberts, 'Samuel Storke: an eighteenth-century London merchant trading to the American colonies', *Business History Review*, XXXIX (1965), pp. 147–70.

[61] Wilson, *Gentlemen merchants*, p. 79.

[62] R. Davis, *Allepo and Devonshire Square. English traders in the Levant in the eighteenth century* (London, 1967), pp. 11–12.

[63] L. M. Cullen, *Anglo-Irish trade 1660–1800* (Manchester, 1968), pp. 98–9.

sort of liquidity they needed in a hurry at various times in their business life. Malynes had warned 'That he who is farthest from his goods, is neerest to his losse.'[64] Getting repayment from sluggish debtors was hard enough in England, but the problems were magnified for overseas debtors. When monetary conditions were tight, merchants could not expect extension from their creditors, and so they found themselves trying to haul in assets which were weighted down by distance in an attempt to keep their own repayments going. 'In fact the ability to command commercial credit in time of duress was more important to success in eighteenth century commerce than any technical or administrative skill the merchant might possess.'[65] In 1773, for example, John Norton & Sons, London merchants trading to Virginia, had outstanding accounts of £64,000. Perkins, Buchanan & Brown, of London, who went under in August 1773 were owed upwards of £70,000 by Virginians. At another time, the Pinneys, trading to the West Indies, were owed between £20–30,000. And in 1792 John Dawson, a Liverpool slave trader, had accumulated debts owed to him of £228,000 in the New World.[66] When James Balliness, a merchant from Bishopsgate Street, went bankrupt in March 1780 owing over £35,000 he declared that he was owed nearly £44,000 from twenty-eight debtors in the West Indies and America.[67] Successfully demanding repayment from overseas debtors was notoriously difficult, for they were beyond immediate moral suasion and quick legal redress.[68] Statutory provision in 1731, which recognised that 'his majesty's subjects trading to... America lie under great difficulties, for want of more easy methods of proving, recovering and levying of debts due to them', failed to solve effectively the problem in the most rapidly growing corner of trade.[69] Indeed, at the end of the century one of the reasons for the institution of the Manchester Commercial Society in 1794 was the acknowledged problem of getting repayment from overseas debtors.[70]

Frequently, merchants got into deep water because they tried to expand too quickly by being over-liberal with credit. In late July 1773 John Norton wrote

---

[64] G. Malynes, *Lex mercatoria* (London, 1622), p. 222.

[65] Rosenblatt, 'Significance of credit', p. 387.

[66] *John Norton & Sons*, p. 293. *Joshua Johnson's letterbook*, p. 93. R. Pares, *A West-India fortune* (London, 1950), pp. 175–8. J. E. Inikori, 'Market structure and the profits of the British African trade in the late eighteenth century', *Journal of Economic History*, XLI (1981), p. 756. Micajah Perry II, M.P. and Lord Mayor of London, was bankrupted in the late 1740s because of the over-extension of credit advances to Virginia planters. Nash, Thesis, p. 209.

[67] P.R.O., B3/178–9.

[68] W. E. Minchinton, ed., *The trade of Bristol in the eighteenth century* (Bristol, 1957), p. 139. Some good examples can be found in [Cruttenden,] *Atlantic merchant-apothecary. Letters of Joseph Cruttenden 1710–1717*, ed. I. K. Steel (Toronto, 1977), especially pp. 7, 9, 11, 34–5, 58–9, 112. J. E. Inikori, 'English trade to Guinea: a study in the impact of foreign trade on the English economy, 1750–1807' (University of Ibadan Ph.D. thesis, 1973), p. 378.

[69] 5 Geo. III, c. 7.

[70] A. Redford, *Manchester merchants and foreign trade 1794–1858* (Manchester, 1934), p. 22.

that another firm, Franck & Bickerton, had just stopped and, more worryingly, 'their only Indiscretion *like most of us* had been in endeavouring to do too much Business & place a Confidence in promised Remittances, in which we are all more or less disappointed'.[71] Problems existed everywhere. In 1744 the Levant Company made factors swear not to trade on credit because of the acknowledged dangers it could involve.[72] And Professor Pares directly related the success of the Pinneys to their manipulation of credit, 'to their extreme hesitation about accepting other people's bills of exchange and their extreme jealousy about letting their own bills get into the hands of any stranger who could dishonour or even discount them; but most of all to John Pinney's caution in taking on new correspondents'.[73]

This credit system must on average have paid its way and generated profits. But its very nature was fraught with problems and difficulties. The path to profitability involved passing through a difficult maze. Merchants took the chance because they were encouraged to do so by the credit system; because without it they would have been hopelessly uncompetitive and because it worked more often than not. It allowed trade to expand, strengthened commercial ties and helped reduce some risks. Price felt that 'The British credit system would thus appear to have resulted in a greater total production of goods and services and in a higher return on risk capital, at the cost perhaps, of a higher failure rate and possible higher retail prices.'[74]

It was not easy to be a successful merchant, particularly as trade expanded in the second half of the century. The volatility of markets coincided with frequent wars and uncertainty was compounded by the dependence of expansion on a valuable but precarious credit system. Of course, if you were skilful or fortunate then the rewards which could be reaped were huge. Little wonder then that successful merchants formed the elite of the eighteenth-century business community. Rich rewards led to rich lifestyles, as successful merchants put down roots in the environs of London by purchasing, as Defoe put it, 'considerable estates', though this was done for reasons both of status and security.[75] But there was a price to be paid by some of their colleagues.

---

[71] *John Norton & Sons*, p. 343. Emphasis in the original.
[72] Davis, *Allepo and Devonshire Square*, pp. 212–13: 'the dangers involved in giving credit had to be learned afresh by each new confident generation'. See also pp. 242–50.
[73] Pares, *A West-India fortune*, p. 176. In a very similar vein see Wilson, *Gentlemen merchants*, pp. 78–83.   [74] Price, *Capital and credit*, p. 122.
[75] D. Defoe, *A tour through the whole island of Great Britain*, ed. P. Rogers (Harmondsworth, 1978), pp. 56–7. J. V. Beckett, *Coal and tobacco. The Lowthers and the economic development of West Cumberland, 1660–1760* (Cambridge, 1981), p. 114. Also the perceptive comments of R. Grassby, 'English merchant capitalism in the late seventeenth century', *Past and Present*, XLVI (1970), pp. 87–107, especially p. 104. Merchants' purchase of estates, often modest, was different from attempts to enter the landed elite. Hence, the strictures of L. and J. C. F. Stone, *An open elite?* (Oxford, 1984), are not always to the point.

Uncovering the patterns and causes of bankruptcy in the three sectors of the economy looked at in this chapter has done much more than stress the significance of those sectors to industry and trade at the time. Examining the relationships between the rise and fall in numbers of bankrupts and businesses and the level of production and exchange has stressed the need to understand the determinants of differential rates of bankruptcy. The explanation of those differences has rested on the idea of the interaction between a hierarchy of risk and variable thresholds of entry. The degree of risk attached to emerging opportunities was determined not only by the natural uncertainty about them but also by the ease with which new entrants could arrive and compete. Consequently, rates of failure in distilling were different from in brewing, just as Liverpool was different from Manchester. The importance of credit and its risks has also become apparent. Beyond that, the variable quality of information at businessmen's disposal heightened risk and insecurity, sometimes leaving them to make guesses rather than calculations. Consequently, merchanting was subject to unwitting speculation because of wars, while the example of the cotton industry showed how difficult it was for merchants to gauge the rate of growth of demand for a new product. Finally, the intensity of short-run dislocations of market conditions has been found sometimes to have had a profound effect on longer-run changes in the fortunes of sectors.

7

FLUCTUATIONS, THE WEATHER
AND CYCLES

So far, numbers of bankrupts have been looked at from a long-term perspective. But most historians have usually adopted a short-term one when looking at bankruptcy, comparing one year's totals with the next. In fact, among certain areas of business enterprise, short-term influences on numbers of bankrupts were large enough to affect longer-term trends. As businessmen operated in a short-term context it is important to see how seasonal and annual bankruptcy totals moved, what the causes of those movements were and what they show about the environment of decision-making.

FLUCTUATIONS IN BANKRUPTCY

Fluctuations in the numbers of bankrupts naturally gain greater meaning when they are compared with fluctuations elsewhere in the economy. Unfortunately, this places some constraints on the way the bankruptcy material can be analysed, largely because of the inconsistency with which fluctuations have been examined in the past – arising from problems associated with the available data and the way historians have handled it. Studies of eighteenth-century fluctuations have been beset by the problem of finding data that have been counted in a suitable way. In particular, this relates to the issue of whether the unit of reference should be the calendar year, the harvest year or the excise year.[1]

To avoid these contentious points and to avoid the impact of seasonality for the time being, the analysis of short-term fluctuations in bankruptcy here uses quarterly totals which have been stripped of their seasonal element.[2] The full data are presented in Appendix 4, where fluctuations are expressed as a percentage deviation from a sixty-one quarter moving average. Such evidence is more easily taken in by charting those deviations, as in Figure 6.

These fluctuations can be described in two broad ways. Firstly, the most

---

[1] For a discussion of these problems see Ashton, *Fluctuations*, pp. v, 31–3. L. S. Pressnell, *Country banking in the industrial revolution* (Oxford, 1956), passim.
[2] The seasonal element has been eliminated by following the method set out in K. A. Yeoman, *Statistics for the social scientist: 1 Introducing statistics* (Harmondsworth, 1980), pp. 224–8.

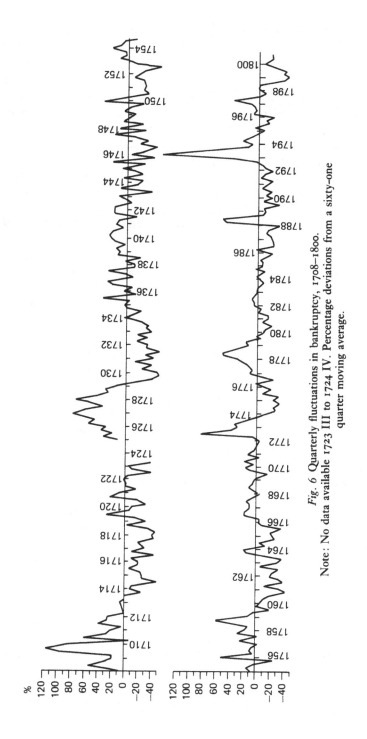

Fig. 6 Quarterly fluctuations in bankruptcy, 1708–1800. Percentage deviations from a sixty-one quarter moving average.

Note: No data available 1723 III to 1724 IV.

extreme variations above and below the trend can be pointed to and, secondly, periods where the deviations were consistently above or below the trend for several quarters can be isolated and discussed. Both approaches will be used here, though only in relation to the period after 1707. Before then, numbers were gravely distorted by the change in the law of bankruptcy in 1706, and earlier still numbers were too small to be meaningful.[3]

In broad terms, the period 1708–34 was marked by a large number of extreme fluctuations in bankruptcy, with longish periods of levels either above or below trend. But there then followed a period of about three or four decades when fluctuations were more settled. This continued after 1770 in some respects, but the tranquillity was periodically broken by very substantial short-term peaks. Altogether, violent fluctuations, quarters with deviations in excess of 30 per cent, occurred in 22 per cent of the quarterly totals. Violent peaks in the level were more frequent and greater than violent troughs. Mild fluctuations, deviations from the trend of between 10 and 30 per cent, characterised 45 per cent of all quarters, while 33 per cent of all quarters fluctuated by less than 10 per cent from normal levels. Obviously, these definitions of violent and mild fluctuations are a little arbitrary, but they show the need to adopt a balanced approach towards interpreting the vicissitudes of eighteenth-century bankruptcy. The absence of fluctuations must be appreciated as well as the violence of those that did occur, even if this section dwells on the latter.

Superficially, it is inviting to think that in Figure 6 short-run peaks in numbers of bankrupts indicate depression and short-run valleys buoyancy. But fluctuations in bankruptcy must not be confused with fluctuations in aggregate economic activity, mostly because modern empirical evidence suggests that there are lags involved between the state of the economy and bankruptcy and because numbers of bankrupts can rise during expansion for the sorts of reasons which have been discussed over the last two chapters.[4] Gluts and shortages of bankrupts do reflect on the business environment, but they cannot be taken as an exact reflection of general economic conditions. On this basis Table 14 can be offered as a summary of Figure 6.

The pattern of fluctuations described in Table 14 can be thought of as a pattern of changing levels of competition and risk. It is very apparent that they were sometimes kind and gentle, but at other times severe and brutal. The reasons for this can be easily summarised, though less easily detailed empirically. Primarily, competition between firms in any area of the market depends on the number of firms that exist there, the way they compete and cooperate with one another, the availability of factors of supply and the size of

---

[3] Numbers in 1706–7 have been examined in some detail in Hoppit, Thesis, pp. 68–70.

[4] Mirowski, Thesis, pp. 521–2. Beveridge, 'The trade cycle in Britain', p. 90. R. G. Rodger, 'Business failure in Scotland 1839–1913', *Business History*, XXVII (1985), pp. 75–99.

Table 14. *Fluctuations in bankruptcy,*
1708–1800

Dates (Year/Quarter)		
From	To	Conditions
1708 I	1713 I	Depression
1713 III	1719 II	Prosperity
1719 III	1723 I	Fluctuations
1725 I	1728 IV	Severe depression
1729 II	1734 IV	Prosperity
1735 I	1743 I	Mild depression
1743 II	1747 II	Mild prosperity
1747 III	1750 I	Stability
1750 II	1753 I	Prosperity
1753 II	1759 I	Depression
1759 II	1766 II	Prosperity
1766 III	1772 II	Stability
1772 III	1773 III	Depression
1773 IV	1776 IV	Prosperity
1777 I	1779 II	Depression
1779 III	1788 I	Mild prosperity
1788 II	1788 III	Severe depression
1788 IV	1792 III	Mild prosperity
1792 IV	1794 IV	Violent depression
1795 I	1796 I	Stability
1796 II	1797 III	Setback
1797 IV	1800 IV	Prosperity

Source: London Gazette; P.R.O., B4/1–20.

the market they are trying to satisfy and win. In practice, only the last two issues are likely to have been significant. Over the short term it is unlikely that the flow of firms into any area fluctuated wildly enough to change the degree of competition. Certainly, there were occasions when this occurred, as in the cotton industry in the middle 1780s, but they were very rare. Nor was it usual for the way competition and cooperation were structured – such as the degree of homogeneity of markets, substitutability, product differentiation or attempts at price fixing – to change decisively and effectively over the short term, though occasionally legislative action might have had some impact. It is likely, then, that it was supply- and demand-side factors that were the most important underlying causes of the toing and froing charted in Figure 6. The former can be grouped into labour, raw and processed materials, plant and finance. In terms of producing fluctuations in the number of all bankrupts only the last of these, finance, is likely to have had a general effect; all the other supply-side factors were usually trade-specific and, in fact, rarely a problem. In all likelihood, changes in the availability of finance and markets were the key determinants of fluctuations in bankruptcy.

Professor Robinson provides a useful framework with which to discuss changes in demand.

Variations of demand may be of four different types. The change may be a permanent one, due to a decline in the popularity of some particular article, owing to the growth of either direct substitutes or of alternative ways of satisfying the same ultimate demand. The change may be a cyclical change, a decline of demand, that is, which is due to a temporary general decline in the power of the community to purchase goods. The change may be a seasonal one, since the particular commodity satisfies needs which arise, or can be met, only at certain times of year. The change, lastly, may be wholly erratic, and due to the failure of individual orders to combine in such a way that they form a single continuous stream. Any actual decline of demand for the products of a firm is likely in practice to be compounded of two or more of these elements of change...[5]

Outside the fashion-based trades it was very rare in the eighteenth century for permanent changes in demand to take place in the way Robinson suggested. Even in the fashion trades, the birth and death of demand was prolonged and hazy, not brief and clear cut. So, on the demand side, causes of fluctuations arose from three possible areas: cyclical, seasonal and random changes. As Robinson said, it would be naive to expect that fluctuations were caused by only one of these; they may well have interacted in a complex and not altogether decipherable way. The first two are looked at here. Commonly, the eighteenth century is characterised as a bridge between an economy that began by dancing to the rhythms of the seasons and the tempi of the weather but ended as one moved by the discordant harmonies of the trade cycle.

BANKRUPTCY AND THE WEATHER

In the eighteenth century, agriculture dominated the economy and the weather dominated agriculture. The passage of the seasons and the change from good to bad harvests and back again could well have influenced conditions facing businessmen, as regular and irregular patterns of demand for labour, patterns of baptisms, marriages and deaths, and patterns of flows of foods and goods were set up. Whether or not bankruptcy was affected by sunshine and showers can best be discussed by separating the pattern of the seasons from the weather in any particular year. The impact of the weather would have affected the quality of the harvest first and foremost so discussion in this section is firstly

---

[5] Robinson, *The structure of competitive industry*, p. 74.

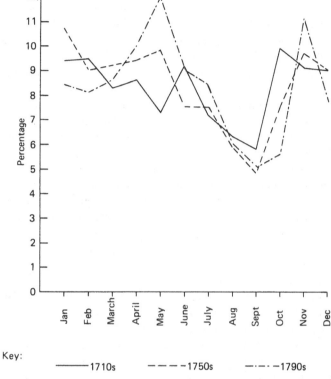

Key:

———1710s   — — — —1750s   — · — · —1790s

Fig. 7 The seasonality of bankruptcy (percentage of all bankrupts in a decade falling in a given month).

of the relationship between bankruptcy and the seasons and secondly of that between bankruptcy and harvests.

Marked seasonality is present in the bankruptcy statistics. Figure 7 shows that businesses did not fail in an entirely random pattern through the year. If they had then each month would have had 8.3 per cent of all bankrupts. Even allowing for some lag between the actual failure of a business and its appearance in the *London Gazette* or Docket Books it is apparent that relatively few businesses went bankrupt between July and October, the main harvest months. Over the whole century, July claimed just 7.9 per cent of bankrupts, August 6.0 per cent, September 5.5 per cent and October 8.1 per cent. Less markedly, November to January and, by the end of the century, April and May were times when numbers of bankrupts were disproportionately high. The summer months were usually ones of intensive employment and production in eighteenth-century England. Not only were harvests gathered, but buildings were

erected and trade active.[6] During these months of frantic activity, payments
and transactions were often deferred.[7] But soon enough, 'Harvest wages, and
the payments which farmers themselves received from their first marketings of
the recently gathered corn crops, gave the economic system its biggest injection
of cash during the course of the year. Outstanding debts were paid off and a
general process of stocking up for the months ahead occurred.'[8] Creditors
appear to have given debtors the benefit of the doubt during the harvest months,
hoping to be paid in the autumn and early winter. If they were then not paid,
bankruptcy proceedings were an obvious tack to take. As Ashton saw, 'There
were two points of time at which what economists call the transactions demand
for money was especially high: in the early autumn, when the crops were being
moved and wages paid out on a large scale, and about Christmas, when merchants and manufacturers made up their accounts and called for payments.'[9]
If unequal seasonal strains on credit and liquidity were essentially a function
of demand for money, then there would be an a priori expectation for bankruptcies also to show a peak in the springtime because the seasonal demands of
pastoral farming – lambing, calving, dairying – and sowing peaked then; a
good deal of labour was paid off in April and May.[10]

It may be that the changing nature of pastoralism and the greater weight to
be attached to market forces as enclosure spread and service in husbandary
declined explains the growing emergence of April and May as important
months for bankruptcy at the end of the century. As traditional forms of
agriculture and employment faltered, and as hiring emerged, so the amount of
wages paid out in the spring increased, with the result perhaps that monetary
conditions tightened.[11] Such changes, along with industrial growth and generally reduced dependence upon agriculture, also led to the emergence of a
seasonal price pattern and, therefore, of seasonal patterns of demand. Bowden's
study of arable crop prices has shown that before 1750 they did not, as has so
often been argued in the past, 'exhibit a general tendency to fall at the beginning
of a harvest year, rising subsequently, but rather they tended to move in a
contrary manner'.[12] By the end of the eighteenth century, the seasonal peak of
prices did come at the close of the harvest year, in the late spring and early
summer, when demand was high relative to supply.

Seasonality of bankruptcy appears to have resulted more from patterns of

---

[6] K. D. M. Snell, *Annals of the labouring poor* (Cambridge, 1985), pp. 20–1, 48, 148–9, 151–4,
156–7, 159, 247–9. F. C. Spooner, *Risks at sea* (Cambridge, 1983), pp. 120–6.

[7] Fairs had some seasonality, for example, with a reduction in July, August and September which,
interestingly, was most marked in the metropolitan counties. Chartres, 'The marketing of
agricultural produce', pp. 435–8.   [8] Bowden, 'Agricultural prices', p. 36.

[9] *Fluctuations*, p. 13.   [10] Bowden, 'Agricultural prices', pp. 34–6.

[11] Snell, *Annals of the labouring poor*, Chs. 2 and 4. A. S. Kussmaul, *Servants in husbandry in early
modern England* (Cambridge, 1981), Ch. 6.   [12] 'Agricultural prices', p. 38.

demand for money and expectations about repayment than violent seasonal swings in the volume of demand for goods. That is not proof that demand for goods is redundant in explaining fluctuations, but it should make us cautious about its role. Whereas we began by thinking that short-run changes in the volume of bankruptcy could probably be explained in terms of variations in final demand, it is now clear that an important associated element to be worked into an argument is again supply and demand for money and credit. This was significant even in the non-seasonal context. In the end, after all, when a debtor fell into the abyss of bankruptcy, the exact timing of his fall could be determined by general credit conditions just as much as by the particular ones between a debtor and his creditors.

In an economy where the bulk of employment, output and income arises from working the land, the variability and uncertainty of the weather sets up both seasonal and harvest fluctuations. Agricultural productivity from one year to the next was fundamentally determined by the weather, especially in arable farming. For most historians, the impact of good and bad harvests on industry has usually been viewed in terms of effects on disposable incomes. Good harvests led to lower grain prices which boosted the disposable incomes of most consumers, though the incomes of farmers may have been cut. Bad harvests had the opposite effect – prices rose, by more than enough to offset the loss of income from the reduced volume of grain available for sale.[13] But just as the seasons were linked to monetary factors, so were harvests. Primarily, this affected the grain trade because very poor or very good harvests could significantly increase or decrease demand for grain imports or even lead to grain exports. In either case, money would no longer flow abroad as it had; indeed the flow could have been reversed. With a good harvest monetary conditions may have eased, leading to falling interest rates and an expansion of credit at home, perhaps encouraging some upward movement in prices of manufactured goods. Professor John argued that the volume of the grain trade was linked directly and intimately with domestic monetary conditions. High exports of corn generated bills of exchange which filtered out from the main ports of the South and East along the channels of internal trade, easing the credit situation as they went. In 1727, for example, following an appalling harvest the Collector

[13] A large literature surrounds this issue. Ashton, *Fluctuations*, Ch. 2. Pressnell, *Country banking*, pp. 448–9. A. H. John, 'Agricultural productivity and economic growth in England, 1700–60', *Journal of Economic History*, xxv (1965), pp. 19–34. J. D. Gould, 'Agricultural fluctuations and the English economy in the eighteenth century', *Journal of Economic History*, xxii (1962), pp. 313–33. R. Ippolito, 'The effect of the "agricultural depression" on industrial demand in England, 1730–1750', *Economica*, xlii (1975), pp. 298–312. M. W. Flinn, 'Agricultural productivity and economic growth in England, 1700–1760: a comment', *Journal of Economic History*, xxvi (1966), pp. 93–8. G. E. Mingay, 'The agricultural depression 1730–50', *Economic History Review*, viii (1955–6), pp. 328–38. Deane and Cole, *British economic growth*, pp. 89–97.

of Customs at Yarmouth wrote to London complaining that 'the small trade we have to Holland [in grains] at present is a great reason for the scarcity of bills'.[14] Such an environment would have left businessmen chasing debts and liquidity, actions that lie well along the path leading to the initiation of bankruptcy proceedings.[15] Certainly, 1727 and 1728 saw depressingly high levels of bankruptcy.

The potential demand and monetary influences of harvests on the business environment can be tested readily by looking at the extent of correlations between bankruptcy and fluctuations in the price of grain and the volume and direction of the grain trade. Because of the relative inelasticity of demand for cereals at home, fluctuations in their supply arising from good or bad weather led to falls or rises in their price. Unfortunately, it is impossible to measure with any accuracy whether such price movements had a significant short-run impact on the general level of demand for non-food items, though we can assume that price movements for grains did lead to shifts in the social composition of demand. Equally, the income effects of harvests – a good harvest usually required more labour – are difficult even to guess at.

Despite the time and effort that has been spent on collecting information about prices in the eighteenth century it is still impossible to make a comprehensive analysis of cereal prices over the whole hundred years. Hoskins, using the building blocks carved out by Thorold Rogers and Beveridge, has analysed wheat prices only down to 1759, and Bowden has looked at all grain prices down to just 1750.[16] Nevertheless, wheat prices can be looked at for the whole period, though it cannot be assumed that they were representative of all cereals.[17] Three series of wheat prices, all from southern England, are available: Eton, Winchester and Exeter.[18] Northern England has failed to provide comparable material.

Following Hoskins's methodology, these series have been detrended, using a fifteen-year moving average, and ratio deviations from the trend calculated. If the bankruptcy material is counted using the same 'year', one beginning and ending at Michaelmas, and analysed in the same way, then direct comparisons

[14] A. H. John, 'English agricultural improvement and grain exports, 1660–1765', in D. C. Coleman and John, eds., *Trade, government and economy in pre-industrial England* (London, 1976), p. 55.

[15] Generally on harvests, the grain trade and monetary conditions see Ashton, *Fluctuations*, pp. 45–8. Pressnell, *Country banking*, pp. 448–9.

[16] W. G. Hoskins, 'Harvest fluctuations and English economic history, 1620–1759', *Agricultural History Review*, XVI (1968), pp. 15–31. W. Beveridge, *Prices and wages in England* (London, 1939). J. E. T. Rogers, *A history of agriculture and prices in England*, 7 vols. (Oxford, 1866–1902). Bowden, 'Agricultural prices'.

[17] C. J. Harrison, 'Grain price analysis and harvest quality, 1465–1634', *Agricultural History Review*, XIX (1971), pp. 135–55.

[18] Reproduced in Mitchell and Deane, *Abstract*, pp. 486–7.

between prices and bankruptcy can be made. Correlation analysis of the ratios shows that bankruptcy had a coefficient of 0.07 against Eton, 0.18 against Exeter, 0.08 against Winchester and 0.11 against an average of all three. On this basis at least, there appears to have been virtually no consistent synchronisation between fluctuations in wheat harvests and bankruptcies. Of course, harvests may sometimes have been linked to bankruptcy, but not frequently enough to establish a clear pattern. It might be argued that extreme harvest fluctuations were more likely to exert an influence. To test this, good and bad harvests were defined as those years when wheat prices deviated more than 20 per cent from the trend. Good harvests were then: 1701–2, 1704–7, 1714, 1718, 1731–2, 1742–4, 1761, 1778–9, 1791 and 1793 (eighteen harvests in all). Bad harvests were: 1708–9, 1713, 1725, 1727–8, 1739–40, 1756–7, 1766–7, 1772, 1795 and 1799–1800 (sixteen harvests in all). But a correlation analysis of these dates produces as small a coefficient as those calculated for the whole period. At the aggregate level, fluctuations in wheat prices had no consistent effect on business failure. Good or bad harvests, on this measure, may have had an effect, but it was not a general or predictable one. Other, stronger, influences must have been at work. The possibility must exist, strengthened by these results, that levels of bankruptcy were erratically and inconsistently influenced by shifts in aggregate demand within the domestic economy. It could be that fluctuations in domestic consumption in the eighteenth century were too small to be of any significance, and that changes in the level of consumption were a consequence rather than a cause of economic fluctuations, as most trade cycle theory in fact states.[19] Or, if bankruptcy levels were to some extent determined by variations in levels of consumption, then such variations were not usually set up by changes in harvest quality, but elsewhere. Finally, it is possible that the effects on demand of harvests at the disaggregate level were influential but tended to cancel one another out in the aggregate, producing no net effect. Here we run up against the problems that, firstly, the quality of harvests affected consumers and farmers in different ways and, secondly, that there was no single national market for agriculture's output, but a collection of overlapping ones.

If harvests did directly influence business failure, it must have been through the second path described earlier, the grain trade, balance of payments and domestic monetary conditions. Between 1650 and 1750, despite the stagnation of England's population, agriculture improved considerably. Productivity was raised through the introduction of new crops, rotations, drainage, irrigation and private enclosure.[20] Increases in food output easily outpaced the growth of

[19] R. C. O. Matthews, *The trade cycle* (Welwyn and Cambridge, 1959), p. 4.
[20] For a recent summary see J. Thirsk, 'Agricultural innovations and their diffusion', in Thirsk, ed., *Agrarian history*, Vol. v, Part ii, pp. 533–89. R. V. Jackson, 'Growth and deceleration in English agriculture, 1660–1790', *Economic History Review*, XXXVIII (1985), pp. 333–51.

domestic demand, producing an increasing surplus available for export. Grain exports mounted and reached a peak in 1750 when some £1.8m worth was shipped abroad.[21] In part, this outflow had been prompted not by natural but by man-made bounty, as the corn laws offered clear-cut encouragement to export grain.[22] After the middle of the century, population growth and urbanisation gathered pace, placing much greater demands on domestic food production. Agriculture just failed to meet this challenge, and grain prices rose; exports dwindled and imports gradually mounted. By the 1790s it was common for more than £2m worth of corn to be imported each year.[23]

Figures on the corn trade are readily available, but not always consistent with one another. Still, John's figures on the export of grains 1700–65 and Schumpeter's on the import of corn products for the whole century have been collected directly from the ledgers of the Inspector-General of Customs and Excise and ought to be reliable.[24] If the export side of the grain trade down to 1765 is compared with levels of bankruptcy by detrending, using a fifteen-year moving average, and ratios of deviations are calculated, then a correlation analysis between the two series of fluctuations provides a coefficient of −0.28. Similarly, for the same period corn imports and bankruptcy have a coefficient of 0.20. There is an indication here of a weak relationship whereby high grain exports show some tendency to coincide with low levels of bankruptcies and vice versa, and high grain imports sometimes coincide with high levels of bankruptcies. The coefficients are small and provide no evidence of a strong or stable relationship, but they hint at an occasional one. The tentative nature of this conclusion is enhanced by what appears to have happened after 1764. Using the wheat and flour export figures in Mitchell and Deane, and Schumpeter on corn imports, the correlations are −0.05 for both corn imports and exports against bankruptcy.[25] Clearly, after the middle of the century swings in the grain trade bore virtually no relationship to bankruptcy.

Harvest fluctuations in the second half of the century were not noticeably weaker than those before 1750, so that if the statistics which have been used are fairly reliable, the complete absence of any relationship after 1764 must arise from changes in the importance of the grain trade itself. Certainly, in the second half of the century, grain exports dwindled away to nothing while

[21] John, 'Grain exports', p. 64. Chartres, 'The marketing of agricultural produce', pp. 448–54. D. J. Ormrod, *English grain exports and the structure of agrarian capitalism 1700–1760* (Hull, 1985).

[22] M. Combrune, *An enquiry into the prices of wheat, malt and occasionally other provisions* (London, 1768). C. Smith, *Three tracts on the corn trade and corn laws* (London, 1766). Smith, *Wealth of nations*, Vol. II, Ch. 5. D. G. Barnes, *A history of the English corn laws from 1660–1846* (London, 1930). C. R. Fay, *The corn laws and social England* (Cambridge, 1932).

[23] E. B. Schumpeter, *English overseas trade statistics* (Oxford, 1960), pp. 58–9.

[24] John, 'Grain exports', p. 64. Schumpeter, *Trade statistics*, Tables XV–XVII.

[25] *Abstract*, pp. 94–5.

imports grew. Yet year to year fluctuations should still have been as fierce as before, thereby influencing the balance of payments, unless either the trade became distorted by changes in the corn laws or, alternatively, the grain trade became a less significant determinant of the balance of payments. Both factors may well have been at work.

From 1764 to 1773 the corn trade was dealt with uncertainly and indecisively by government and parliament. Incentives and restrictions on the trade were applied in an ad hoc fashion in an attempt to provide flexibility while marking time. In 1773, however, a new act governing the trade for most of the remainder of the century was introduced.[26] One innovation it made was to allow imported grain to be warehoused in Britain, with duties being paid only when it was finally sold. This means that the import data on the grain trade are liable to be much less accurate than before in terms of when grain was being shipped in.[27] Any relationship between the grain trade and bankruptcy would thereby appear to have been weakened. But there may also have been a real weakening as the share of the grain trade in total trade shrank. This is difficult to test accurately using the trade statistics because of the considerable difficulties of converting official to current prices, which is especially important for the corn trade.[28] Nevertheless, it seems probable that the grain trade did become less significant towards the end of the eighteenth century, as the import–export economy around raw materials and finished goods grew rapidly. In particular instances, the relationship between net exports and eased monetary conditions, and net imports and tighter monetary conditions, might well have existed. Ashton argued, for example, that in the 1790s large imports of food were partly responsible for a lack of credit.[29]

There were several occasions in the first six decades of the eighteenth century when bad harvests, large grain imports or a sharp drop in exports and a peak in bankruptcy coincided with one another. In 1708–9, very poor harvests saw the price of wheat and rye rise especially sharply; grain exports died away and bankruptcies were very high. A similar picture was repeated in 1727–8. And the very poor harvest of 1740 led to a slump in grain exports and a small, but marked, peak in bankruptcies.[30] But it is impossible to unravel the actual causations that may have been at work. Whether the quality of harvests in such years had any effect on the business environment, be it through the demand or the monetary side, is still an open question, though the correlation coefficients incline us to put more weight on the monetary side. The absence of any consistent relationship between wheat prices or the grain trade and bankruptcy makes it likely that harvests were of marginal significance and only occasionally

[26] 13 Geo. III, c. 43.
[27] Barnes, *English corn laws*, pp. 42–5.
[28] Ormrod, *Grain exports*, pp. 70–5.
[29] Ashton, *Fluctuations*, pp. 46–8.
[30] Bowden, 'Agricultural prices', pp. 830–1. John, 'Grain exports', p. 64.

important, perhaps by reinforcing other stimuli. Other factors were more prominent causes of fluctuations, though the effect of the seasons and harvests on monetary conditions has once again emphasised the attention that has to be paid to the state of credit and liquidity over the short term. Indeed, the prominence of seasonality makes it impossible fully to accept Mirowski's claim that 'The conception of a premodern "natural" economy that fluctuates because of shocks external to social and market processes does not hold up well under scrutiny.'[31]

The weather made a rhythmic rather than disruptive contribution to fluctuations in bankruptcy. Seasons appear to have been more important than good or bad harvests. From this finding we can move on to see whether there was any regularity behind fluctuations that might be laid at the door of trade cycles.

BANKRUPTCY AND BUSINESS CYCLES

Not the least of the worries that faced early-nineteenth-century attempts to reconcile widespread evidence of poverty in the midst of plentiful material progress was the problem of the trade cycle. Regular cycles were seen as a new curse that bewitched the economy's efforts to grow steadily and surely. To Carlyle, English commerce suffered 'convulsive fluctuations' that made 'life a bewilderment'.[32] 'For times are really strange...times here of half-frantic velocity of impetus, there of the deadest-looking stillness and paralysis.'[33] And Coleridge saw that 'the spirit of commerce will occasion great fluctuations' which 'Within the last sixty years...have occurred at intervals of about 12 or 13 years each.'[34] What was new in these generally held views was a belief in the inevitability and regularity of fluctuations. Eighteenth-century onlookers believed good times followed bad, but always unpredictably and erratically. Most historians of the origins of trade cycles would agree with this. Few believe cycles existed much before 1780 and Gayer, Rostow and Schwartz remarked that 'the very existence of business cycles...before 1825' has been questioned.[35] But they, along with others, have found cycles of a sort from about the end of the American War of Independence in 1783.[36] Recently, though, attempts have been made to push back into the early eighteenth century not just the conception but the birth of the business cycle.[37]

[31] P. Mirowski, 'Macroeconomic instability and the "natural" processes in early neoclassical economics', *Journal of Economic History*, XLIV (1984), p. 354.
[32] T. Carlyle, *Selected writings* (Harmondsworth, 1980), p. 175.
[33] T. Carlyle, *Past and present* (London, 1978), p. 18.
[34] S. T. Coleridge, *Lay sermons*, ed. R. J. White (London, 1972), pp. 161, 202–3.
[35] Gayer, Rostow and Schwartz, *Growth and fluctuation*, Vol. II, p. 568.
[36] Silberling, 'British prices and business cycles'. Beveridge, 'The trade cycle in Britain'.
[37] Mirowski, Thesis. R. V. Eagly and V. K. Smith, 'Domestic and international integration of the London money market, 1731–1789', *Journal of Economic History*, XXXVI (1976), pp. 198–212.

Common sense would give more credence to the argument that cycles were born in the later, rather than the earlier, years of the century. After all, 'cycles are not characterised by their uniformity in duration or amplitude or by their initiating causes; the essential feature is the way in which the economy responds to a given set of stimuli by magnifying them into cumulative movements which may or may not be self-sustaining'.[38] Before the end of the century a 'national economy' hardly existed in the macro-economic sense. Rather, the national economy was the sum of regional economies whose borders were permeable and shifting. The absence of a truly national economy early in the eighteenth century is partly evidenced by regional price differentials.[39] Basic infrastructural developments – coastal shipping, turnpike roads, canals, newspapers and the marketing network – helped to forge a more national economy during the eighteenth century, with significant developments taking place after *c.* 1730. All in all, then, not until the end of the first phase of canal building, say, was the economy united enough to behave in a cyclical way.

Cyclical fluctuations in national income are usually thought to be caused by changes in the level of aggregate demand, possibly in either consumption or investment, though 'It is fluctuations in investment that are generally held to lie at the heart of the cycle.'[40] From this, it also seems unlikely that the cycle would have emerged in England until the volume of investment reached significant levels at the end of the eighteenth century.[41] If investment was slight, then changes in its total would have affected aggregate economic activity only marginally. Crafts, for example, has estimated that Gross Domestic Investment as a proportion of Gross National Product rose from 4.0 per cent in 1700 to 6.0 per cent in 1760, 7.9 per cent in 1801 and 11.7 per cent in 1831.[42] On this basis Gayer *et al.* were right to believe that 'major' investment cycles were intermittent before 1850.[43] Of course, if investment in particular sectors was disproportionately important, then it could seem as if cycles were at work before *c.* 1780. Perhaps this explains the stance adopted by Mirowski, and Eagly and Smith. Their evidence for the existence of cycles early in the eighteenth century derives from large, usually metropolitan, business corporations and from the London money markets. But what was happening there can hardly be taken as representative of enterprise elsewhere and of the general level of economic activity. Mirowski is particularly reluctant to confront the limitations of his

[38] D. H. Aldcroft and P. Fearon, 'Introduction' to Aldcroft and Fearon, eds., *British economic fluctuations 1790–1939* (London, 1972), p. 4.
[39] Chartres, 'The marketing of agricultural produce', pp. 459–65. Bowden, 'Agricultural prices', pp. 16–33.   [40] Matthews, *Trade cycle*, pp. 3–4.
[41] Ashton, *Fluctuations*, pp. 136, 173. Aldcroft and Fearon, *Fluctuations*, pp. 2–3. W. W. Rostow, *British economy of the nineteenth century* (Oxford, 1948), pp. 36–7, 41.
[42] Crafts, *British economic growth*, p. 73.
[43] Gayer, Rostow and Schwartz, *Growth and fluctuation*, Vol. II, Chs. 1 and 2.

evidence, despite his willingness to apply such tests to other historians.[44] Large corporations accounted for a very small fraction of economic activity and were atypical of business enterprise as a whole, which was open to related but different opportunities and difficulties. Swift had complained, it is worth remembering, that 'It is the Folly of too many, to mistake the Eccho of a *London* Coffee-house for the Voice of the Kingdom.'[45]

Gayer, Rostow and Schwartz, who have made the most careful and systematic study of early business cycles in Britain, found signs of both minor and major cycles at the end of the eighteenth century. Minor cycles, lasting about four years, were created by rhythmic fluctuations in exports associated with inventories. Major cycles of about nine years rested on investment in fixed capital projects such as construction, transport and plant.[46] The chronology they suggested was that from the trough of 1788 the economy expanded as part of a major cycle to a peak in 1792, with heavy investment taking place in canals between 1791 and 1793. A slump followed quickly in 1793 and a minor cycle ran through to the next trough in 1797, with the peak occurring in 1796. A major cycle then bridged the troughs of 1797 and 1803. When this timetable is compared with the fluctuations in bankruptcy described in Figure 6 it is clear that peaks in the economy did coincide with low numbers of bankrupts and troughs with high numbers. But it is also worth stressing that the troughs were marked by very extreme peaks in the numbers of bankrupts. The violence of such depressions in the bankruptcy figures after 1772 has already been noticed and may in itself point to the greater integration of the economy which, it has been argued, was vital to the emergence of the business cycle. In fact, 1772, 1778, 1788, 1793 and 1797 were all years of financial crisis and it might be that large numbers of bankrupts in those years were less a sign of cyclical depression than an indication of the collapse of the monetary system. Certainly, between 1772 and 1800 periods when the economy was known to be booming, such as 1783–8, tended to show only small variations around and below the trend line of bankruptcies.

Even so, before 1772 it is difficult to find evidence from fluctuations in bankruptcy of wave-like motions of economic activity. High levels of bankruptcy at the close of the War of the Spanish Succession were followed by low levels, just as high levels in the late 1720s were followed by low levels in the early 1730s. But from 1719 to 1723 numbers of bankrupts flitted back and forth

[44] Thesis, pp. 520–2. His evidence has been published in two articles: P. E. Mirowski, 'The rise (and retreat) of a market: English joint stock shares in the eighteenth century', *Journal of Economic History*, XLI (1981), pp. 559–77; 'Adam Smith, empiricism, and the rate of profit in eighteenth-century England', *History of Political Economy*, XIV (1982), pp. 178–98.

[45] J. Swift, *The conduct of the allies*, ed. H. Davis (Oxford, 1951), p. 53.

[46] *Growth and fluctuation*, Vol. II, Chs. 1 and 2. This is a crude summary of their argument. See the critique by R. C. O. Matthews, 'The trade cycle in Britain, 1790–1850', *Oxford Economic Papers*, VI (1954), pp. 1–32.

across the trend line, something repeated in 1734–50, 1753–7, and 1766–71. According to the bankruptcy material, periods of prosperity were rarely followed by periods of clear depression, and vice versa. On the basis of Figure 6, Hoffman's conclusion that during the eighteenth century 'An examination of the number of bankruptcies shows clearly the existence of long waves of between 18 and 20 years duration' is unsupportable.[47]

If Gayer, Rostow and Schwartz are right to ascribe exports and investment a central role in the causation of early business cycles in England, then it need not hold that the lack of evidence of cycles before *c.* 1780 means that these factors were irrelevant in generating instability. Rather, the economy was probably unable to magnify these stimuli to create cumulative movements or, alternatively, the stimuli only attained their full weight late in the century. Given that Gayer *et al.* put more weight on exports in the formation of cycles in the late eighteenth century it is sensible to begin by looking at their relationship with bankruptcy.

Data on exports are available from 1697.[48] By employing the same method for finding fluctuations as that which was used for wheat prices and the grain trade (ratio deviations from a fifteen-year moving average), we can use correlation analysis to test the degree of coincidence between fluctuations in exports and bankruptcies. The expectation is that high levels of exports would coincide with low levels of bankrupts but in fact when the two series are compared over the century a coefficient of only −0.23 is produced. However, remembering that exports as a proportion of national income changed over the century – 8.4 per cent in 1700, 14.6 per cent in 1760, 9.4 per cent in 1780 and 15.7 per cent in 1801 – it seemed wise to test the data for the two halves of the century.[49] Down to 1750 the correlation coefficient of fluctuations in bankruptcy and exports was just −0.09, but for the second half of the century it was −0.40. The expected inverse correlation between the two became moderately true as the economy grew and trade's involvement became that much greater, hardly surprising given that growth and bankruptcy were especially strongly connected to the expanding colonial trade and the increasingly export-orientated textile industries of Lancashire and the West Riding. To use the jargon, the export multiplier rose. In large part, the impact of exports was probably felt via demand, but the monetary influence, acting through balance of payments and credit conditions, cannot be forgotten, as the pattern of failure among merchants discussed in the last chapter showed.

---

[47] Hoffman, *British industry*, p. 154. His waves were 1741–59, 1759–80, 1780–98 and 1798–1819: p. 155.

[48] Schumpeter, *Trade statistics*, Table II. Deane and Cole, *British economic growth*, pp. 319–21. McCusker, 'Current value of exports', pp. 620–2.

[49] Crafts, *British economic growth*, p. 131. I. Mintz, *Cyclical fluctuations in the exports of the United States since 1879* (New York, 1967), p. 6.

It is not hard to find instances in the second half of the eighteenth century when a slump of exports coincided with a peak in bankruptcy, and vice versa. For example, the collapse of exports with the outbreak of war in 1776 was associated with a substantial surge in numbers of bankrupts, just as it was in 1793. But the extent to which these movements in exports can be ascribed to cyclical causes rather than erratic influences is open to doubt. Evidence of a broadly based export-led inventory cycle is hard to find, though its existence in specific trades has already been referred to.[50] War probably had a more general impact than such a cycle, affecting many areas of trade.

Judging the relationship between investment and fluctuations in bankruptcy is far less easy than for exports because of the lack of reliable evidence. Year by year totals of capital formation are lacking and only partial evidence can be called upon. Superficial comparisons can be made between bankruptcy and investment in building and some points can be made in relation to parliamentary enclosure, turnpike roads and canals. Fortunately, construction has been looked at in some detail by a number of historians, all of whom are confident that imports of deal and fir provide a good surrogate measure of building activity.[51] According to Lewis, peaks in the building cycle were reached in 1705, 1724, 1736, 1753, 1776 and 1792. Troughs were reached in 1711, 1727, 1744, 1762, 1781 and 1798. Looking back to Figure 6 it appears that the building cycle barely coincided at all with fluctuations in bankruptcy. Although the construction slumps of 1711 and 1727 were periods when bankruptcies were unusually high, at other times cyclical peaks and troughs show no discernible relationship with bankruptcy.

If imports of deal and fir provide a reasonable measure of the amount of investment taking place in construction from one year to the next, comparable material is sorely lacking on turnpikes, canals and enclosure. Although projects in all three areas required an act of parliament to proceed, it is impossible to tell when the finance was raised and utilised. For example, the Leeds and Liverpool Canal was begun in 1770, but work was suspended in 1777 before being resumed in 1790 and finished in 1815. Consequently, numbers of acts authorising turnpikes, canals and enclosures are a better measure of confidence and expectations in the near future than of the reality of fixed capital formation. On that score, it is interesting that all three areas were barely active in the early 1780s when the economy was feeling the full effects of the American War of Independence.[52]

[50] Rostow, *British economy*, p. 41. See above, Ch. 6, n. 56.
[51] Ashton, *Fluctuations*, Ch. 4. J. P. Lewis, *Building cycles and Britain's growth* (London, 1965), Ch. 2. Thomas, 'The rhythm of growth', pp. 11–14.
[52] E. Pawson, *Transport and economy: the turnpike roads of eighteenth century Britain* (London, 1977), pp. 113–15. W. Albert, *The turnpike road system in England 1663–1840* (Cambridge, 1972), Appendix B. J. R. Ward, *The finance of canal building in eighteenth century England*

Fluctuations in bankruptcy bear out the usual view that business cycles emerged only towards the end of the eighteenth century. Moreover, the evidence supports the belief that it was the volatility of exports rather than investment which was the most decisive driving force at work making for cyclical activity. But whether exports moved in the fashion of an inventory cycle or were the function of external factors, most particularly war, is unclear. What is clear is that the eighteenth-century presumption that trade was unusually important and naturally unstable has been fully borne out both here and in the previous chapter.

In attempting to come to terms with short-term fluctuations in the number of bankrupts, this chapter has had more negative than positive achievements. For while seasonality and exports have been found to have been of some importance it would be easy to exaggerate their significance. They hardly explain all fluctuations, nor do they appear to explain any fluctuation completely. On the negative side, the role of harvests and cycles has been played down, leaving the way open for an investigation of the impact of the erratic and supposedly random factors of wars and financial crises. Perhaps they, along with exports, hold the key to the pattern of bankruptcy drawn in Figure 6.

(Oxford, 1974). M. Turner, *Enclosures in Britain 1750–1830* (London, 1984), p. 18. B. J. Buchanan, 'The evolution of the English turnpike trusts: lessons from a case study', *Economic History Review*, XXXIX (1986), pp. 223–43.

8

BANKRUPTCY, WARS AND FINANCIAL CRISES

Wars and financial crises ravaged eighteenth-century England and it was widely recognised that businessmen bore the brunt of the dislocation they caused. But how far did such destructive powers lead to the downfall of businesses and cause the fluctuations in the numbers of the bankrupts uncovered at the start of the previous chapter?

WAR

Between 1700 and 1800 England was involved in five major wars, covering a total of forty-six years: the War of the Spanish Succession (1702–13); the War of the Austrian Succession (1739–48); the Seven Years War (1756–63); the American War of Independence (1775–83); and the Revolutionary War (1793–1802).[1] Some of these wars were more serious than others and conflict was never continuous or consistently destructive. At the very least, it is sensible to remember the distinction introduced earlier between the threat of war, the waging of war and the making of peace. Within this broad chronology, wars need to be looked at in terms of their impact on domestic and overseas trade on both the supply and the demand sides of economic activity. All these concerns centre on the impact of war on the competitive balance in the business world and the changing nature of risk and uncertainty produced. This is not to forget that wars created as well as destroyed opportunities, but just to emphasise that they increased the degree of unpredictability. If financiers or ironmasters could make their fortunes from war, plenty of other businessmen could lose them.

On the demand side, the most obvious impact of wars was felt in the closure of foreign markets, especially in Europe and America. War usually destabilised exports and, as we have seen, exports in turn had some influence on fluctuations in levels of bankruptcy, especially after the middle of the century. Foreign markets which were not actually shut by war might, even so, be reached only

---

[1] I have counted the War of the Quadruple Alliance (1718–20) as a minor war and also not included local conflicts with France over India.

via new and more expensive routes. Similar problems existed on the import side. Domestic demand was also altered by war as the armed forces cried out for men, food, drink, clothing, arms, ammunition and transport. Morally, wars may have been the devil's work, but they were a godsend to those who supplied the combatants. Finally, wars had to be financed and this led to short- and long-term changes in the nature of government financing. Customs, excise and taxation were altered to raise more revenue, and the substantial shortfalls between income and expenditure were met through the institution and development of the national debt. In wartime, therefore, the government competed with businessmen not just for supplies of labour and goods, but also for finance.[2]

The effects on the economy of war were neither uniform nor predictable, 'For clearly the conditions, economic and otherwise, in which war takes place will vary from country to country, and from war to war; even the character and extent of wars are important in such estimates.'[3] Nevertheless, the impact of eighteenth-century wars on levels of bankruptcy did produce some sort of pattern. Specifically, looking back to Figure 6, there was usually a rise in the number of bankruptcies in the early part of the five wars before they fell back, sometimes to a low point before the formal conclusion of fighting, sometimes just after. Leaving aside the War of the Spanish Succession because of the difficulties in interpreting numbers of bankrupts arising from the change in the law in 1706, we can begin by looking at the War of the Austrian Succession. From a low point in 1739, Quarter III, levels of bankruptcy rose to a peak in 1740 II, when they were nearly 30 per cent above trend. After 1742 levels dropped off and were below trend in 1746 and 1747. In the Seven Years War, the peak was reached in late 1758, two years after the declaration of war. But after 1759 II levels were consistently below trend for the rest of the war. Indeed, in 1760 IV they were 46 per cent below average. War with the Thirteen Colonies saw levels rise from a low point in 1774–5 to a peak in 1778 II when they were 53 per cent above trend. But between 1779 III and 1783, when the war ended, levels were either well below normal or only just above. In 1793 the outbreak of war coincided with and partly caused a financial crisis that sent levels rocketing. Distinguishing the one cause from the other is impossible. And in 1797 there was another financial crisis that complicates attempts to pick out a pattern of bankruptcy.

In terms of bankruptcy, wars tended to cause their greatest problems earlier

[2] For a discussion of war and the economy see A. H. John, 'War and the English economy'. Ashton, *Fluctuations*, Ch.3. P. Deane, 'War and industralisation', in J. M. Winter, ed., *War and economic development* (Cambridge, 1975), pp. 91–102. Davis, *The rise of the English shipping industry*, Ch. 15. P. G. M. Dickson, *The financial revolution in England* (London, 1967).
[3] John, 'War and the English economy', p. 330.

rather than later in their course. In most of the wars during the eighteenth century, the problems they caused made an immediate impact but they then either were solved by businessmen or they actually weakened. Yet it was found (see Chapter 6) that merchants tended to suffer more and more relative to other occupations as wars continued, relief coming only a few years into peace. Any explanation of the impact of war on the business environment needs, therefore, to take into account the experiences of different sectors and occupations.

One possible explanation for the distinctive chronology of bankruptcy during wartime is the impact of altered monetary conditions. It has already been shown that demand for money and liquidity were of considerable importance in helping to determine the timing of business failure, so there is some prior expectation that heavy government borrowing could influence rates of bankruptcy. Wars were partly financed by the government gaining access to the reservoirs of savings which existed in the nation, and which usually irrigated local ecomonic activity and business enterprise. 'More than four-fifths of the "extra" cost of military expenditure in wars fought by Great Britain in the eighteenth century was met by borrowing; through one of the great British inventions of the period – the permanent, funded National Debt.'[4] Between 1688 and 1815 some £671m was raised by government borrowing to finance wars.[5] Raising such large sums placed considerable pressure on the availability of money elsewhere. As Swift saw, 'the Bait of large Interest would draw in a great Number of those whose Money by the Dangers and Difficulties of Trade lay dead upon their hands'.[6] In part, this can be assessed by looking at what was happening to discòunting and balances at the Bank of England as they reflect on monetary conditions. In 1739, the value of the Bank's notes in circulation plus balances in drawing accounts had fallen by 7 per cent from the previous year, demonstrating a search for liquidity and monetary pressure. Between 1756 and 1759 the fall was 12 per cent; between 1775 and 1778 it was 13 per cent and between 1792 and 1794 it was 9 per cent.[7] Such falls were not totally caused by government borrowing but they must have been partly caused by it. Yet, after these falls at the start of each war the amount of money usually readjusted and returned to previous levels or sometimes actually grew. Part of the reason for this successful realignment of monetary conditions, before 1783

---

[4] P. Mathias, 'Taxation and industrialization in Britain, 1700–1870', reprinted in his *The transformation of England*, p. 121.

[5] F. Crouzet, 'Editor's introduction', p. 40. Dickson, *Financial revolution*.

[6] J. Swift, *The history of the last four years of the Queen*, ed. H. Davis (Oxford, 1951), p. 68. H. J. Habakkuk argues that government borrowing in war soaked up sources of funds for the mortgage market: 'The rise and fall of English landed families, 1600–1800. II', *Transactions of the Royal Historical Society*, 5th series, xxx (1980), pp. 206–7.

[7] The data are taken from J. H. Clapham, *The Bank of England. A history*, 2 vols. (Cambridge, 1944), Vol. I, pp. 295–7. I am grateful to Professor Pressnell for suggesting this approach to me.

at least, was the willingness of the Dutch to invest in the British national debt in wartime.[8] In the early years of wars monetary conditions tightened, squeezing liquidity and putting pressure on the structure of debts, making repayment more difficult and a willingness to accept deferment of payment less likely.[9] Creditors became more anxious and debtors less able. Fortunately though, these conditions did not last because government 'borrowing resulted in credit inflation, sometimes slight and sometimes considerable'. Extensions of the unfunded debt led fairly directly 'to increases in the circulating medium'.[10] If the government borrowed from the Bank of England's funds this helped put reserve currency into circulation, but if it borrowed directly from the money market there would be some siphoning off of credit from the private sector.[11]

Governments raised money to pay for wars not just by borrowing but by increasing income via customs and taxation. Ralph Davis showed some time ago how Marlborough's successes were supported financially by the erection of customs barriers. And the land tax and excise were always liable to rise during war.[12] Increases in these financial burdens obviously affected some businesses more than others by raising costs and cutting markets. A clear example of this more specific financial burden arising from war can be seen in the case of the building industry in the American War. A building boom in 1775–7 was partly brought to a halt by increased duties on glass and stained paper (wallpaper), imposed to help finance the struggle. But the war also hit insurance and freight rates, and vital supplies of overseas timber increased in cost. Clearly, conditions for the construction industry were becoming difficult, and this is reflected in the bankruptcy figures. In the five years leading up to the imposition of the new duties in July 1777, bankruptcies in the construction sector averaged just fifteen per annum. But in 1777 itself, there were thirty, and in the following year fifty-eight, a level not surpassed until the disasters of 1793. Indeed, much the same pattern recurred in 1793. Yet the depression in the construction industry in

---

[8] L. D. Neal, 'Interpreting power and profit in economic history: a case study of the Seven Years War', *Journal of Economic History*, XXXVII (1977), pp. 31–5. A. C. Carter, 'The Dutch and the English public debt in 1777', reprinted in her *Getting, spending and investing in early modern times* (Assen, 1975), pp. 20–41.

[9] The War of the Austrian Succession produced far less pressure in this respect and others compared with the other wars. See D. M. Joslin, 'London bankers in wartime, 1739–84', in Pressnell, ed., *Studies in the industrial revolution*, pp. 160–2.

[10] E. B. Schumpeter, 'English prices and public finance, 1660–1822', *Review of Economic Statistics*, XX (1938), pp. 31, 29.

[11] P. K. O'Brien, 'Government revenue, 1793–1815 – a study in fiscal and financial policy in the wars against France' (University of Oxford D. Phil. thesis, 1967), p. 25.

[12] 'The rise of protection in England 1689–1786', *Economic History Review*, XIX (1966), pp. 306–17. P. Mathias and P. K. O'Brien, 'Taxation in Britain and France, 1715–1810. A comparison of the social and economic incidence of taxes collected for the central governments', *Journal of European Economic History*, V (1976), pp. 601–50. W. R. Ward, *The English land tax in the eighteenth century* (Oxford, 1953).

1777–8 was not simply the result of the increased costs that came with war, but also arose from financial insecurity characteristic of such a highly speculative sector.[13]

The third way in which wars proved financially disruptive was through the interruption of international settlements. Necessarily, the deterioration of communications caused by war made the repayment of overseas debts much more difficult, leading to longer credit, despite the general wish to shorten it and reduce risks. Credit was pulled in two opposing directions, shaking the international edifice of credit and debt, and thereby exposing the bedrock of confidence that underlay the whole system. At the start of the Seven Years War Robert Plumstead, a London merchant, confessed that 'the situation of the times obliges Every prudent man to press for Remittances'.[14] But whether or not money was forthcoming is another matter. Some merchants were obviously more successful and fortunate in these situations than others. It was possibly James Symes's failure effectively to squeeze his correspondents in the West Indies and Thirteen Colonies which led to his bankruptcy in August 1777 because 'he hath been much distrest for money to enable him to carry on his Business for six months and upwards'.[15] Simple dishonouring of debts was always more likely in wartime and became very serious during the American War of Independence. By 1783 about £5m was owed to British traders by the Americans, much of it many years overdue.[16] At the start of the war, in 1776, 'a large capital was locked up in that country, by which the trade of London, Bristol, and Liverpool, was considerably injured, and at Glasgow, and Whitehaven, a very extensive bankruptcy took place'.[17] In fact, anywhere connected with the colonial trade was liable to get caught out. One solicitor, pleading to the creditors of a Leeds merchant, stressed that his client had

ye greatest part of his effects in ye Colonies of Virginia and [blank], and all trade & intercourse with those Colonies being prohibited during their present unhappy state, he is thereby rendered incapable of making that speedy payment of his debts, which otherwise he would have done, and which some of his Creditors have endeavoured to obtain by legal diligence.[18]

[13] Ashton, *Fluctuations*, pp. 100–3. Chalklin, *The provincial towns*, pp. 270–4, 279–84. J. R. Ward, 'Speculative building at Bristol and Clifton, 1783–1793', *Business History*, xx (1978), pp. 3–18.

[14] Cambridge University Library, Add. Mss. 2798, The Plumstead letterbook, 1756–8, fo. 160.

[15] P.R.O., B3/4433–5.

[16] K. A. Kellock, 'London merchants and the pre-1776 American debts', *Guildhall Studies in London History*, I (1974), pp. 109–49. E. G. Evans, 'Planter indebtedness and the coming of the revolution in Virginia', *William and Mary Quarterly*, 3rd series, xix (1962), pp. 510–33. Gibbon's father lost many debts in the war with Spain, 1740–8. Gibbon, *Memoirs*, p. 58.

[17] J. Wilson, i.e. J. Currie, *A letter commercial and political, addressed to the Rt. Honble. William Pitt, in which the real interests of Britain in the present crisis are considered...* (London, 1793), p. 29.   [18] Leeds Archive Office, Carr Mss., CA3, fo. 332.

Apart from finance, another main way in which wars led to uncertainty and bankruptcy was through the dislocation of exports and imports. But, as was pointed out in Chapter 6, it would be wrong to think that war led only to the collapse of trade. In fact, although exports usually slumped with the outbreak of hostilities, they gradually recovered and by each war's end were above pre-war levels. Exports peaked at levels higher than ever before in the war years of 1708, 1746, 1748, 1759, 1760, 1796, 1798, 1799 and 1800.[19] One study has even concluded that 'war generally had a stimulating effect on London's exports'.[20] Nevertheless, there were industries and products which were vulnerable to the collapse of export markets during war, such as Norwich worsteds.[21] Imports were certainly worse affected than exports, being especially badly hit by war in 1702–13 and 1739–48. The Seven Years War had no appreciable effect, while the war with the American colonies saw imports fall and then recover. In 1793, imports stagnated for a few years before resuming their upward trend.[22] Obviously, members of import-dependent occupations, such as wine merchants, silk dealers or linen drapers, were all especially likely to be affected by these movements. But it is far easier for the historian to sit in his warm study and, looking at tables of trade statistics, analyse the course of trade during war than it was for businessmen at the time to understand what would happen to markets, prices and profits. What struck them most forcefully was that war created uncertainty and risk.

A measure of the escalation of that insecurity during wartime can be found by looking at insurance rates. In February 1756, for example, three months before the formal start of the Seven Years War, the French began to seize British ships which, naturally, 'had a sudden Effect upon Insurance'. This, and the expectation that privateers would soon be unleashed into the Channel, pushed up insurance rates by 25 per cent. But, even in March, with tensions continuing, rates were 'not yet Got Quite to War price'.[23] Yet, a year later, with war in full flight 'Wee have such a Great Number of french privateers Out, that Increases the Risque prodigiously, & many ships have lately fallen into their hands which makes it verry difficult to get Insurance Compleated.'[24] The risks had reached such heights that insurance was difficult to get at all.[25] In the previous war,

[19] Deane and Cole, *British economic growth*, pp. 319–21.   [20] French, Thesis, p. 91.
[21] Clapham, 'The transference of the worsted industry', p. 196.
[22] Deane and Cole, *British economic growth*, pp. 46, 319–21.
[23] Plumstead letterbook, fos. 25–6, 50. In 1792 economic war broke out in advance of military conflict. Redford, *Manchester merchants*, p. 15.
[24] Plumstead letterbook, fo. 237. P. G. E. Clemens has argued that one reason for the emergence of Liverpool as a major port was that it was relatively remote from the ravages of privateers in wartime: 'The rise of Liverpool, 1665–1750', *Economic History Review*, XXIX (1976), pp. 215–16.
[25] Early in the century, rates rose from a peacetime level of 2.5 per cent to a wartime level of 15 per cent. [Cruttenden,] *Atlantic merchant-apothecary*, p. xx.

Thomas Newson lost his ship to Spanish privateers and found himself 'not Insured soe full as I should have by some hundred pounds, and my being taken is considerable Loss to me moore than I care to own'. But it was a risk he had chosen to take because three months earlier he had confessed that 'Warr with france is att Last proclaimed...Freights are higher, Insurance is higher and all Sorts of goods is dearer.'[26] His attempt to cut costs in an unstable environment had been punished, and he paid the price. Merchants were in a clear dilemma in war. They could hardly leave their ships to rot at the quayside or in dry dock, for income had to be generated if debts were to be repayed. But escalating insurance rates or, at times, the unavailability of insurance, made trade either too expensive or too risky. Moreover, the convoy system, which offered reassurance and protection, led to highly distorted markets because of the way the system encouraged gluts.[27]

It has become clear that businessmen found it hard to judge the real extent of dislocation engendered by war. Unreliable, patchy or non-existent information meant that headline news probably exerted undue influence on their decisions. In many ways, therefore, it is inappropriate to distinguish between the actuality of war and the threat of war. But unless this is done, then important fluctuations in the bankruptcy series are liable to be misunderstood. Most significantly, the threat of war is a factor to be worked into an explanation of the enormous peak in bankruptcy that lasted for four years, from 1725 to 1728.[28] The height of this peak, and the depth of the distress it demonstrates, can hardly be underestimated. The extent of the fluctuation in bankruptcy between 1726 and 1728 was vast and surpassed only once in the remainder of the century, in 1793. Early in both 1727 and 1728 bankruptcies were about 80 per cent above normal; Lord Bolingbroke referred to 'the *daily Bankruptcies* that we find in all our News Papers'.[29] This crisis coincided with, and was partly caused by, tensions in Anglo-Spanish relations. Active preparations for war were made from February 1727 and threat of hostilities did not dissolve until late in 1729. Naturally, the very threat of war exerted an influence on freight costs and insurance rates, as well as draining confidence and encouraging a search for liquidity and the realisation of credit assets. A brief doubling of the

---

[26] P.R.O., Chancery Masters Exhibit, C104/78. Letters of 16 July 1744 and 5 April 1744.

[27] P. Crowhurst, *The defence of British trade 1689–1815* (Folkestone, 1977). G. N. Clark, *The Dutch alliance and the war against French trade 1688–1697* (Manchester, 1923). G. N. Clark, 'War trade and trade war, 1701–1713', *Economic History Review*, I (1927–8), pp. 262–80. R. Pares, *War and trade in the West Indies 1739–1763* (Oxford, 1936), pp. 497, 515. Nash, Thesis, Ch. 3. R. Bourne, *Queen Anne's navy in the West Indies* (New Haven, Conn., 1939), Ch. 4. Davis, *The rise of the English shipping industry*, Ch. 15.

[28] The threat of a French invasion in early 1797 lay behind the liquidity crisis that bankrupted many businesses and led to the suspension of cash payments.

[29] *Contributions to the Craftsman*, ed. S. Varey (Oxford, 1982), p. 81.

land tax must have put some additional strain on monetary conditions.[30] But as we saw earlier, when the fate of the victuallers in these years was examined, other factors were also at work apart from the threat of war (see p. 95). Harvests were very bad in 1727 and 1728; there was a serious downturn in joint-stock activity which was presumably associated with the collapse of a boom in turnpike road projects; and severe crisis mortality afflicted the nation.[31] The English economy can hardly have been subjected to an unhappier series of coincidences over the century.

If the threat of war caused problems, then the threat and reality of peace also demanded readjustments. Peace was often effectively restored well before a war was formally wound up. The most significant response at the macro-economic level was the surge of exports that arrived with the end of fighting. Usually, the bankruptcy figures respond with some post-war reduction, though this is true to a lesser extent of the conclusion of the Seven Years War. Opportunities expanded quickly and this expansion was all to the good for businessmen, so long as the speculative element was not too great – which may have been true of the merchant sector, but not of others. Unavoidable government deficit financing may also have helped with reconstruction.[32] It is worth remembering, however, that certain industries, iron and steel in particular, suffered with the making of peace and the loss of government contracts.[33]

War substantially destabilised the eighteenth-century economy, producing prosperity and depression in an unpredictable mix. Certainty was eroded, confidence ebbed and the prospect of stability vanished. With the heightening of risks, the less bold, more nervous and cautious trader might cut commitments. Others would have looked to new sources of supply and to new markets. Merchants might choose to lessen their investment in trade, and to redirect it to government finance with its secure returns. Competition in trade may have weakened if the numbers pulling out were proportionately greater than the reduction in actual trading activity. But risks were undeniably greater, as privateers and hostile navies provided a different sort of competition, so while those who remained in trade would reap greater profits if they actually reached their markets, the possibility of failure was also greater. Adam Smith argued that 'The ordinary rate of profit always rises more or less with the risk. It does not, however, seem to rise in proportion to it, or so as to compensate it completely.'[34]

[30] D. Marshall, *Eighteenth century England* (London, 1962), pp. 142–3. W. A. Speck, *Stability and strife* (London, 1977), p. 217. Ashton, *Fluctuations*, p. 59.

[31] Bowden, 'Agricultural prices', p. 831. Mirowski, Thesis, pp. 527–46. Pawson, *Transport and economy*, p. 113. Wrigley and Schofield, *The population history of England*, p. 333.

[32] Ashton, *Fluctuations*, p. 67.

[33] T. S. Ashton, *Iron and steel in the industrial revolution* (2nd edn, Manchester, 1951), Ch. 6.

[34] *Wealth of nations*, Vol. I, p. 124.

If the discussion of the effect of war has concentrated on the financial damage it caused, which seems natural in a study of failure, then its benefits should certainly not be forgotten. Businessmen did adjust to changes between war and peace but it was not easy and, because of poor or unreliable information, instability was the order of the day. As Richard Plumstead complained in 1756, war 'Renders human Affairs verry uncertain and may throw the Best of us into Confusion'.[35] In a similar vein, a merchant at the end of the War of the Spanish Succession was sure that 'losses must be expected this war time, which if one should happen the profit of many years would be gone att once'.[36] The onset of war and peace necessitated changes and adjustments that some handled well and others fumbled. War upset the applecart by putting pressure on the edifice of peacetime credit, by dislocating markets and sources of supply and by imposing new costs on trading and production. Each firm's production schedule was altered and requirements for success or failure changed. Over the short term, the coming and going of war fostered conditions which weakened and strengthened competition and magnified risks.

FINANCIAL CRISES

The second major erratic influence that haunted the eighteenth-century English economy was financial crisis. Periodically, contemporaries bewailed the collapse of monetary order as a tidal wave of panic drowned confidence. Creditors furiously chased debtors in the rush for assets, attempting to gain buoyancy to weather the storm. This itself suggests that bankruptcy should be very helpful in describing the appearance, disappearance and form of financial crises, for bankruptcy is precisely a measure of a debtor's inability to meet his creditors' just demands. In fact, such crises go a long way towards explaining many of the most dramatic peaks in numbers of bankrupts shown in Figure 6.[37]

Financial crises are not easy to define, mainly because they are not exact phenomena which might be identified simply by looking at movements in financial series. Essentially, they are moments when confidence in some financial mechanism evaporates and is followed by an intense demand for liquidity; fear and impatience become the order of the day.[38] In 1772, for example, as Dr Johnson witnessed: 'Such a general distrust and timidity has been diffused through the whole commercial system that credit has been almost extinguished and commerce suspended...It can, however, be little more than a panick terrour

---

[35] Plumstead letterbook, fo. 30.
[36] [Cruttenden,] *Atlantic merchant-apothecary*, p. 12.
[37] I have dealt with this topic more fully in 'Financial crises in eighteenth-century England', *Economic History Review*, xxxix (1986), pp. 39–58.
[38] A recent discussion of the nature of financial crises can be found in C. P. Kindleberger and J. P. Laffargue, eds., *Financial crises: theory, history, and policy* (Cambridge and Paris, 1982).

from which when they recover, may well wonder why they were frighted.'[39] A month earlier, someone closer to trade noticed that 'Distress seems pictured in each countenance on Change.'[40] Fear about the soundness of certain financial instruments lay at the heart of financial crises. That fear was much more likely when financial instruments were novel or being used in a speculative fashion.

Because crises cannot be precisely defined there has been some debate about when they happened in the eighteenth century. In large part, this has arisen because the variety of crises has not been acknowledged. But Ashton, who has made the most careful and thorough study of them, was well aware of the differences that existed when he suggested that there were thirteen crises in the century: 1701, 1710, 1715, 1720, 1726, 1745, 1761, 1763, 1772, 1778, 1788, 1793 and 1797.[41] Looking back to Figure 6, three of these crises (1715, 1745 and 1761) had a negligible impact on the numbers of bankrupts. In 1720 and 1763 crises coincided with a slight surge in numbers. But in 1710, 1726, 1772, 1778, 1788, 1793 and 1797 bankruptcies rose very substantially when the crises struck. What is most marked about this pattern is that the last five crises of the century all coincided with a violent peak in numbers of businesses going to the wall. Before then, the impact was usually either mild or non-existent. An important first starting point in explaining this is that crises could be crises of public, corporate or private finance; consequently, one crisis might be like the next, or it might not. Secondly, because the financial systems, particularly in the public and private spheres, were changing and developing over the century crises at the start tended to be different from those at the end in both their geographical and occupational impact.

Because bankrupts were private businessmen using private finance, we would expect crises of private finance to be shown up much more clearly than those of public finance by numbers of bankrupts. Moreover, we know that the system of private finance was evolving very significantly over the course of the eighteenth century, making general crises in that sector much more likely. The last five crises, all of which were linked with exceptionally high levels of bankruptcies, would seem, at first glance, to show that crises of private finance were weak or non-existent before 1770. It would also seem that crises of public and corporate finance were either very weak in the century or, alternatively, had little impact on the business community when compared with crises of private finance. These differences in the nature of crises through the century are partly evidenced by the degree of concentration in the capital in crisis years, largely

---

[39] Quoted in P. Mathias, 'Dr Johnson and the business world', reprinted in his *The transformation of England*, p. 298.   [40] *Joshua Johnson's letterbook*, p. 40.
[41] The first of these, 1701, will be left out of the following discussion because of the problems associated with the change in the law of bankruptcy in 1706. Ashton, *Fluctuations*, Ch. 5.

Table 15. *Bankruptcy and financial crises, 1710–97 (London bankrupts as a percentage of all bankrupts in given years)*

Pre-crisis	Percentage from London	Crisis	Percentage from London
1707–9	48.8	1710	44.8
1712–14	52.0	1715	65.0
1717–19	47.8	1720	53.8
1742–4	40.7	1745	50.7
1758–60	34.6	1761	35.6
1760–2	33.1	1763	40.7
1769–71	50.2	1772	52.6
1775–7	45.2	1778	45.2
1785–7	34.1	1788	38.8
1790–2	42.3	1793	34.4
1794–6	36.9	1797	35.9

Note: The crisis of 1726 has been excluded because of the gap in the evidence for 1723–4.
Source: London Gazette; P.R.O., B4/1–20.

because public and corporate finance were very heavily concentrated in the capital. Table 15 shows a clear enough picture.

The crises of 1715 and 1745 were especially limited to London, though there was also a marked concentration in 1720, 1763 and, to a lesser extent, 1788. All but the last of these were crises of public finance and appear to have had a very limited impact on the general business environment. In 1788, it was the infant cotton industry, with its trading links in the capital, which collapsed.[42] The crises of 1772, 1778, 1793 and 1797, all of which caused great numbers of failures, had either a neutral geographical impact or, as in 1793, an impact that hit the provinces rather than the capital. In short, after 1772 bankruptcy provides clear evidence that crises were, firstly, much more disruptive of business enterprise than before and, secondly, much less limited to London.

Crises in public finance hardly affected the general business climate at all. This is conclusively demonstrated by the lack of response the bankruptcy figures showed to the crises caused by the Jacobite rebellions in 1715 and 1745 and the speculative activity associated with the South Sea Company and the national debt in 1720. Slumps in the price of stocks and panic in Exchange Alley cannot be equated uncritically with widespread dislocation. Before 1770, if crises were associated with general distress, then that distress arose from a

---

[42] See my 'The use and abuse of credit', pp. 67–71, for a discussion of 1788. Also, see above pp. 84–5.

coincidence of several factors rather than from the power of shock waves sent out by financial collapse. Until the last third of the eighteenth century, private finance was too poorly integrated to suffer a general destruction and for the whole century links between public and private finance were too weak to allow panic in the one to cause panic in the other. So, the high levels of bankruptcies in 1710 and 1726 are explained by non-monetary factors such as bad harvests and the threat of war.

The emergence after 1770 of crises that racked the business community at large bears witness to its increasing dependence on confidence, and on bills of exchange and accommodation notes, and the more complete integration of the various realms of the world of private finance. In particular, the crises were caused by the extensive use of credit, in the form of bills of exchange and accommodation notes, to fund expansion. During the seventeenth and eighteenth centuries the use of credit mechanisms, which was already a commonplace in overseas trade, spread through the domestic economy in an attempt to bypass the problems caused by an inadequate coinage, delays between production and consumption and the risks involved in moving money about the countryside. Middlemen played a pivotal role in the process, but by 1770 the infant country banks were also becoming important. The bill on London came to link provincial financial fortunes to one another through their mutual reliance on the capital's discounting facilities.[43] By the end of the century 'scarcely a transaction now takes place in the mercantile world but it produces a bill of exchange'.[44] But because bills relied on personal security, relationships in such networks were absolutely dependent upon confidence. The accommodation note, an even less stable form of bill, also suffered from these problems. Consequently, marriages between creditors and debtors were always likely to be stormy and the risks of default high. It was the nature of credit, the way it was structured and the ever-increasing extent of its use, along with a general environment of economic growth, which generated the crises of private finance that were so catastrophic for the general business community.

England's economy could grow in the late eighteenth century only as a result of firms expanding in size or of more firms coming into being, or both. Either way, the demand for venture capital increased and was in large part met by the expansion of credit. Businesses and prospective businesses could raise only limited funds from friends and relations or, once trading, from profits. Resorting to credit was the easiest alternative route forward. On an individual level, when David Boyn, a London merchant, failed during the hurricane that swept the business world in 1793, an acquaintance of his reported that Boyn 'began business without a Capital, and borrowed money of other persons'. And when things started to go wrong, he kept himself afloat not by a permanent loan

[43] Pressnell, *Country banking*, Chs. 2 and 4.
[44] W. Roscoe, *Thoughts on the causes of the present failures* (London, 1793), p. 9.

but through 'temporary accommodation...by means of the circulation of bills'.[45] At the final count, his debts amounted to £185,000. This was a common enough way of getting and keeping going in business, even if the scale of this particular undertaking was not.[46]

Credit was used by all businessmen. Another unifying theme, therefore, was that everyone who used credit to fund expansion was essentially indulging in risky speculation. Naturally, a confident and buoyant environment, with credit readily available, encouraged the formation of greater and less easily fulfilled expectations than a depressed and sullen environment where credit was tight. At various points during the last thirty years of the century, growth and credit combined to call forth from businessmen decisions that were over-ambitious and ill founded. This was the root cause of the five crises after 1770. In 1772, for example, a merchant in London noticed that at first 'Money Matters were very easy & Credit & a general Confidence was established beyond anything you ever knew, but all of a sudden the very Reverse took place & the most rigid Diffidence & Suspicion...was established everywhere.'[47] Instability had been heightened in 1772 by the fabrication of credit and the drawing and redrawing of bills – so-called accommodation notes – to create a 'fictitious Circulation'.[48] False bills and credit became common just before the onset of the 1788 crisis as well.

Usually what happened was that growth began by being well founded but that gradually the speculative element increased and the dependence on credit, especially dubious credit, was magnified. Before 1772, for example, heavy investment had been taking place in turnpikes, canals, enclosures, overseas trade and manufacturing. Growth encouraged roguery and stupidity, with the most culpable being Alexander Fordyce and the Ayr Bank.[49] Prophetically, a correspondent to the *London Chronicle* argued before the crisis storm had broken that credit is good 'under due regulation, kept within the bounds of moderation, and where the persons, having recourse to it for the enlargement of trade, have real property and foundation to depend on...but 'tis an evil of the first magnitude, when applied to the encouragement of such perpetual forgeries; furnishing men of no property with most fallacious appearances, and

[45] P.R.O., B3/195.
[46] Another example is William Blenden of Clifton, Bristol, a carpenter and builder, who went bankrupt in 1794 having started out twelve years earlier 'intirely on Credit'. P.R.O., C110/151.
[47] Quote in J. M. Price, *France and the Chesapeake*, 2 vols. (Ann Arbor, Mich., 1973), Vol. 1, p. 640.
[48] Smith, *Wealth of nations*, Vol. 1, pp. 327–35. Clapham, *Bank of England*, Vol. 1, pp. 242–3. John Norton & Sons, p. 254.
[49] See my 'Financial crises' for a fuller discussion of the gestation of the 1772 crisis.

putting them on a line with Merchants of unquestionable fortune'.[50] Calmly surveying the scene from the peace and comfort of Strawberry Hill Horace Walpole complained that 'the Scotch bankers have been pursuing so deep a game by remitting bills and drawing cash from hence, that the Bank of England has been alarmed'.[51]

The particular causes of the collapse of credit puffed up by growth and speculation varied from one crisis to the next. In 1772 it was caused by the fall of Fordyce and the Ayr Bank. In 1778 it was the collapse of trade with the New World, as war cut off Britain's most dynamic overseas market. In 1788 it was the bankruptcy of Livesey, Hargreaves, Anstie, Smith & Hall, calico printers and bankers from Clitheroe in Lancashire and London.[52] In 1793, it was the outbreak of war. And in 1797 it was the suspension of cash payments that followed the threat of a French invasion.[53] But behind each of these lay a common medium-term cause, the failure to fulfil expectations which had grown with growth and been fuelled by credit. Risk-taking had got out of hand and all five crises after 1770 can be seen as the growing pains of the first industrialising nation.

It is obvious that financial crises and the nature of credit explain many of the waves of bankruptcy which periodically swept the business community during the early decades of the Industrial Revolution and were, in fact fostered by the generally sunnier economic climate in those years. These crises may also help explain the evidence of growing rates of bankruptcy after *c.* 1760. As might be expected, contemporaries frequently came to view bankruptcy in terms of the experience of financial crises. Their explanations of failure were increasingly framed in terms of an understanding of crises and their moral response to bankruptcy influenced by the speculation and fraud that those crises exposed to view.

In the first place, what struck onlookers was the way trust and confidence disappeared during crises, producing a 'general consternation'.[54] The scale and extent of the distress were widely reported in the papers, with stories about notable failures, suicides and the cessation of all business. Crises were especially newsworthy if they could be individualised as they were in 1772 when Alex-

---

[50] 28–30 April 1772, p. 412. This analysis is similar to J. Steuart's in 1767, *An enquiry into the principles of political oeconomy*, ed. A. S. Skinner, 2 vols. (Edinburgh, 1966), Vol. II, p. 439.

[51] *The Yale edition of Horace Walpole's correspondence*, Vol. XXIII, ed. W. S. Lewis, W. H. Smith and G. L. Lam (London, 1963), p. 420.

[52] 'The leviathan of the industry...[who] employed between 700 and 1,000 printers shortly before their bankruptcy': Chapman, *The cotton industry*, p. 24.

[53] See Ashton, *Fluctuations*, Ch. 5, for a discussion of all these.

[54] Words used both by the *London Chronicle*, 20–3 June 1772, p. 598, and *Gentleman's Magazine*, June 1772, p. 293.

ander Fordyce became something of a folk anti-hero. Moral lessons were most easily drawn from noisy and flamboyant crashes. Fordyce's career was offered up as an example to all. He was a Scot (the 1772 crisis invoked considerable anti-Scottish feelings), who had arrived in London as a hosier. A born speculator, he made his first successful venture when he heard before most others of the end of the Seven Years War in 1763. He moved on to gamble on the future market in hops, a crop whose price was notoriously unstable.[55] 'The capricious goddess still favoured him, and he seemed so infatuated with her kindness, as to think she was intirely at his command.' Ambition drove him on socially as well as commercially. He bought an estate, married well and pumped £14,000 into an unsuccessful attempt to become an M.P. But he was finally undone by the stock market slump caused by the rumpus with Spain over the Falkland Islands in 1770.[56] Although he managed to keep things going by dealing in fictitious bills, this only delayed and increased his ultimate failure.[57] One report put his debts at £550,000, another at £350,000.[58] Either way, the scale of his failure was enormous and attracted condemnation and morbid curiosity on an equally grand scale. His bank (Fordyce, Neale, James & Down) owed £150,000. Dividends totalling 14s 6d in the pound were repaid by 1794.[59] When he went before the bankruptcy commissioners, huge crowds collected outside the Guildhall to catch a glimpse of him surrendering his last possessions, a snuff box and a few coins in his pocket.[60]

Failures like Fordyce's served as examples of the evils of speculation and gambling in trade. Each crisis was followed by a torrent of moral censure of the over-eager desire for riches. Colquhoun's fair-minded belief 'that the spirit of speculation ...[is]...necessary to give energy to trade' was a very unrepresentative response to a crisis.[61] Most onlookers preferred to curse all ambition and avarice on such occasions, condemning either businessmen or society as a whole. Speculation and ambition were often chastised in terms of the damage they did to the social order. Typical of this perspective was Boswell's belief that

A few men of enterprize may be of use in a country, but what must become of that country where all are men of enterprize? The consequence must be, that labourers, mechanicks, traders, and farmers, by all struggling to get into a situation higher than

---

[55] Bowden, 'Agricultural prices', p. 42.
[56] *London Chronicle*, 30 June–2 July 1772, p. 1.
[57] Ibid., 22–4 September 1772, pp. 292–3.
[58] Ibid., 9–11 July 1772, p. 35. The second figure is from an unidentified newspaper cutting at the British Library in a volume entitled *Collection of ballads, broadsides, etc*. In the same volume there is a poem about Fordyce's collapse, 'A new song on a late remarkable occasion'.
[59] P.R.O., B3/3675–6.
[60] *London Chronicle*, 12–15 September 1772, pp. 258–9.
[61] Colquhoun, *An important crisis*, p. 26.

that to which they have any probable means of attaining, must, like the frog in the fable, burst in the attempt.[62]

Consequently, he believed that the crisis would have the good effect of 're-storing just notions of subordination, frugality, and every other principle by which the good order of society is maintained'.[63] Crises were also worked here into commonplace complaints about the luxury and extravagance of the times, another way in which social disorder was often viewed, explained and con-demned. Henry Fielding complained that a 'vast torrent of luxury...hath poured into this nation' and he associated this with excessive social fluidity.[64] The infant 'Thunderer' was told that 'The nobility game with dice – the ladies with cards – the linen-drapers with bills – and the lower class with lottery tickets...and the consequences are proportioned to the quality of the gamblers, being in four words, SUICIDE, ADULTERY, BANKRUPTCY, and the GALLOWS!'[65] It was a small step from here to linking individual with national bankruptcy in just the ways in which public and private credit were condemned.

Given that financial crises in the last third of the eighteenth century centred on the collapse of private credit and bill networks it is to be expected that contemporaries should have found fault with the monetary system as well as with public and private morals. A steady stream of complaints poured forth to chide credit inflation and fictitious bills. In particular, the country bankers were blamed. This was not surprising, because in any crisis they were bound to be at the centre of the frenetic activity. But that is hardly the same thing as being the cause of such panic. Collapse, and collapse they did, is no proof of guilt.[66]

The failure of country banks, or of anyone for that matter, was not always a cause for regret, however, even if it was a cause of censure. From Hume onwards, each crisis was greeted by some observers as a necessary storm which cleared a muggy atmosphere. Crises cleansed the business soul. Usually, this was expressed in terms of a crisis checking exaggerated credit and providing an example for future behaviour. In a sense, this replicated in a more specific context Boswell's hopes that crises would restore the order of things and check the erosion of natural patterns of subordination. Early in the crisis of 1772, for instance, Hume wrote to Adam Smith that 'On the whole, I believe, that the

---

[62] J. Boswell, *Reflection on the late alarming bankruptcies in Scotland* (Edinburgh, 1772), p. 18.
[63] Ibid., p. 23. A very similar view of the same crisis is expressed in the *London Chronicle*, 28–30 April 1772, p. 412.
[64] *The late increase of robbers*, p. 21. See also J. Brown, *An estimate of the manners and principles of the times* (Dublin, 1757).
[65] *The Times*, 9 June 1788, p. 3.
[66] See especially Macpherson, *Annals of commerce*, Vol. IV, pp. 266–7. Pressnell, *Country banking*, pp. 457–9.

Check given to our exhorbitant and ill grounded Credit will prove of Advantage in the long run, as it will reduce people to more solid and less sanguine Projects.'[67] Sixteen years later *The Times* and the *London Chronicle* carried the same report on the same day to the effect that 'Ruinous as the recent failures will be in their immediate operation, it may justly be said that they were absolutely necessary to restore trade to its proper channel.'[68] But in fact, as crisis followed crisis into the nineteenth century, lessons were not learnt and the denunciations were repeated.[69] Speculation returned time after time because an element of growth was speculation, which was intensified by the type of credit instruments used.

What crises did demonstrate was the centrality of confidence to the normal workings of business life, and it was on this issue that the Treasury and Bank of England were drawn into the fray. The Bank was always sure to know as soon as anyone when a crisis was breaking because it would increase its discounting and also accept deposits from those too nervous to keep their money in their usual banks.[70] By its discounting policy, particularly the care it took in uncovering dubious bills, the Bank could materially affect the progress and extent of crises. In 1772 it let the Ayr Bank continue for a while before refusing to discount its bills any further.[71] In 1788 the directors sat every day to sort the good from the bad paper, presumably because they were 'determined to let the Fire burn out. It will in the End purge the Mercantile Atmosphere of a great deal of foul Air.'[72] But, as Lovell has shown, the Bank also played a positive role in crises by supporting well-founded houses.[73] The Bank well knew the importance of restoring confidence and by 1788 realised that it and the government had an important part to play in that process. In 1788 the directors visited Pitt at least twice during the early days of the crisis, perhaps attempting to get the Prime Minister to agree to the issue of some form of short-dated instruments or smaller denominations of Bank of England notes.[74] In 1793 the directors were instrumental in organising the issue of Exchequer Bills which miraculously restored credit and confidence overnight.[75] These bills simply assured business-

[67] *The correspondence of Adam Smith*, ed. E. C. Mossner and I. S. Ross (Oxford, 1977), p. 163.

[68] *The Times*, 13 May 1788, p. 2.

[69] B. Hilton, *Corn, cash, commerce. The economic policies of the Tory governments 1815–1830* (Oxford, 1977), pp. 227–30.

[70] *London Chronicle*, 20–3 June 1772, p. 599.

[71] F. Baring, *Observations on the establishment of the Bank of England, and on the paper circulation of the country* (London, 1797), p. 14. *Scots Magazine*, June 1772, p. 316. *London Chronicle*, 15–17 September 1772, p. 269.

[72] *Manchester Mercury*, 20 May 1788, p. 4.

[73] M. C. Lovell, 'The role of the Bank of England as lender of last resort in the crises of the eighteenth century', *Explorations in Entrepreneurial History*, x (1957), pp. 8–21.

[74] *London Chronicle*, 3–6 May 1788, p. 433; 6–8 May 1788, p. 443.

[75] Clapham, *Bank of England*, Vol. I, pp. 258–65. Baring, *Observations on the Bank of England*, pp. 32–3. J. Ehrman, *The younger Pitt. The reluctant transition* (London, 1983), pp. 385–7.

men that liquidity was ultimately available, thereby cutting the ground from under the feet of those who clamoured for payment. If you knew that you would be paid in the end, then there was no rush to get paid now. The central support of crises was swept away. Indeed, Thornton noticed that it was as much the decision to issue Exchequer Bills as their actual appearance which closed the floodgates of bankruptcy.[76] While those gates had been open, however, bankrupts had poured through in greater numbers than at any other time in the century.

Reactions to financial crises ranged then from moral outrage to sound economic analysis. Whatever their opinions, contemporaries' sense of financial crises fundamentally influenced their reaction to bankruptcy and enterprise in the last third of the eighteenth century. And in terms of crises determining major peaks in the numbers of bankrupts after 1770, this preoccupation was right and proper. The importance of financial crises to bankruptcy reinforces the importance of monetary influences on the short-term business environment. In particular, the importance of confidence to the success of credit networks and good relations between creditors and debtors has been clearly outlined.

Both wars and financial crises were major causes of the short-term swings in the number of bankrupts. Wars created a high degree of uncertainty by cutting flows of information, money and goods and disrupting access to markets. But, financial crises caused distress 'not so much from a failure of the usual markets for the goods, as from the difficulty in discounting...the long-dated bills received for the goods'.[77] Together, wars and financial crises show how businessmen could wittingly and unwittingly become more or less speculative in their decision-making and risk-taking because of sudden changes in external conditions beyond their control. Short-run vicissitudes posed many of the problems which businessmen had to solve in order to succeed. In 1772, Josiah Wedgwood achieved this by tightening his grip on his firm and improving his methods of cost accounting.[78] But lesser mortals, lacking his ability and foresight, found themselves exposed to the tides of economic fortune and, every now and then, the failure rate dropped and then rose. It was within this short-term environment that decisions were taken by businessmen helping to forge the first Industrial Revolution. A central factor determining short-term levels of failure was monetary conditions and the availability of credit.

[76] H. Thornton, *An enquiry into the nature and effects of the paper credit of Great Britain*, ed. F. A. von Hayek (London, 1939), p. 98.

[77] Cobbett, *Parliamentary history*, Vol. xxx (1817), p. 744.

[78] N. McKendrick, 'Josiah Wedgwood and cost accounting in the industrial revolution', *Economic History Review*, XXIII (1970), pp. 45–67.

9

*

DEPTHS OF FAILURE
AND THE ROLE OF CREDITORS

Thus far, one bankrupt has been distinguished from another only in terms of time, geography and occupation. But it would be fallacious to believe that bankrupt merchants, say, were different in these ways only. Obviously, some bankrupts failed for just hundreds of pounds, others for hundreds of thousands of pounds. Some had few creditors, some many. The exploration of these differences is vital to a proper appreciation of bankruptcy in the eighteenth century. The role of creditors – in terms of who they were and how their actions determined patterns of failure – is also important. After all, in an age when voluntary bankruptcy was not available to insolvents, creditors were fundamentally important in deciding just how indebted a bankrupt became and just when he was closed down.

PATTERNS OF INDEBTEDNESS

Some examples of different depths of bankruptcy have already been uncovered. Alexander Fordyce, the speculator who went bankrupt in 1772, reputedly sank for £500,000 or £350,000 (see pp. 135–6). But the law allowed you to be classed as a bankrupt if your debts were more than just £100. So, how big and how small were eighteenth-century bankrupts? Unfortunately, evidence on the depths of failure is limited. This is not because it was not collected at the time – the commissioners and assignees knew well enough how much each bankrupt owed and to whom. But few of their files have survived. All in all, only 152 files out of the 33,000 originally compiled have been found which allow the depth of failure to be calculated for eighteenth-century bankrupts. Of these 152 files, moreover, some may not be complete records. Certainly, eleven allow only a summary total of the debts to be calculated.[1] The 152 files usually provide information of who the creditors were, what they did and how much they were owed. They also give details of the dividends awarded from each bankrupt's

---

[1] Most of these records are held at the P.R.O. in class B3; some in Chancery Masters Exhibits. A few have been found in provincial record offices. These sources are cited fully in the bibliography.

estate. But in most cases they give no details of the bankrupt's estate, just a summary of how much it realised. Detailed assignees' accounts are virtually non-existent.[2] Yet without such records it is impossible accurately to fashion explanations of particular bankruptcies. Circumstantial and coincidental information is helpful, but can only be employed in a general way, creating impressions rather than irrefutable arguments. However, because neither the commissioners nor the assignees were required to investigate the causes of a bankrupt's collapse it is not clear that if all their deliberations and the bankrupt's books had survived it would be possible to do more than speculate on the reasons behind any failure. In 1813, an M.P. complained to the House of Commons that 'The commissioners ought to be told how the bankrupt obtained credit, with what capital he had commenced business, whether he had preyed on the property of others, how he himself had lived.'[3] But they did not, and we are the poorer for it.

The 152 files that have survived can be described in various ways, relating to their chronology and the depth and patterns of indebtedness they reveal. Taking the first of these, some 90 per cent of the files relate to bankruptcies that happened in the period 1780–1800, while only four files relate to bankruptcies in the first half of the century. Yet only 40 per cent of all bankruptcies in the century happened in the last twenty years. For the century as a whole, therefore, only 0.46 per cent of the commissioners' files have survived, but for the two decades 1780–1800 the proportion is 1 per cent. The reason for this chronological imbalance is clear enough. When the original files were sorted out – with the vast majority being consigned to oblivion – those which were kept and stored were commissions which had often been protracted and difficult. And given that the sorting out of the files took place some time in the nineteenth century, commissions from the first half of the eighteenth century had, by then, usually run their full course. Moreover, a corollary of this factor is that large commissions – with many creditors being owed large sums of money – and complicated ones were difficult to draw to a conclusion and therefore play a disproportionate role in the files which have survived. The 152 files are chronologically skewed and heavily biased in favour of the big, problematic and spectacular bankruptcies. Consequently, they can hardly be used as representative examples of eighteenth-century bankruptcy as a whole.

Nearly 78 per cent of the 152 files cover London bankrupts, a proportion that rises to 82 per cent if the immediately adjoining areas of Surrey, Kent and Middlesex are added. This marked geographical bias, which is much greater

---

[2] I have found only one such set: Guildhall Library, Ms. 8601, 'The account book of the assignees of Alexander Hog, grocer and bankrupt'. Also, Ms. 8623, 'Correspondence concerning Hog's bankruptcy'.

[3] *Hansard's parliamentary debates*, Vol. xxv (1813), p. 609.

Table 16. *Gross debts of 152 bankrupts*

Amount of debt (£)	Number of firms	Amount of debt (£)	Number of firms
100–1,000	28	10,000–15,000	13
1,000–2,000	16	15,000–20,000	7
2,000–3,000	5	20,000–30,000	18
3,000–4,000	4	30,000–40,000	7
4,000–5,000	3	40,000–50,000	5
5,000–10,000	15	50,000–100,000	19
		100,000 +	12

Source: Manuscripts cited in Bibliography.

than for bankruptcy as a whole, partly reflects the ways in which the files have survived. Most were originally in the Lord Chancellor's office, which held the files of London-based commissions. Country commissions, however, were undertaken by specially appointed commissioners who probably held on to the papers. And because provincial commissioners were private individuals their papers have almost all been lost. In London, on the other hand, the chance of the survival of the papers was always much greater because commissioners were part of a permanent bureaucracy. But the geographical imbalance in the files also reflects the fact that London bankruptcies tended to be larger and more difficult, with their papers 'active' well into the nineteenth century when the original sorting out took place. On the basis of insurance records, which have their own biases, Schwarz and Jones concluded that 'Within the manufacturing and commercial sector the predominance of London-based wealth is apparent.'[4]

Table 16 presents information about the gross debts of the 152 bankrupts.[5] Roughly half of the 152 bankrupts failed with debts of under £10,000, half with more. Of those owing more than £10,000 nearly 90 per cent came from London, bearing out the conclusion that the biggest failures as well as the biggest businesses were located there. Of that select body failing for more than £100,000, all came from London, three-quarters of them merchants and one-quarter bankers. Indeed, of those owing more than £30,000 or more some 65 per cent were London merchants, while only two merchants failed for less than £4,000. At the other end of the scale, those twenty-eight bankrupts with debts of less than £1,000 showed no occupational pattern – twenty separate occupations were covered by them. Apart from five tailors, the absence of occupational

[4] Schwarz and Jones, 'Wealth, occupations, and insurance', p. 370.
[5] Gross debts are total debts proved. Net debts are gross debts minus the value of assets. Lack of evidence does not permit the calculation of net debts.

Table 17. *Size of debts of sixty-seven bankrupts*

	£10–1000 (small)	£5,000–10,000 (medium)	£30,000–50,000 (large)	£100,000 (giant)
Number	28	15	12	12
Average number of creditors	11	47	70	205
Average size of debt	£53	£154	£492	£1,017

Source: Manuscripts cited in Bibliography.

bunching among these 'poor' bankrupts is very marked. In short, large bankrupts invariably came from London and were invariably merchants. Small bankrupts came from anywhere and did anything but merchanting.

As Table 17 shows, bankrupts failing for small amounts owed money to fewer creditors and in smaller amounts than those failing with large total debts. Such summary measures of course conceal as well as reveal and within the four categories of size of firm used in Table 17 the numbers of creditors varied considerably. Among the small firms, for example, two firms had just two creditors while one had as many as forty-one. Among the medium-sized firms the range was from sixteen to 232; for the large firms nineteen to 167; and for the giants it was fifty-three to 493. The bankruptcy with the biggest number of creditors was that of the Bury St Edmunds bank of Robert Carss, gazetted during the financial crisis of 1797, who failed owing debts of £56,000 to 940 creditors.[6] As one of Carss's competitors, the Bury banker James Oakes, had noticed, 'Mr Carss's Affairs are in a very perplexed state & apparently a large Number of Creditors.'[7] If the number of creditors of firms had varied considerably then the size of their average debts was similarly dispersed. Among the small firms the range of average debts was from £19 to £223; among medium-sized firms, £57 to £743; among large firms, £181 to £2,351; and for giant firms, £362 to £2,525. In short, a hierarchy of failure can be described in terms of simple indebtedness, which roughly corresponds to changes in the hierarchy of size and number of debts, but with both patterns masking a considerable range of possibilities. Big firms did tend to fail in big ways all round, and small ones in small ways, but the relationship was neither simple nor uniform.

[6] P.R.O., B3/821–2. This commission, not untypically for those in B3, was not concluded until October 1842, by which time dividends totalling 17s 9d in the pound had been repaid.
[7] Suffolk Record Office (Bury St Edmunds branch), HA 521(5), Diary of James Oakes, entry for 17 March 1797.

The representativeness of the 152 files which have been analysed here can, at least in terms of the number of creditors bankrupts had, be tested for a short period at the start of the eighteenth century. Between September 1710 and May 1714 information has survived of the signatories of 504 bankrupts' certificates of discharge.[8] A certificate of discharge, which freed a bankrupt from any obligation for his debts and set him loose to begin life anew, needed the agreement of four-fifths of the creditors (see Chapter 3), so by looking at the number of signatories on them it is possible to get a rough idea of the numbers of creditors these 504 bankrupts had. Of these bankrupts, 229 (45 per cent) had between one and ten creditors signing their certificates. A further 137 (27 per cent) had between eleven and twenty signatories. So, over seven out of ten bankrupts had between one and twenty creditors assenting to their discharge. Only one in ten had more than forty.

Running this pattern against that in Table 17 seems to show that between 1710 and 1714 the bulk of bankrupts failed for sums ranging from £100 to £10,000, and that failures for more than £10,000 were very rare indeed.[9] In most cases it seems likely that bankrupts traded on a modest scale, that the evidence of the 152 files exaggerates the large failures, and that most bankrupts had less than fifty creditors and many just twenty or thirty.

CREDITORS AND BANKRUPTS

Problems over credit were one of the main factors determining changing volumes of bankruptcy over the short term. Extensions of credit caused indebtedness, and the loss of patience by creditors was a cause of bankruptcy. Yet despite the widely acknowledged significance of credit in eighteenth-century England, little is known about who creditors were and what they did. We know more about systems of credit than we do about the creditors themselves. Apart from some work by Holderness on probate inventories and by Anderson on the general structure of credit in Lancashire, creditors remain an anonymous group, praised for their investments but rarely described or portrayed in a general way.[10] Fortunately, the bankruptcy records allow some outlines to be sketched of creditors.

[8] P.R.O., B5/20. These certificates represent all those issued in that period.

[9] The comparison cannot be precise because certificates were signed by between 80 and 100 per cent of the creditors and because inflation at the end of the century probably changed the size of bankruptcies.

[10] B. A. Holderness, 'Credit in English rural society before the nineteenth century, with special reference to the period 1650–1720', *Agricultural History Review*, XXIV (1976), pp. 97–109; 'Credit in a rural community, 1660–1800', *Midland History*, III (1975), pp. 94–115. B. L. Anderson, 'Aspects of capital and credit in Lancashire during the eighteenth century' (University of Liverpool M.A. thesis, 1966); 'Money and the structure of credit in the eighteenth century', *Business History*, XII (1970), pp. 85–101; 'Provincial aspects'.

In 1710, the clerks to the Lord Chancellor began to keep the Docket Books and until 1764 these recorded the name, occupation and address of those petitioning creditors who struck the docket. Over those fifty-four years a little over 22,000 creditors were involved in the striking of dockets and, although they were not necessarily typical of debtors' creditors as a whole, an analysis of them does allow some assessment to be made of who creditors were just before the onset of industrialisation.[11]

Most debtors in the Docket Books were there because of the actions of just one creditor. Some were there because of two or more, but for the most part formal proceedings were initiated by a single creditor. For instance, in 1737, which was a peacetime year when the number of dockets struck was very close to the trend calculated for the year, some 260 dockets were struck of which only one failed to list the petitioning creditor. Out of the remaining 259, some 214 (83 per cent) had just one petitioning creditor. The vast majority of these 214 creditors were individuals, with only twenty-six being partnerships. Only nine debtors had more than five petitioning creditors and none had more than ten. In this year, therefore, each debtor had an average of 1.38 petitioning creditors, though for the period 1710–64 the proportion was a bit higher at 1.57.

Information from the Docket Books says little about any individual's network of indebtedness but it does allow some assessment to be made of substantial creditors owed more than £100 who took an active role in initiating bankruptcy proceedings. As with the bankrupts, in the first instance creditors can usefully be described in terms of their occupations and locations. Table 18 compares the sectoral composition of creditors and bankrupts for the five decades 1711–60. Three sectors – textiles, wholesale and miscellaneous – provided two-thirds of all creditors. The food, drink and agricultural sectors accounted for some, though not many, and other sectors were of virtually no significance. Comparing the creditors with the debtors is equally revealing here. Firstly, agriculture was the home of over 1,000 petitioning creditors but, over the same period, of virtually no debtors. Of course, this was largely the product of the legal restrictions which sought to keep the jurisdiction of bankruptcy off the land and confined to trade and industry: farmers and the like could be creditors but not bankrupts. Yeomen and corn dealers accounted for a large part of agriculture's share of petitioning creditors, with yeomen being particularly important.[12] Such people were able to accumulate pools of savings because of the inequalities of landownership and income, so long as their expenditure was lower than their receipts. They did not spend all their savings through conspicuous consumption and lending money to business could be productive, though risky. It is possible,

---

[11] P.R.O., B4/1–20. All discussion of creditors in this section comes from this source.
[12] Terminologically, 'yeoman' was an imprecise occupational designation. See G. E. Mingay, *English landed society in the eighteenth century* (London, 1963), p. 88.

Table 18. *Sectoral composition of debtors and creditors, 1711–60 (per cent)*

Sector	Creditors	Bankrupts
Agriculture	5.6	1.6
Fuel	0.4	0.5
Food	8.0	12.7
Drink	7.8	12.2
Construction	2.4	3.6
Textiles and clothes	26.1	26.2
Finance	1.1	1.2
Transport	2.4	3.9
Metal	3.2	3.6
Wood	0.9	1.5
Retail	1.4	9.9
Wholesale	17.9	15.7
Miscellaneous	22.9	7.2

Source: P.R.O., B4/1–20.

moreover, that the first half of the eighteenth century saw an expansion of lending from the agricultural to the industrial and commercial sectors as perceptions of investment opportunities improved from the late seventeenth century.[13]

Although the food and drink sectors provided significant numbers of petitioning creditors, they made a markedly smaller contribution than they had done in bankruptcy. Probably this resulted from the fact that whereas traders in these sectors found it relatively easy to become indebted for at least £100 they rarely gave out credit in large enough amounts to allow them easily to become petitioning creditors. Indeed, in these trades credit was characteristically given in small amounts to retail customers or small shopkeepers. Such traders stood not at the head but at the foot of lines of credit, taking credit from suppliers in reasonably large amounts but giving it out in relatively small amounts. A similar explanation applies more generally to the retail sector in Table 18 – the shopkeepers, dealers and chapmen. Because they were small traders, operating on an insubstantial bedrock, with limited savings or 'stock', to use the eighteenth-century term, they usually gave out credit in small amounts. If they had chased debtors it would have been via the small debt and insolvent debtor procedures outlined in Chapter 3, not bankruptcy.

Wholesalers and those in the miscellaneous occupations made a more signifi-

[13] Certainly, landowners and the agricultural sector of the economy played an important role in financing canals. Ward, *The finance of canal building.*

cant contribution to the ranks of the creditors than they had to the ranks of bankrupts, presumably because they did give out credit in large lumps. Among the wholesale creditors, merchants were especially important, partly bearing out Anderson's belief that 'The central figure in the whole structure of credit and debt was the merchant, typically the man who bought in bulk, financed stocks and sold in smaller quantities often on long credits.'[14] Between 1711 and 1760 12.8 per cent of all bankrupts were merchants, but over the same period 15.7 per cent of petitioning creditors were merchants, making them easily the most important single occupation among both groups. Over half a century ago Lucy Sutherland noticed that, depending on one's viewpoint, the eighteenth century could be considered 'either as the zenith of an old system of capitalism, where the merchant was the "spring and centre of trafic," or as the forerunner of a new age when the merchant prince saw his place usurped by the industrial magnate'.[15] It seems clear now that the princes were still in command. Certainly, the importance of merchants in bankruptcy, be it on the credit or debt side of the divide, makes the neglect they have suffered from historians impossible to understand. Aside from discussions of overseas trade, the role of merchants as coordinating businessmen, so amply illustrated by their role as creditors, has been badly neglected.[16] They were vital not only to the development of the import–export economy but, through the provision of credit, to the state of liquidity within a much more general area of business enterprise. Standing at the peak of the business hierarchy, they had accumulated reserves that were widely used in the provision of credit. Their beneficence improved the fertility of the soil from which all business enterprise sprang.

The greatest difference between the sectoral compositions of bankrupts and creditors came in the miscellaneous sector: only 7.2 per cent of bankrupts but 22.9 per cent of creditors came from this area. For the bankrupts, the most influential occupations were tallow chandlers, perukemakers and similar craft occupations. But among the creditors it was much more specifically gentlemen, widows and spinsters. Of course, a bankrupt could not go into the *Gazette* as a 'gentleman', whereas for creditors such general descriptions could readily be used. But this only partly explains the importance of 'gentlemen' etc. as creditors; their role in the supply of loans and credit to business points to a more considerable influence. Some 10.4 per cent of petitioning creditors were

[14] Thesis, p. 123.

[15] L. S. Sutherland, 'The law merchant in England in the seventeenth and eighteenth centuries', *Transactions of the Royal Historical Society*, 4th series, XVII (1934), p. 149.

[16] Minchinton, 'The merchants of England', is more concerned with their background than their role. C. P. Kindleberger, 'Commercial expansion and the industrial revolution', *Journal of European Economic History*, IV (1975), pp. 613–54, is about trade rather than merchants. There are some general points in Westerfield, *Middlemen in English business*, pp. 349–62. Wilson, *Gentlemen merchants*, is an excellent study of the Leeds merchant community.

gentlemen, 4.0 per cent widows and 1.7 per cent spinsters. All three groups were capable of accumulating funds, often through inheritance, which had to be invested to produce income. Business was just one area they turned to, for agriculture and the national debt were other attractive outlets for their capital. Undoubtedly, among such social groups there were those who preferred to keep their money away from trade, but their importance as petitioning creditors shows just how heavily involved they were with enterprise during the eighteenth century.[17]

Before 1764, some 19.2 per cent of petitioning creditors were gentlemen, yeomen, widows or spinsters. These four groups formed vital links between savings and enterprise. They put money out to those whom they knew, of course; to businessmen who were close, whether because of friendship, geography, family, religion or 'professional' advice. Outside the most developed areas of the economy, most credit was given and taken fairly locally and non-trading petitioning creditors lent within the local context.[18] As Professor Mathias has noticed, 'Many gaps had to be spanned between those groups receiving most of the savings and those requiring most of the credit. There was no national capital market in eighteenth-century England, in the sense of a coherent, nationally organized entity with flows responding quickly throughout the economy to changes in the supply and demand for funds.'[19] The gentlemen, yeomen, widows and spinsters who were so significant as petitioning creditors must, then, have lent locally, often using attorneys as intermediaries in the ways Anderson has described.[20] Of course, the significance of these four groups as creditors may reflect not only on their wealth but also on their nervousness, inexperience and inflexibility in handling debtors. It is possible that, once debtors began to shuffle and postpone repayment, those outside trade were less patient and confident with them than were those inside and were quicker to shut down businessmen by striking a docket. In 1791, for example, William & Samuel Atherstone, hosiers, buying and selling worsted and cotton 'and· making and converting the same into stockings', from Loughborough, had a commission begun against them by a gentleman from Staffordshire. But during the following weeks only one other debtor, a toymaker from Birmingham, proved a debt against them. Obviously, the extent of their indebtedness was limited and the implied foolishness of their gentleman creditor considerable.[21]

Sectorally, just over a quarter of petitioning creditors came from textiles, a proportion that matches this sector's contribution to bankruptcy. Among the

---

[17] For background see Crouzet, 'Editor's introduction'.
[18] See Anderson, 'Provincial aspects'. Also Holderness, 'Credit in a rural community', p. 102.
[19] P. Mathias, 'Capital, credit and enterprise in the industrial revolution', reprinted in his *The transformation of England*, pp. 91–2.
[20] B. L. Anderson, 'The attorney and the early capital market in Lancashire', reprinted in Crouzet, ed., *Capital formation in the industrial revolution*, pp. 223–55.   [21] P.R.O., B3/5452.

Table 19. *Main counties of creditors and bankrupts, 1711–60*

	Percentage from given county	
County	Creditors	Bankrupts
Devon	2.6	2.4
Glos.	7.3	4.7
Lancs.	4.0	3.5
London	51.8	45.6
Middx.	2.9	3.9
Norfolk	3.9	4.7
Surrey	2.1	2.5
Yorks.	4.2	4.3
Total	78.8	71.6

Source: P.R.O., B4/1–20.

creditors, five occupations were especially prominent: woollen manufacturers, cloth dealers, linen dealers, mercers and haberdashers. Of these, the linen dealers were the most important, something that is easily explained. 'The draper kept a shop, but was much more than a mere shopkeeper; he was often his own wholesaler, travelling into the countryside to procure goods.'[22] As such, they frequently supplied credit to country manufacturers and, acting as wholesalers, they usually sold goods on credit to retailers. Richard Campbell thought that linen drapers were in 'the first Rank of Tradesmen', potentially able to accumulate substantial profits and provide loans.[23] Indeed, in time, many went on to become country bankers.[24] Initially, they had been both wholesalers and retailers but 'The retail function became less and less and was given over to the mercers.'[25]

We move on now to the geography of creditors to see whether the patterns which have so far been uncovered were replicated there. Again, although creditors came from similar areas to bankrupts there were differences in emphasis which reinforce the basic points already made. In the first place, the creditors were more concentrated than the bankrupts, with the dominance of London especially marked. Second, in only two counties, Gloucestershire and London, was their share of the respective categories different by more than 1 per cent. In this period, London and Bristol (which largely accounts for Gloucestershire's position among the creditors) controlled the great majority of England's over-

[22] Pressnell, *Country banking*, p. 51.   [23] *The London tradesman*, p. 282.
[24] Pressnell, *Country banking*, p. 51.
[25] Westerfield, *Middlemen in English business*, p. 309 and also p. 322.

seas trade, lending weight to the importance of merchants as creditors. The capital handled much of the nation's international trade, was the focal point in England for overseas and inland bills of exchange, had a large and wealthy community and, finally, organised a large part of domestic economic activity either directly or indirectly. All of these factors meant that the capital was bound to be the centre of credit networks. If a very large proportion of the produce of the domestic economy flowed through the streets and wharves of the metropolis then equally many provincial trades were dominated by middlemen there.[26] Bristol also had a vibrant and wealthy community of merchants in these years who seem to have willingly supported enterprise in the surrounding areas. They, like their colleagues in London, shouldered many of the difficulties – and reaped many of the rewards of course – of economic life in eighteenth-century England. After all, the turnover of goods was usually slow, money often unavailable and the necessity for book debts and bills of exchange commensurately great.[27]

Creditors tended to be located socially and economically above bankrupts. Merchants, gentlemen, yeomen, widows, spinsters and large wholesalers all played a vital role in the provision of credit to businessmen. From them flowed the life-giving funds, the venture capital in a sense, that was instrumental in the expansion of enterprise in the century. But from them also flowed bankruptcy proceedings. They offered life, but they sometimes demanded death. With their personal commitment in the gladiatorial contest of eighteenth-century business enterprise, it was their thumbs which decided the fate of the fallen.

FOUR CASE STUDIES

Patterns of indebtedness and the role of credit and creditors can be taken a step further by looking at four specific bankruptcies. Firstly, a comparison will be made of two provincial shopkeepers who failed. Secondly, two London merchants will be examined. The network of debts that these four businesses became entangled in will give some idea of the range of such networks that existed.

In 1782, William Symonds, a shopkeeper from Herstmonceux, Sussex, was declared bankrupt. His bankruptcy was gazetted in August, but the commission had actually got under way in July.[28] With sixteen creditors, proving debts totalling just £902, his average debt was a modest £56. These debts varied in value from just over £4 to the largest debt of £263, owed to a surgeon at Lewes

---

[26] Pressnell, *Country banking*, Ch. 4.
[27] W. E. Minchinton, 'Bristol – metropolis of the west in the eighteenth century', *Transactions of the Royal Historical Society*, 5th series, IV (1954), pp. 69–85.
[28] P.R.O., B3/4436.

in the same county. Six of the debts were for sums over £50. Geographically, Symonds had two sorts of creditor, those from nearby in Sussex and those from London. Five of his creditors, or nearly a third, came from the capital, though they were owed only one-fifth of his total debts. The five were an ironmonger, tobacconist, haberdasher, linen draper and hosier. Local creditors therefore provided a disproportionately large share of his credit. Half of these local sources – a surgeon, grocer, tallow chandler, banker, linen draper, ironmonger and the executor of a will – came from Lewes, about fourteen miles from Herstmonceux. The remaining four all came from villages close to Symonds. Two of these were yeomen, owed £118 and £106, and the other two were farmers, owed £37 and £65. Naturally, Symonds's debts could either have been trade credits or they could have been straight loans. Unfortunately, when creditors proved their debts they rarely said what sort of debt it was, and loans can only be distinguished from credits on the circumstantial evidence of the occupations of creditors.

Symonds was a small shopkeeper operating in a rural environment. His customers would have been agricultural labourers, farmers, landowners, parson and squire. In many ways, his business may have been very similar to that of Thomas Turner, whose shop was at East Hoathly, just eight miles away – though both of them traded on a more modest scale than either Abraham Dent or William Stout.[29] Symonds stocked cloth, clothing, ironware, candles, grocery goods and tobacco. And the farmers and yeomen to whom he was indebted may have supplied him with grain, flour, meal or meat – though it is perhaps more likely that the yeomen at least had lent him money. Though he was supplied primarily from London, the bulk of the credit had been raised locally.

We can guess at several reasons for Symonds's failure. Firstly, perhaps he had set up a shop with too small a market to serve. The area around Herstmonceux had always been thinly populated. In the 1801 census there were just 961 inhabitants spread over the parish's 5,000 acres. Whether a market of about 200 households was enough for a small shopkeeper is debatable, not the least because we know nothing of the competition he faced.[30] He may have fallen, secondly, because he had over-extended himself. Clearly, he had borrowed several large sums of money from people within the local community, while some of the Lewes debts and all of the London ones were more straightforward trade credits. These local creditors were particularly important in allowing Symonds to operate on the scale he was attempting, and it was their confidence in his ability to repay which was critical to the survival of his business. Maintaining their confidence was a major priority for him. This he could do by

[29] *The diary of Thomas Turner*. T. S. Willan, *An eighteenth century shopkeeper. Abraham Dent of Kirkby Stephen* (Manchester, 1970). *The autobiography of William Stout*.
[30] *Victoria county history of Sussex*, Vol. II, ed. W. Page (Oxford, 1907), p. 222.

having enough trade to repay some of his debts, or by persuading them that repayment would be forthcoming. Once that confidence was lost, either when he realised that his business was a failure or when one or more of his creditors believed so, then bankruptcy ensued. Over the short term, Symonds failed because he was unable to support the credit and loans he had taken on. In all likelihood, the amount of trade he carried on was insufficient to generate the money necessary to placate his creditors. This suggestion is supported by the fact that a solitary dividend of just 2s 3d in the pound was paid to his creditors in 1788, six years after his bankruptcy. Unless there had been a substantial fraud, it seems clear that when Symonds failed he had meagre assets and that his trade had been a losing one for some time.

The second bankrupt shopkeeping business to be considered is the partnership of Elizabeth and John Sanderson from Staithes in Yorkshire, some six miles up the coast from Whitby. They were gazetted in June 1788 and owed 132 creditors a total of £7,478, or on average £57, strikingly close to Symonds's average debt.[31] Only fifteen of these creditors came from London, but they accounted for 44 per cent of the total value of the debts. An Irish factor from King Street, running off Cheapside, dominated these metropolitan debts, being owed £2,300, though there were two other large London debts, one to a gentleman for £437 and one to a grocer for £253.

In terms of numbers, most creditors came from within the immediate vicinity of Staithes. Nearly two-thirds of the creditors lived within fifteen miles of the village. The small port itself provided thirty, Whitby twenty-two, Loftus, lying just over four miles from Staithes, had ten and other small settlements had a handful each. Although numerous, these local creditors were only owed a total of £3,423, or an average of £43. Beyond them and the London creditors, there were another thirty-seven provincial creditors. They included merchants from Newcastle, Hull, Sheffield, Bradford, Leeds, Halifax and Manchester and creditors in Carlisle, Durham, Gainsborough, Birmingham, Nottingham, Great Yarmouth and elsewhere. All of these were owed small sums. Nevertheless, it is clear from the pattern of these debts that the Sandersons had trading connexions which spread up and down the east coast, infiltrating the manufacturing heartland of the Midlands and north. By implication, therefore, they were no mere 'shopkeepers' as advertised in the *London Gazette* but middlemen who were enmeshed in the internal trade of northern England. Moreover the presence, among the creditors from Whitby, of members of various shipbuilding occupations suggests that the Sandersons were intimately linked to the coastal trade. They almost certainly acted in the capacity of wholesalers, dispersing goods shipped into Whitby and Staithes from the coastal traffic that plied the edge of the North Sea.[32]

---

[31] P.R.O., B3/4440–1.
[32] T. S. Willan, *The English coasting trade 1600–1750* (Manchester, 1938), Ch. 8.

The Sandersons' undoing was probably the result of trading ties and debts. The London debts were dominated by the one owed to the Irish factor, which might have been a trade credit or a loan, akin to an injection of capital by a sleeping partner. It is impossible to say which, though the latter seems more likely. In that case, the raising of the loan must have been possible because earlier successes made them appear creditworthy, and that loan was meant to allow them to expand.[33] The expansion might have meant a widening of the inland market they served – which would have been physically difficult because of the poor communications Staithes and Whitby had with their hinterlands – or, more probably, was linked to the coastal trade they were involved with. This single large debt may have caused them to fail. Certainly, the Irish factor struck their docket. Perhaps the financial crisis of the spring and early summer of 1788 made him seek liquidity and hurry his debtors. If that were the case, then the Sandersons were being questioned more in relation to their short-term liquidity than their long-term solvency.

It is possible, but unlikely, that the Sandersons' demise was initiated locally. Local creditors probably had more to lose than gain from initiating bankruptcy proceedings. Seven of their creditors from Staithes were widows and two were spinsters. These nine women were owed £1,435, or an average of £159. The Sandersons also owed money to seven fishermen, five mariners, two boat-builders and two innkeepers in the tiny port. But the bulk of their local sources came from the women just mentioned. This supports the findings of earlier in the chapter and confirms the view of Holderness to the effect that 'The widow ...had always been a centrally important personage in the economics of village life, and despite fundamental changes in inheritance customs since the Middle Ages, her function in redistributing idle capital towards the economically active in the community was by the seventeenth century predicated upon her provision of credit.'[34] In the Sandersons' case it is unlikely that these widows would have contemplated initiating bankruptcy proceedings.

In the *London Gazette* both William Symonds and the Sandersons were described as 'shopkeepers'. But they were very different. Symonds was a petty trader, exclusively local, with few commitments and a restricted range of ambitions. The Sandersons, however, were linked to a very wide sphere of trading, and attempted to make some headway in the east-coast trade that was thriving in this period. Symonds and the Sandersons failed for different reasons, reasons that reflect the sort of business they conducted and the financial implications of their aspirations. The Sandersons' business drowned in much

---

[33] They owed a round sum of £400 to a gentleman in Bedford Square which was almost certainly not a trade credit.

[34] Holderness, 'Credit in English rural society', p. 105; 'Credit in a rural community'; 'Elizabeth Parkin and her investments, 1733–66. Aspects of the Sheffield money market in the eighteenth century', *Transactions of the Hunter Archaeological Society*, X (1973), pp. 81–7.

deeper waters than did Symonds's partly because they had access to credit and loans that allowed them to wade further out. Creditors rightly judged that they were in a far better position than Symonds to drive a larger trade. In short, recalling Chapter 1, it was as important for the creditors to recognise opportunities as it was for the businessmen to try to seize them using capital and credit. But during the financial storms of 1788, the Sandersons came to grief. Yet it would be wrong to assume that, because they were more ambitious and their indebtedness greater, their business acumen was correspondingly less. Compared with the paltry dividend of 2s 3d in the pound paid on Symonds's estate the Sandersons paid out 11s 4d. While the Sandersons were in deeper water, they had judged the risks and opportunities better and taken along more, though not enough, equipment for survival.

The first of the two London merchants to be examined is Leslie Grove of Crosby Square, gazetted in January 1789 as a 'merchant, banker, dealer and chapman'.[35] He failed with debts totalling £6,127 to forty-three creditors. The average debt was £142, roughly three times as large as those of the shopkeepers just looked at. Before Grove was declared bankrupt, the commissioners examined his clerk who swore that Grove not only traded with Ireland and other countries but was also a banker. Yet only ten of his creditors came from outside London, though they were owed 56 per cent of the value of his total debt. He owed small debts to an apothecary and a stable keeper in Mitcham, Surrey – which suggests that he lived or visited there. A surgeon from Gravesend was owed £104 and a gentleman from Walworth in Surrey £163. He also had a creditor at Falmouth and another at Wareham, which lies at the west end of Poole harbour in Dorset. Both of these creditors lay en route for Ireland and may have been staging posts for Grove's business there. He owed them £261 and £294 respectively. Two of the non-metropolitan creditors came from Ireland, both esquires, owed £500 and £300. He had only two other overseas creditors – which casts some doubts on the claim that he traded with several countries – an esquire in Jamaica owed £305 and an official in the East India Company in Bengal owed close to £1,500. This last debt was easily the largest he owed, over twice the value of the second biggest.

The largest London creditor was a Viscount from Stanhope Street owed £713. But Grove had only five other creditors in the capital who were owed more than £100 each. An insurance broker was owed £450, a gentleman £250, an esquire £628, a linen draper £111 and, finally, a wine merchant £112. Twenty-five of his London creditors were owed less than £50 each, which suggests that these were living expenses. These small debts were not the cause of his collapse; creditors in such a position have little to gain by pursuing bankruptcy proceedings. Grove, moreover, would not have found it too difficult

[35] P.R.O., B3/1849.

to keep their confidence. His downfall must have come from his big debts, those fourteen that were in excess of £100. Over the short term, it was the way he managed these which probably accounted for his failure.

Grove was declared a bankrupt on 9 January 1789, and at the first meeting to prove debts, held eight days later, only four creditors turned up. At the next meeting, on 24 January, another twelve creditors proved or claimed debts. Fifteen out of these first sixteen debts proved were large ones. It was not until April that the small creditors began to prove their debts. So, substantial creditors were the quickest to establish their presence in the commission, and this sense of urgency reflects both the size of the debts involved and their importance in Grove's demise. The large debts were of two main sorts: those owed to the well-to-do of London society who appear to have been using Grove as a bank and perhaps as an investment; and then there were those debts owed to trading connexions, usually to do with Ireland. The first of these groups was the quickest to establish the proof of their debts, both because they were best situated to do so and because it may well have been a member of this group whose 'nerve' broke and initiated bankruptcy proceedings.

Whether Grove failed because of a failure on the banking or merchanting side of his business is impossible to say. Certainly, as a banker, he had very few depositors compared with other bankrupt banks, and this side of his business was the least important, probably supplementing and providing liquidity for the merchantry.[36] However, his inexperience in banking, along with the problems of 1788, could have caused his collapse. The acute liquidity problems that were typical of overseas trade at the time would also have been damaging – his largest creditor, after all, was in Bengal. Much of his capital would have been caught up in ships and stores, either on the seas or in warehouses. It is possible that he began his banking operations in an attempt to circumvent the difficulties he was finding in funding his trading. Moreover, a schedule of his estate presented to the commissioners in April 1789 listed only four substantive assets, all of them illiquid ones. Firstly, he had an estate in Ireland worth £304 per annum, but with two annuities totalling £90 due on it. Secondly, he had a portion of real estate near Dublin worth £45 per annum. Thirdly, he claimed to have a navy pension of £150 per annum, though he confessed that he had no right to enforce the payment of it. Finally, he was owed, or claimed to be owed, an unspecified amount from a partnership he was involved in with John Hood of Crosby Square. Hood, for his part, put in a counter-claim.

Grove's failure was not a catastrophic one. Not only was the size of his total debt modest by the standards of other merchant bankrupts, but he also owed

---

[36] See above, the example of Robert Carss, p. 143. The London bank of Gibson and Johnson, which failed in 1788, had around 200 creditors: P.R.O., B3/1845-8. Neal, James, Fordyce and Down, another bank, which failed in 1772, had 441 creditors: P.R.O., B3/3675-6.

money to a limited number of creditors. Moreover, a reasonably good first dividend of 8*s* in the pound was paid in September 1789. Clearly, not all of his assets had been tied up and his business had rested on some sort of bedrock. But the second dividend, for 2*s* 6*d* in the pound, was not made until June 1795, a delay caused by a contest in Chancery over Grove's Irish estate. A final dividend of 5*d* in the pound was paid in June 1828, thirty years after his bankruptcy. In the end, therefore, his estate realised nearly 11*s* in the pound, which was average to good by the standards of the day, and it would have been greater of course had the assignees not fought in Chancery over his estate. The immediate cause of Grove's failure probably arose because he had insufficient liquidity to satisfy one or more of his creditors, probably from among the London well-to-do. That creditor initiated bankruptcy proceedings either because he was being pressed himself or because his nervous suspicions about Grove were intensified during the difficult conditions of 1788.

Grove was a merchant operating a fairly restricted trade. He had few overseas commitments, and in terms of credit and debt he was poorly linked to the London mercantile community. This is in stark contrast to the second merchant firm to be examined, the partnership of Batter and Zornlin, operating from Devonshire Square, close by Bishopsgate.[37] They were declared bankrupt in November 1799 and were gazetted as 'merchant, dealer and chapman'. Fortunately, however, their clerk was called upon to give evidence before the commissioners to prove that they were traders, as the law demanded. He said that Batter and Zornlin were merchants 'by exporting sugar and coffee and manufactured goods and importing raw cotton and other commodities and did Trade from this Kingdom of England to Germany and divers other Places'. Evidence that they owed debts above £100 came from Manchester and, indeed, when the assignees were chosen, early in December, one was from London and the other from Manchester.

By the end of the commission, debts proved against the partnership totalled £81,621. They had 142 creditors, owed on average £575 each. While not the biggest merchant failure, Batter and Zornlin were in the top league. They traded on a large scale, with substantial commitments, to many people. Their creditors can be categorised in three ways: those coming from London, those from the provinces and those from overseas.

London was the home of fifty-three out of the partnership's 142 creditors, but they were owed just £11,034, or 13.5 per cent, of the value of their debts. Only eleven London creditors were owed more than £100. Of these eleven four stand out. Three merchants were owed £2,000, £2,094 and £1,502, while an insurance broker was owed £1,666. These debts were probably loans.

37 P.R.O., B3/205–6.

There were twenty-four provincial creditors, 17 per cent of the total, who were owed £24,932, or 30.5 per cent, of the value of the total debts. But this picture was heavily influenced by a single debt of £14,245 owed to the Holywell Cotton Twist Company. Although the company had its factory at Holywell in Flintshire, it also had a warehouse in Manchester and was both a spinning and merchanting concern.[38] Geographically, the partnership had clear links with the north. The partners owed a total of £3,929 to four Manchester merchants, £200 to a Glasgow merchant, £400 to a factor in Birmingham and £2,661 to merchants in Leeds. Their other main link with the provinces was with Exeter, where they owed five merchants a total of £1,288. If the debt to the Holywell Company is ignored, the average debt of Batter and Zornlin to provincial creditors was £465, whereas in London it was just £208. However, the largest debts lay overseas.

Just under a half of their creditors were overseas and they were owed just over half of their total debts. The average overseas debt was £697. Twenty-four of the creditors were in Germany, half in Augsburg, the remainder coming from Hamburg, Dresden, Leipzig and elsewhere. German creditors were owed on average nearly £900. The second main area of Batter and Zornlin's European business was Switzerland, where they owed sixteen creditors a total of £6,880, an average of £430. Most of these were from Basle. The partnership had less numerous and significant connexions with Italy and Austria, along with two creditors in Lisbon, two in the Dutch provinces and one in St Petersburg. On the other side of the Atlantic, they had four creditors: two from New York, one from Philadelphia and another in Halifax, North Carolina. These four were owed an average of £1,055 each.

We can use this pattern of indebtedness to reconstruct a picture of how Batter and Zornlin probably traded. They obtained supplies of raw cotton, sugar and coffee from America, the bulk of it going to England with some perhaps destined for re-export. Finished cotton goods and cotton yarn were bought from Lancashire alongside woollen goods from the West Riding and Exeter which were all shipped to Europe from their London warehouses. Most went into Europe via Hamburg, from where the cotton yarn, which made up the bulk of their business on the export side, moved in two directions. Some flowed into Saxony and Silesia, supplying their infant cotton industries. But most flowed south, to Frankfurt and Augsburg. In the Rhine valley the partners found some business but most of the yarn was destined for Switzerland. This Swiss market focused on Basle, and was primarily served from the north. Batter and Zornlin offer specific confirmation of the general statement that 'From 1780 onwards Switzerland had been an important market for British cotton

[38] E. J. Foulkes, 'The cotton-spinning factories of Flintshire, 1777–1866', *Journal of the Flintshire Historical Society Publications*, XXI (1964), pp. 91–7.

textiles.'[39] The Austrian market, with Vienna at its centre, was probably supplied via Augsburg and the Danube. Had the supply route been overland from Dresden, we would have expected creditors in Prague, but there were none.

Quite what Batter and Zornlin imported from Europe in return for their heavy cotton exports is unclear. Perhaps they included 'raw materials... from the more backward parts of Europe, the lands bordering the Baltic and Mediterranean that produced the surpluses of timber, iron, hemp and flax, silk, oil and many dyestuffs'.[40] Given the substantial debts Batter and Zornlin had in Augsburg, Dresden, Hamburg and Leipzig, they may well have imported linens or other textiles from Silesia and other parts of central Europe. The trade with America was probably more straightforward: the partnership exported cotton and woollen manufactured goods and imported raw cotton, sugar and coffee.

Batter and Zornlin were deeply committed to trading with Europe, providing vital export markets for the rapidly growing Lancashire cotton industry. To do this they took and gave large amounts of credit on both the import and the export sides, working a delicate balancing act as they went along. The more creditors and links they acquired the more difficult that balancing act became though, equally, the greater the trade they drove, the more confidence they could expect from their creditors. In fact, they did not go bankrupt because they were desperately insolvent. Within just three weeks of their declaration of bankruptcy a dividend of 12s in the pound was paid, while a year later another 2s in the pound was awarded. By the end of the commission in 1826, nearly 16s in the pound had been repaid. Given the expense of administering such a large commission, it is quite likely that when they were bankrupted their assets were very close to the value to their liabilities. Francis Baring's comment, distinguishing insolvency from bankruptcy, seems apt in this case:

A state of insolvency is correctly understood, and is irretrievable; that of bankruptcy is more indefinite, for there are many instances where they are not insolvent... I apprehend the name attaches more to a legal form of proceeding, than to a correct definition of real capacity or incapacity of the party to fulfil his engagements...[41]

Batter and Zornlin failed because they lost the confidence of their creditors

[39] B. M. Biucchi, 'The industrial revolution in Switzerland', in C. M. Cippola, ed., *The Fontana economic history of Europe*, Vol. IV, Part ii (Brighton, 1976), p. 627. For a general discussion of European industrialisation in the late eighteenth century and potential markets for British cotton goods see S. Pollard, *Peaceful conquest. The industrialization of Europe 1760–1970* (Oxford, 1981), Ch. 3, especially pp. 100–3. Davis, *British overseas trade*, p. 17. Edwards, *British cotton trade*, Ch. 4.   [40] Davis, *British overseas trade*, p. 37.

[41] *Further observations on the establishment of the Bank of England, and on the paper circulation of the country* (London, 1797), p. 15.

rather than because they were operating an obviously unprofitable trade; they were unable to convince some creditors, or themselves in fact, that they were reasonably sound at bottom. It was the petitioning creditors, two Manchester merchants, who were unconvinced and decided to call it a day. There were probably two short-term causes of the partners' failure: first, the loss of patience among some creditors and, second, their mismanagement of liquidity.

The Manchester merchants had good reason to be apprehensive of businesses trading with central Europe in 1799. Britain, at war with an expansionist France, was unsuccessfully trying to establish diplomatic authority in the area, when first Austria and then Russia made this increasingly difficult. The Swiss market may have appeared to be particularly threatened by a powerful, revolutionary France. While Napoleon was occupied elsewhere in 1799, it seemed likely that central Europe would become a battleground at some stage.[42] With such political uncertainty, creditors of those trading to the area may have judged that, if a firm was stalling for time in any case, then the sooner it was brought to an end by bankruptcy, then the more chance there would be of getting complete and unfettered access to the estate. If that was the supposition of the two Manchester merchants, then their judgement was soundly based, given the dividends that were paid out. They had played a part of the competitive game well; they had taken a sort of risk and it had paid off.

In their own eyes, Batter and Zornlin may well have believed that they had failed. Yet from the dividends it is clear that theirs was not a complete and utter failure. In all probability, they had confronted a massive liquidity problem to which they could see no answer given the uncertainty of their markets. Without a list of who their debtors were it is impossible to judge this issue. Clearly, they had contracted too many debts relative to the credit they had given, in terms of the timing of the flows of income that would be accruing to the business. The size of their first dividend and the speed with which it was paid suggests, perhaps, that they had a large amount of stock (cotton goods?) lying on their hands. This left them in a position where they were temporarily insolvent, a condition which some creditors reacted to because of their assessment of the medium- and long-term prospects of the firm. It is unlikely that Batter and Zornlin had made mistakes over pricing policy; the cheap Lancashire cotton yarn they exported would have assured them of European markets under normal conditions. But 1799 provided peculiar, not normal, conditions. They may also have made mistakes on the import side of their business where they were involved in sugar and coffee. Demand for both these commodities was being influenced by the sharp inflation in prices for basic foodstuffs that

---

[42] For a summary see I. R. Christie, *Wars and revolutions. Britain 1760–1815* (London, 1982), pp. 244–8.

characterised England in the 1790s, though demand for sugar proved surprisingly inelastic.[43]

In the end, it seems most likely that Batter and Zornlin simply miscalculated the 'pace' of their trade such that the delicate balancing act in the giving and taking of credit could no longer be performed. That balancing act was obviously more tricky than the one Grove had failed to perform. They had far more variables and unknowns to take into account. Batter and Zornlin were also operating in a competitive domestic environment in the 1790s because they found new, forceful, competitors from Liverpool coming onto the scene. 'London was the principal port for cotton until at least 1795, and after that time London merchants and their agents were active in Liverpool, Manchester and other northern centres. Towards the end of the century Liverpool superseded London.'[44] Perhaps Batter and Zornlin should have moved their business from Devonshire Square closer to the hub of their trade, industrial Lancashire.

Four bankruptcies have been examined, ranging from one for under £1,000 to one for over £80,000. The evidence has not survived to assess these businesses' purchasing, pricing and marketing policies. But in the eighteenth century, failure ultimately focused on the giving and taking of credit and debt. Failure did not arise from mistakes in one area but in a series of areas – industrial location, purchasing and pricing policy, financial underpinning, quality control, marketing and so on. The decisions of bankrupts in reference to these areas are lost from view because of the absence of evidence, but in the end the businesses that survived had liquidity and arguments for creditors while those that did not failed. In that light, creditors might also be culpable.

Most businesses at the time had little room for manoeuvre. The marketplace, over which they had no control, determined what prices they should pay and demand. Most businessmen imitated successful competitors in most of the areas over which they had a choice. It was on marketing – where goods should be sold, at what price, to whom and how – and the establishment of trading connexions that businessmen were called upon to make truly critical judgements. Given this, the sorts of factors that have been uncovered in these four case studies appear more relevant. Choice of creditor and choice of debtor, and there was real choice here, were central to the success of a business. Creditors and the nature of debts took many forms and behaved either passively or actively when it came to insolvency, temporary or permanent, and the possibility of bankruptcy. Without creditors there would have been no debtors, and without debtors there would have been no bankrupts. Moreover, without credit there would have been far less chance for growth in eighteenth-century England. All businessmen were both debtors and creditors, but not all creditors were businessmen.

[43] Davis, *British overseas trade*, pp. 43–4.   [44] Chapman, *The cotton industry*, p. 45.

10

CONTEMPORARIES AND FAILURE

How did people in the eighteenth century understand bankruptcy and what sort of advice did they offer to businessmen to help them avoid it? Such opinions have already been examined in the context of the legal mechanisms for dealing with failure and of the significance of financial crises as causes of failure. What becomes clear from the following, more concerted analysis, is that historians' preoccupation with the heroes of the Industrial Revolution has helped them to ignore or forget the considerable worries and reservations that were expressed at the time about the balance between success and failure, about the way businesses were conducted and about the achievements of the business world.

EIGHTEENTH-CENTURY PERCEPTIONS OF SUCCESS AND FAILURE

Perceptions of business enterprise in the eighteenth century, and of the route towards success and away from failure, have to be reconstructed from a variety of sources. Opinions about the job, role and aims of businessmen were rarely expressed methodically and have more usually survived as a series of piecemeal and disjointed reflections. Nowhere were the causes of success and failure clearly detailed, but business letters, the law of bankruptcy, economic pamphlets and the so-called 'advice books' can all be used to piece together a picture of opinions at the time.[1]

Over the course of this book many causes of bankruptcy have been discussed. Some businessmen obviously failed because of their avarice or luxury; others because of circumstances beyond their control such as wars, fires or storms; others simply because they were bad businessmen who made uncompetitive decisions given the conditions of supply and demand they were faced with; others because of monetary pressures, sometimes self-inflicted; and, finally, some collapsed on purpose to exploit loopholes in the law of bankruptcy. Although no single eighteenth-century observer produced a comprehensive discussion of these broad causes they were all, nevertheless, raised at one time

[1] Advice books were written to guide the young businessman away from the rocks and towards calm waters as he set out on his business life.

161

or another. Interestingly, however, failure was often thought of in terms of issues adjacent to these causes as much as in terms of the causes themselves. Most commonly, these were the issues of credit, risk, extravagance and morality – the four main pivots around which ideas of the determinants of success and failure rotated in the century.[2] What unites these issues and led to considerable overlap between them was that failure was often seen as avoidable rather than accidental – though it was not necessarily blameable. Naturally, bankruptcy was frequently viewed in terms of mischance, by 'Losses, Crosses and Misfortunes'.[3] But the obvious and undeniable truth of this meant that it often took the form of an unwritten assumption when success and failure were examined. One elaboration of the accidental theme was made: that everyone, rich or poor, weak or strong, could be devastated by its impact. To Defoe, 'The best and most flourishing Tradesmen fall into Disasters. We have had fatal Blows to Men of Fortune in *England*...and such Men are standing Instances of the little Guard great Estates are to the surprises of Trade.'[4] Postlethwayt balanced the good with the bad when he proffered the maxim that 'As people in trade are never too low to rise, so they are never too high to fall.'[5] But, beyond this, the accidental motif was only really raised in relation to the balance the law of bankruptcy should strike in the degree of culpability to be attached to bankrupts. The plea of accident was one of the main ways by which debtors and insolvents could hope to find sympathy. It was the principal way in which the personal tragedy of bankruptcy was successfully understood.

Credit was the most important peg on which ideas of bankruptcy in the eighteenth century were hung. Indeed, we have already seen the many ways in which it was central to expansion and collapse, to bankruptcy and fortune. This was one basis of the eighteenth-century concern with credit, but it was also seized on by contemporary onlookers because, as an increasingly vital commodity to businessmen, it inspired some feeling of novelty. In particular, a system of credit evolved, bound together by a web of bills of exchange and banks. Together, credit and bills allowed businessmen to cope with the acute shortage of ready money at the time, the problems of moving money about the country and the delays that haunted exchange.[6] By 1790, and much earlier in developed areas of the economy, it was said that '*ready money* is never employed

---

[2] Some writers did try to analyse the broad causes of failure in a systematic way, but there were always gaps in their vision. See Petty, *The Petty papers*, Vol. i, p. 249. *The compleat tradesman: or the exact dealers daily companion* (London, 1684), Ch. 4. T. Goodinge, *The law against bankrupts: or, a treatise wherein the statutes against bankrupts are explain'd* (3rd edn, London, 1713), Preface.

[3] *The case of the poor prisoners for debt and damages* (London, 1711 ?).

[4] Defoe, *Defoe's review*, 15 January 1706, p. 25

[5] Postlethwayt, *Universal dictionary*, Vol. i, p. 212.

[6] Generally see Anderson, 'Money and the structure of credit'. Pressnell, *Country banking*.

but in regard to trifling demands'.[7] Indeed, as early as 1730 it was reported that 'From a Deficiency of Money in our Nation have proceeded the general Use and Length of Credit, which is such, that we deal by Ink altogether, as if Money was a useless unfashionable Thing.'[8] Credit gave flexibility to an economy which had only imperfect flows of money, resources and information. Its availability enabled the threshold of entry into many branches of trade and industry to be lowered, easing business formation by allowing production and distribution to be extended upon expectations of possible markets, thereby being speculative and a partner of growth. And it reflected the highly personal basis of exchange, where credit and debt were usually given to and taken from known faces.

Bankruptcy was related to credit in terms of the ways in which credit worked or was meant to work. It was widely felt that 'Credit...is no more than a *well established* confidence between men, in what relates to the fulfilling of their engagements.'[9] A general consensus existed as to what constituted 'well established' here, relating firstly to the actual act of giving and taking credit, and secondly, to the purposes for which it was being used. Theoretically, it was meant to be given to those who had proven their creditworthiness. Although there was some onus on creditors to assess accurately the means and character of any potential debtor, there was a greater onus on the debtor to establish and prove his creditworthiness. Obviously, this was most successfully achieved when the pair were close enough to assess and impress one another. They were meant to stand eye to eye, to make sure that they knew what they were letting themselves in for. After all, trade credit rested 'entirely...upon the debtor's personal security' – the simple *expectation* that a debt would be repaid.[10] Personal experience of a debtor, or at least a strong recommendation from a mutual friend or correspondent, was seen as the best foundation for credit. 'True credit I call that which is founded on a right Principle, the knowing and considering whom is trusted by his Character and Abilities.'[11] Creditors had to enquire into a man's financial worth and his character; financial and personal issues were impossible to separate. Obviously, well-established businessmen could point to their earlier successes when looking for credit, but new entrants to business were less fortunate and had only their character and background to recommend them. And young men were also seen as being especially dependent on credit, both because previous profits were unavailable for ploughing back into the firm and because they were able to draw on only limited funds

[7] M. D'Archenholz, *A picture of England* (Dublin, 1790), p. 256.

[8] *London Journal*, 11 July 1730.

[9] Steuart, *Principles of political oeconomy*, Vol. II, p. 440.

[10] *An honest scheme, for improving the trade and credit of the nation* (London, 1727), p. 2.

[11] *A dissertation upon credit* (London, n.d.), p. 1.

from kith and kin. Young men, '*by Reason of the Smallness of their own Fortunes, are very often obliged to borrow Money, in order to enable them to set up*'.[12] Some writers in fact felt this itself was the main cause of many bankruptcies, arguing that it was impossible to set up a business on the basis of credit and be able to generate sufficient profits to meet repayments: 'men starting on CREDIT, soon becoming bankrupts and unhappy felons'.[13]

With credit especially important to infant business, and good character essential to attracting it successfully, young men were swamped with moral as much as financial or business advice. For page after page, advice books chastised indolence, debauchery and extravagance and extolled virtue, industry and frugality. They repetitively took their readers through courses of character building, whipping up indignation and fear within a standard moral framework. In the aftermath of the South Sea Bubble, Bishop Berkeley felt it necessary to revive 'those old-fashioned trite maxims concerning religion, industry, frugality, and public spirit'.[14] By doing this, the Anglican life and the surviving remnants of a more austere Puritanism could be commended at the same time as a well-founded preparation for business life was being provided. If this was not religion and the rise of capitalism, the conjunction between ethics, morality and credit does nevertheless need stressing.[15] An especially frequent line of attack in the struggle for men's business souls was the argument linking credit and honesty. Bankruptcy, except in clear-cut instances of misfortune, involved an element of immorality because of the failure of a debtor to justify the confidence that had been placed in him by his creditors. As credit was a personal bond, based on trust and confidence, this helps explain the continued stigma attached to bankruptcy through the century.[16]

The inability of a debtor to satisfy his creditors was, aside from misfortune, most frequently put down to excessive risk-taking and luxury. Contemporaries often attempted to draw a distinction between the ordinary hazards of trade, generating unavoidable 'natural' risks, and unnatural risks that had been generated by unreasonable adventurousness. In practice, of course, such distinctions were difficult to maintain because of the problems of finding a point at which reasonable gave way to unreasonable. The Whiggish, modernising view, was that

---

[12] *A proposal for rendering bankruptcies less frequent*, p. 13. (Emphasis in original.) Also R. Courteville, *Arguments respecting insolvency* (London, n.d.), p. 29.

[13] *London Chronicle*, 28–30 April 1772, p. 412.

[14] *An essay towards preventing the ruin of Great Britain* (1721), in *The works of George Berkeley Bishop of Cloyne*, ed. T. E. Jessop, 9 vols. (London, 1953), Vol. VI, p. 69.

[15] For some interesting observations see P. Seaver, 'The Puritan work ethic revisited', *Journal of British Studies*, XIX (1980), pp. 35–53. Campbell, *The London tradesman*, p. 317.

[16] Though it was sometimes remarked that the fault lay with creditors for having misjudged debtors.

in all Trading Nations, Numbers of People are undone by *new Projects*, and by what is commonly called, *Pushing a Trade*. As to *new Projects*, tho' they generally prove *unlucky* to the first Projector, yet they often prove *beneficial* to the Country, because others perceive the Rocks upon which the first Projector split...Every Man knows, that large Sums of Money may often be laid out, or expended in that way *very reasonably*, and with a *probable* View of Success...[17]

Certainly, hindsight was fundamental to much of the chastisement bankrupts suffered at the hands of their betters, but there were other factors at work. In particular, many commentators were worried by the excessive ambitiousness of some businessmen, an ambitiousness driven on by the reprehensible desires for wealth, power or reputation. One advice book noticed 'The ambition of being rich too soon'.[18] Quite correctly, it was remarked that heightened desire for success could only be satisfied by increasing the risks involved in one's decisions, thereby raising the chances of failure. One writer ironically reflected that 'A worthy friend of the author's, used to say, the traders of London were too industrious, and took a deal of pains to ruin themselves.'[19]

Businessmen would only come to grief as a result of such expansiveness if they lacked the reserves to cover their adventure. But it was frequently remarked that this was not the case, largely because risk-taking was funded by credit rather than savings. Once again, the young were seen as especially vulnerable to this problem. Because they were particularly dependent on credit and lacked the requisite experience to handle it successfully, along with the fact that they were seen as more foolish risk-takers, youngsters were prime candidates for bankruptcy in many people's eyes.[20] Although credit could 'supply the place of a large fortune' there were inescapable problems associated with a greater dependence on it, quite apart from the issue of whether the expectations it was financing were ultimately fulfilled.[21] A high ratio of credit in any business increased its vulnerability to the sort of liquidity problems that dogged eighteenth-century business enterprise. Defoe caustically proclaimed that because of credit 'there are more tradesmen undone by having too much trade, than for want of trade'.[22] Usually, this was explained in terms of the idea of 'overtrading', where a firm's interests were extended beyond the point at which sudden demands or upsets could be accommodated. Because credit often rested on personal security, and more particularly character, it could be readily

[17] There was an element of special pleading here. *The case of bankrupts and insolvents considered*, p. 51.
[18] *The management and oeconomy of trade*, p. 21. *Instructions for masters, traders, labourers, &c. also for servants, apprentices, and youth* (London, 1718), p. 21.
[19] Ibid., pp. 20–1.
[20] *James Claypoole's letterbook. London and Philadelphia 1681–1684*, ed. M. Balderstone (San Marino, Calif., 1967), pp. 119–20.
[21] *The compleat compting-house companion: or young merchant and tradesman's sure guide* (London, 1763), p. 11.   [22] Defoe, *The complete English tradesman*, p. 70.

obtained, allowing businessmen to wade into deep waters only to find that the tide had turned. At such moments they were impotent. Difficulties might arise either because of the failure of a single adventure or, more usually, because of the failure to balance and compensate the varying fortunes and liquidity problems of a firm's various operations.

Through overtrading the weaknesses of businesses heavily dependent on credit were exposed firstly to the difficulties of synchronising transactions and revenue into and out of a firm, and secondly, to the problems caused by the interdependence of businesses on one another through credit networks. Because businessmen's connexions were widely spread, it was always difficult for them to keep a tight rein on the flows of money between the component parts of their trading empires. Because every businessman was a debtor *and* a creditor it was critically important to ensure that income was balanced with expenditure if one's solvency was to remain unquestioned. This was especially difficult and important when general credit conditions tightened, because prompt repayment of debts under ordinary circumstances was the exception rather than the rule. So, when overall monetary conditions were tight, creditors would redouble their efforts to be paid on time, thereby eliminating slack within the system. Financial flexibility, which allowed many to survive the problems of temporary insolvency, was lost and bankruptcy could ensue.

Synchronisation was also difficult individually because personal security was naturally precarious. If one's credit depended on confidence, ability and character, then it was just as easily destroyed as created. The fragility of credit, either at the general or the individual level, was a commonplace at the time and its fickleness compared to stereotyped portraits of coy ladies.[23] Postlethwayt offered this non-sexist example, however:

> If the trader shall borrow money to the extent of his credit, and launch out into trade, so as to employ it with the same freedom as if it were his own proper stock; such a way of management is very precarious, and will be attended with dangerous circumstances; for, as trade is liable to unforeseen accidents, if such a trader shall meet with losses or disappointments, and bring his credit into doubt, this may and will draw the demands of all his creditors upon him at once, and render him incapable of drawing in so much of his scattered effects as will pay his debts, and thereby will ruin his credit, although he might believe that he had more than enough to satisfy all the world.[24]

Credit might collapse about a businessmen if a single bill were protested or if there was the slightest hint that he was to suffer a writ for debt. Any dent in his armour of virtue could bring down upon him repeated blows from his credi-

---

[23] Defoe, *Defoe's review*, 5 August 1710, p. 221. The delicacy of credit was discussed in similar ways, both linguistically and conceptually, in regard to public and private credit.

[24] *Universal dictionary*, Vol. 1, p. 574. See also *An alphabetical list of the names, places of abode, and occupations of those persons who have appeared in the London Gazette to be discharged out of prison under the compulsive clause of the late insolvency act* (London, 1761), p.v. *The remembrancer: addressed to young men in business* (London, 1794), p. 6.

tors.[25] Obviously, at such moments whether a businessman was permanently or temporarily insolvent hardly mattered. The law of bankruptcy made no distinction between the two and neither did worried creditors. Such imprecision worried some people, though, who felt states of permanent insolvency and temporary illiquidity were different and ought to be treated differently.[26]

Businessmen were brought down by credit via another route, interdependence. Links between businessmen were inevitable of course, but the extensive use of bills of exchange, especially with numerous endorsements, meant that indebtedness and collapse could spread from one point in a credit network to another and perhaps distant one. 'Bills turn the Lenders into Debters.'[27] Contemporaries used several analogies here: of a drowning man pulling others down with him; of a line of dominoes collapsing because of the fall of just one; or of a chain of credit shattered by the breaking of a single link. In that way, the stability of credit networks depended on the strength of the weakest as well as the strongest members. As Defoe put it, 'the contingent nature of trade renders every man liable to disaster that is engag'd in it'.[28]

One Capital Blow has its infinite Dependencies in Trade. *A.* is a great Merchant; the *French* fall in with the *Turkey* Fleet, and take them, and he loses 20 or 30 thousand pound; and the consequence is, he breaks; his Breaking falls heavy upon *B, C, D, E,* and others; perhaps 5 or 6 Tradesmen in *London*; and their Reputation being not able to bear them up under the Publik Report, as well as Burthen of such a Loss, *Break too*: As he broke six, they break 20; and those 20, a hundred; and so it goes on without any prospect of a Conclusion and all this is the Effect of Credit of Men trading beyond their Stocks, and both giving and taking exorbitant Credit.[29]

As Defoe suggested, the failure of some businessmen caused bigger waves than that of others, though even small ripples could initiate sufficient momentum for multiple collapses. Even though his suggested multipliers were exaggerated, it is nevertheless true that the breaking of a large merchant was especially damaging and dangerous. The 'Failure of one principal Merchant is commonly attended with the Ruin of Several *Tradesmen* who necessarily depended upon him.'[30] The extent of the impact of a single failure depended on an individual's

[25] J. Dornford, *Seven letters to the Lords of the Privy Council on the police* (London, 1785), p. 51. Steuart, *Principles of political oeconomy*, Vol. II, pp. 567–8. E. Farley, *Imprisonment for debt unconstitutional and oppressive, proved from the fundamental principles of the British constitution* (London, 1788), p. 28.

[26] Baring, *Further observations*, p. 15. Also the comments by Lord Mansfield in 1781 quoted in Cadwallader, Thesis, p. 478, n. 14.

[27] J. Swift, 'The run upon the bankers', in *Poetical works*, ed. H. Davis (Oxford, 1967), p. 193.

[28] *The complete English tradesman*, p. 198.

[29] *Defoe's review*, 15 January 1706, p. 21. One London merchant claimed to have lost £15,000 by the 'Breaking of his Correspondence abroad, and of Shopkeepers and other Tradesmen at home'. *A bill to impower the Lord High Treasurer...to compound with Benjamin Nicholl* (London, 1706?), p. 2.

[30] *Proposals for promoting industry and advancing proper credit; advantageous to creditors in particular and the nation in general* (London, 1732), p. 31.

importance within the credit network he belonged to. This is evidenced by the frequency with which merchants both were bankrupted and initiated bankruptcy proceedings as petitioning creditors. An individual's importance within his credit network was in turn, not merely a function of his financial weight but also of the strength of the ties that constituted the network he was part of. The greater the erosion of confidence, then the greater the speed and the more dramatic the impact of the domino effect. Over the century, as connexions between the component parts of the economy became stronger and more reliable, so the widespread influence of the domino effect grew. By the 1780s and 1790s, with a very extensive system of bills and accommodation notes operating and the increasing importance of country banks, interdependence became more likely and more dangerous, clearly evidenced by the pattern of financial crises uncovered earlier (see Chapter 8).

Excessive use of credit, especially when linked to over-adventurous risk-taking, most commonly amongst the young, was the main way in which onlookers at the time described and analysed bankruptcy. But a second way that failure was confronted was through the idea of luxury and extravagance. At several points credit and luxury overlapped as issues and it would be foolish to separate them in an exaggerated fashion. Yet for some authors, excess and extravagance were primary and not secondary causes of bankruptcy. The accusation of 'luxury' was used in two ways, one which cursed the extravagance of the businessmen themselves, the other which cursed the indulgence of society more generally. There was nothing very complicated in the first argument: extravagant businessmen neglected their business in the pursuit of expensive social pleasures, straining their financial resources to breaking point; alternatively, the desire for the good life made businessmen over-ambitious and foolhardy, increasing the chances of failure. Luxury was an explanation of bankruptcy that was particularly appealing to the more moralising observer. In 1718, the Bishop of Ely condemned 'The living above and beyond your true Abilities'.[31] Later in the century, the City suffered another clerical onslaught on its lifestyle: 'the *Extravagance, Luxury,* and *Corruption,* that so forcibly prevail now-a-days, put men on grasping at Riches by the most sudden and unjustifiable means! They plunge headlong into *Engagements* immense, distant, and dangerous.'[32] Just as the nation was periodically accused of excessive luxury, expecially at times of peril, so was the business community at times of crisis. If there were variations on this aspect of the luxury theme they were little more than reflections of the bigotry of the age. Wives were sometimes blamed for their husbands' fall, for having badgered them into conspicuous consump-

---

[31] W. Fleetwood, *The justice of paying debts. A sermon preach'd in the City* (London, 1718), p. ii.
[32] W. Scott, *A sermon on bankruptcy, stopping payment, and the justice of paying our debts, preached at various churches in the City* (London, 1773), p. 2.

tion and expensive elegance.[33] Sometimes it was straightforward social emulation and insubordination that was seen as the root of the problem. Finally, the cause of luxury could always be laid at the door of atheism or the devil.

If you were in trade, then the spectre of luxury could haunt you in other ways. Thomas Turner, the Sussex shopkeeper, complained in September 1763 that

> I think I never in my life knew any place so much gone off for trade as is this place since I have lived in it. Most of the principal inhabitants...being dead and the remaining reduced, trade is got to be very trifling. The occasion of poverty's being so frequent proceeds from luxury and imprudence, I fear, too often. For custom has brought tea and spirituous liquors so much in fashion that I dare be bold to say they often, too often, prove our ruin. For by the frequent and continual use of them we increase our expenses, bring on idleness and render ourselves less able to struggle with the world...[34]

Businessmen concerned with making and selling domestic manufactures would, so this quasi-mercantilist stance went, suffer from import substitution just as society would suffer from rampant effeminacy. There were many other strands to the debate over luxury.[35] Interestingly, it was sometimes complained that the very evident luxuries to be found in the nation were more than a sign of mere avarice, rather they were an indication of 'the Spirit of Trade in its Excess', allowing the commercial spirit and luxury to be condemned in the same breath.[36] Fielding reflected that trade 'hath given a new face to the whole nation, hath in great measure subverted the former state of affairs, and hath almost totally changed the manners, customs, and habits of the people'.[37] And he would have agreed that 'The Spirit of Commerce, now predominant, begets a kind of regulated Selfishness, which tends at once to the Increase and Preservation of Property.'[38]

Naturally, the remedy for luxury was parsimony and hard work. Hogarth's 'Industry and idleness' characterised a stock response. But the remedy was recommended both because excessive desire was a road to ruin and because of assumptions about normal and acceptable standards of living for businessmen and their families. Notions of social hierarchy and social obligations played a role in this, impressing on some authors, such as Fielding, the need to vilify the dislocation caused by acquisitiveness. Bankruptcy was sometimes seen as being caused by socially as well as economically aberrant behaviour.

---

[33] Defoe, *The Complete English tradesman*, p. 160. 'Butterfly spouses...run the husband in debt, 'Till his name...help fill the Gazette': 'The modern tradesman', in *Collection of ballads, broadsides, etc.* held at the British Library.
[34] *The diary of Thomas Turner*, p. 280.
[35] See the secondary works cited in Ch. 5, n. 34.
[36] Brown, *An estimate of the manners and principles*, p. 104.
[37] Fielding, *The late increase of robbers*, p. 14.
[38] Brown, *An estimate of the manners and principles*, p. 16.

Credit, not luxury, held pride of place in discussions of bankruptcy. Perhaps this simply reflected the fact that the widespread use of credit among all businessmen was a more complicated and a more novel issue. Consequently, the remedies for and precautions against bankruptcy were more widely discussed in relation to credit. In particular, avoidance of failure was seen firstly in terms of the acceptable limits to risk-taking and, secondly, in terms of the careful judgement of a firm's condition. Examples have already been cited of friendly and hostile opinions about risk-taking as a cause of failure. In practice, trading inevitably involved risk-taking and a more pertinent concern among onlookers was to try to judge realistic limits to it, limits that allowed for expansiveness but not recklessness. The usual response was to counsel caution and moderation, stressing that risk-taking should be kept within bounds. Where those bounds were located was rarely made clear, but in general the slow expansion of the riskiness of the business was encouraged. More specifically, some writers argued that risks should always be underwritten by the individual's own capital rather than borrowed credit. 'The sudden and rapid accumulation of fortunes in trade is a striking proof of that unbounded and dangerous extent of credit which at present prevails; and which enables a man to trade for twenty times his worth; or, in other words, prompts him to grasp at sudden affluence, by staking the fortune of his friends and relations.'[39] The cautious use of credit and the controlled taking of risks were common solutions suggested. Postlethwayt felt that an honest man should 'be careful not to involve the estates of other men in his personal trading adventures'.[40] In practice, this was virtually impossible in many lines of business, where thresholds of entry were high and markets distant. More commonly, it was assumed that using a certain amount of credit was right and proper, so long as moderate profits, not greed, was the motivating factor. Although the more traditional onlookers occasionally condemned credit in the language of usury and stockjobbing, more frequently it was seen as both good and bad: good when taken in moderation, bad when taken in excess. 'If Credit sometimes encourages an extravagant Person to become a Bankrupt, it will on the other Hand save Hundreds of industrious Men from being so, by rescuing them from Oppression, and enabling them to carry on a successful Trade.'[41]

Among contemporary observers there was a striking harmony about the way to reduce numbers and rates of bankruptcy: businessmen should be more circumspect, careful and cautious. Profit maximisation was not the proper goal of businessmen, rather they should pursue profits and security. It was never

---

[39] *London Chronicle*, 7–9 July 1772, p. 28. This idea had been expressed in a similar form in J. Burgh, *The dignity of human nature* (London, 1754), p. 41.
[40] *Universal dictionary*, Vol. 1, p. 574.
[41] *A short case of the charitable corporation* (London, 1730?).

said that there was too little risk-taking, but often remarked that there was too much. Restraint and control, it was argued, would produce success more surely and predictably than ambition and speculation. Defoe specifically wrote his advice book, *The complete English tradesman*, because he believed tradesmen were insufficiently cautious.[42] Elsewhere, he thought 'Caution...is the best Advice can be given to a young Tradesman; and Moderation is a useful Vertue in Trade...not to let every Prospect of Advantage draw him out.'[43] Thomas Turner's hope that God 'bless me with only enough to pay everyone their own and to maintain my family in an indifferent manner' would have been warmly applauded, though perhaps in practice most businessmen felt differently.[44] In 1720 the Bishop of Carlisle argued, like Turner, that a businessman's acquisitiveness should be restricted to 'So much as is necessary to supply all his real, not imaginary wants, in the station in which Providence hath placed him.'[45] Such attitudes stressed the need for conservatism among businessmen, in particular the need for risk avoidance as much as risk-taking. Knowing which risks to take and which to leave well alone depended on skill, experience, knowledge and judgement. What especially concerned contemporaries was that many businessmen failed to take even rudimentary precautions against risks. In particular, this related to the question of the quality of a businessman's accounts.

Many onlookers during the eighteenth century believed that business enterprise was a hit or miss affair. They felt that businessmen were either unwilling or incapable of judging the relative security of their firms, in particular the financial obligations to be met from fluctuating revenue. Risks were bound to be assessed inaccurately. It was argued that businessmen inadequately comprehended the full variety of vicissitudes under which their firms laboured. Because prompt repayment of debts was rare it was difficult for businessmen to balance income and expenditure and to know the state of their enterprise. The stock response was that good accounts offered information upon which intelligent and ultimately successful decisions might be based. Many writers counselled young merchants to keep their accounts punctually. It was axiomatic that declining businesses had very poor accounts and that the businessmen who ran them had, either consciously or unconsciously, little idea of the firm's profitability. As Defoe put it, 'a sinking tradesman cares not to look into his books, because the prospect there is dark and melancholy'.[46] Richard Steele hit the nail more squarely on the head, relating the issue to overtrading, synchronisation and credit:

---

[42] p. iv.
[43] *Defoe's review*, 15 January 1706, p. 25.   [44] *The diary of Thomas Turner*, p. 35.
[45] S. Bradford, *The honest and the dishonest ways of getting wealth* (London, 1720), pp. 6–7.
[46] *The complete English tradesman*, p. 342.

When a Man happens to break in *Holland*, they say of him that *he has not kept true Accompts*. This Phrase, perhaps, among us would appear a soft or humorous way of speaking, but with that exact Nation it bears the highest Reproach; for a Man to be mistaken in the Calculation of his Expence, in his Ability to answer future Demands, or to be impertinently sanguine in putting his Credit to too great Adventure, are all Instances of as much Infamy, as with gayer Nations to be failing in Courage or common Honesty.[47]

Samuel Kershaw, a bankrupt cotton manufacturer from Lancashire, would have got little sympathy from his creditors when he confessed before the commissioners in February 1801 that 'he kept no Books of Account but transacted his affairs by the Invoices made out to him by his Creditors'.[48] Nor would Thomas Allcock, an innkeeper, who despite having been in business for seven years admitted that 'he hath no particular account[s] thereof'.[49] One bankrupt, and there must have been many such others, confessed to illiteracy.[50] Some sank even with the buoyancy provided by accounts, of course. Peter and James Grant, bankrupt merchants from London, handed over thirty-six account books to their commissioners in 1783.[51]

The moral obligation to keep accounts was stressed time after time. Without accounts, a businessman deceived both himself and his creditors. Without accounts, a business would have to drift with the wind, tides and instinct, and everyone appreciated that the economic climate was too variable and harsh to allow such an uncertain course. Soon after the law of bankruptcy was changed in 1706 there was a proposal from one critic that those who failed to keep good accounts should be excluded from the benefit of the law.[52] It was the relationship between keeping accounts and the control of risk and uncertainty that many stressed. Without accounts, the businessman 'never knows how to proportion his expence to the state of his affairs, he must leave his debts to accumulate, he knows not what may embarass him, and he often finds himself upon the brink of ruin, at a time he expected no such matter'.[53]

There were literally dozens of guides to bookkeeping written in the eighteenth century. Many sold extensively and ran through several editions. This in itself shows some of the concern over one perceived cause of failure. Moreover, implicit in such concern was, firstly, the belief that the bulk of businesses did not keep good accounts and, secondly, that a very thin line existed between business life and business death. Consequently, we can see that risk-taking was more akin to rough sport than fine art. Indeed, one of the things which may well have helped set the great businessman apart from his lesser colleagues was the

---

47 *The Spectator*, Vol. II, pp. 187–8.   48 P.R.O., B3/5521.
49 P.R.O., B3/5451.   50 P.R.O., C110/151.   51 P.R.O., B3/1839.
52 *Remarks on the late act of parliament to prevent frauds*, p. 6.
53 *Essays on the spirit of legislation, in the encouragement of agriculture, population, manufactures, and commerce* (London, 1772), p. 380.

degree of control he exerted over his firm. Wedgwood, for example, carefully adjusted his accounting techniques in 1772 at a time of considerable pressure.[54] But even if accounts had been more widely and more carefully kept, it is unlikely that they would have greatly increased the control businessmen exerted over their firms. Good accounts could not eradicate the chance of temporary insolvency.[55]

In essence, eighteenth-century perceptions of bankruptcy, and the ways to avoid it, were uncomplicated. Youth, excessive risk-taking and speculation and over-dependence on credit were the most frequently cited causes. Luxury might also be to blame. Success could be won and failure avoided by the slow accumulation of experience, the moderate expansion of activity, the conservative use of credit, the detailed filling of accounts and a modest way of life. 'Steady and sure' was the motto, though the necessity of risk-taking to enterprise and economic growth was stressed from time to time. Yet this has all concentrated on what was actually discussed and there are interesting gaps in the contemporary perception of bankruptcy which need looking at. Issues such as costing, labour discipline, advertising, purchasing policy, economies of scale and the division of labour rarely came to the fore and, if they did, it was usually within the context of credit and risk. Doubtless, this silence arose partly from the greater attention given at the time to trading rather than manufacture – the advice books were usually directed at merchants and tradesmen for example – which meant that issues such as the price, quality and quantity of such inputs as labour, technology and raw materials were largely irrelevant. But nevertheless, apart from that relating to credit, accounts and parsimony, most of the advice flowing from the pens of observers was general, imprecise and somewhat desultory.

These gaps are not perhaps so surprising when we think of how bankruptcy actually caught the eighteenth-century eye and imagination. Concern over bankruptcy was bound to be greatest when failure overflowed its normal banks and drowned large numbers of businesses. But interpreting failure on the basis of peak levels alone was bound to lead to the detailed appreciation of some causes of bankruptcy and the ignorance of others. Highlighting credit and over-ambitious risk-taking was a valid response to bankruptcy viewed from a short-term perspective. Issues such as costing or scale economies were less pressing

---

[54] McKendrick, 'Wedgwood and cost accounting'.
[55] On the importance of accounts see B. S. Yamey, 'Accounting and the rise of capitalism: further notes on a theme by Sombart', *Journal of Accounting Research*, II (1964), pp. 117–36. R. Bloom, 'Reflections on uncertainty in accounting from historical and current literature', *Accounting History*, IV (1980), pp. 6–14. Pollard, *The genesis of modern management*, Ch. 6. K. H. Burley, 'Some accounting records of an eighteenth-century clothier', *Accounting Research*, IX (1958), pp. 50–60. R. Grassby, 'The rate of profit in seventeenth-century England', *English Historical Review*, LXXXIV (1969), pp. 737–48.

at such moments. So, the lack of a concerted long-term view of bankruptcy necessarily robbed onlookers of valuable insights into the eighteenth-century business world. Nevertheless, one or two people at the time did try to see bankruptcy from such a position.

In 1788 the *London Chronicle* carried an article that looked at annual totals of bankrupts since 1740.[56] Despite some obvious inaccuracies in the data the figures were close enough to the truth to allow the author justly to conclude: 'One thing is evident, that upon the whole the number of bankrupts is increasing – but it is also to be considered, that population and trade are increasing.' But that well-based view soon gave way to yet another complaint 'that while gaming and every species of luxury so much prevail among men of business, we are not to be surprised if bankruptcies continue more frequent than when men were contented with a more simple mode of living, and did not grasp at riches beyond the fair returns of trade'. Far from developing the relationship between growth and bankruptcy, therefore, this article preferred to retreat into a rehash of standard interpretations of bankruptcy. Six years later, the opportunity for a more incisive analysis became available when Chalmers presented his own figures of annual totals of bankrupts since 1700. But although he failed to condemn luxury, indolence, speculation and credit, he also failed to go further than the simple statement that 'the number of bankruptcies, at every period, bore a just proportion to the amount of our trade, and the frequency of our commercial dealings'.[57]

Silence on some of the issues we would regard today as central to an understanding of risk, competition and failure does not in itself prove a lack of concern or ignorance of them among onlookers. James Burgh argued that

To succeed in trade, it is necessary, that a man be possessed of a large capital; and he be well qualified (which alone comprehends a great many particulars;) that his integrity be unsuspected; that he have no enemies to blast his credit; that foreign and home-markets keep nearly according to his expectations; that those he deal with, and credits to any great extent, be both honest and as sufficient as he believes them to be; that his funds never fail him, when he depends on them; and that in short, every thing turn out to his expectation.[58]

This argument, although putting considerable weight on monetary factors, nevertheless acknowledged – with 'he be well qualified' – that businessmen had to have a sure grasp of other factors. But he chose not to discuss further 'those great many particulars'.[59] Generally, issues such as advertising and costing were probably seen as far less frequent or less problematic causes of failure and collapse, largely because the bulk of businessmen were imitators. If

[56] 30 October–1 November 1788, p. 427.
[57] Chalmers, *An estimate*, p. xliii. [58] *Human nature*, p. 41.
[59] Daniel Defoe was exceptional in that he did discuss them. See *The complete English tradesman*.

most firms bought, sold and produced goods and services in similar ways to their competitors, then the degree of risk or speculation attached to their decisions and the extent of their command of credit could rightly be seen as principal determinants of bankruptcy.

By and large, contemporaries viewed bankruptcy as resulting from incaution and excessive desires of one sort or another, tending to bypass more sophisticated determinants of competitiveness. Although the limitations of such an approach cannot be ignored, their appreciation of credit and risk was considerable and showed good awareness of the short-term liquidity problems that beset firms. It would be wrong to imagine that all bankruptcies were caused by such difficulties, but evidence has mounted over many chapters now of the thin line that existed at the time between success and failure and of how short-term access to funds was often a major determinant of which side of that line a business found itself. Not only was concern expressed with the monetary causes of bankruptcy but also with the business frame of mind which, it was believed, created it. Especially striking among contemporaries was the concern with excessive risk-taking and speculation and the desire for caution, control and conservatism among firms. For them, risk-taking created abundant failures and it was a moot point whether the commensurate growth produced by successful risk-taking offset them sufficiently.

11

*

CONCLUSION

In Chapter 1 some seeds of doubt were sown about the traditional ways in which historians have approached eighteenth-century enterprise. Although the crop is not yet fully ripe and ready to be harvested, some attempt might be made to judge its quality and yield. How does the history of bankruptcy that has been described help us understand the role of businessmen during the early stage of industrialisation?

Bankruptcy was an eighteenth-century growth industry. The sheer volume of bankruptcy demands some rethinking of the place of enterprise in growth. More especially, there was a profound discontinuity in trend levels of failure at about the middle of the century, just at the point at which the economy began visibly to impress contemporaries with its fecundity. But that fruitfulness was associated with higher rather than lower levels and rates of bankruptcy. Prosperity, far from banishing or subduing failure, coincided with the blossoming of business collapses. Clearly, the intensifying insecurity of the business environment during early industrialisation considerably damages uncritically optimistic and Whiggish visions of eighteenth-century businessmen and the business world. Explaining the stagnant or improving bankruptcy rates before 1760 and the worsening rates thereafter needs to be related to the interconnected issues of opportunities, market imperfections, competition, risk and uncertainty discussed in Chapter 1.

The geographical and occupational dynamics of eighteenth-century bankruptcy show a clear relationship between growth and failure. Stagnant areas of the economy, such as the Norfolk cloth industry, had steady or declining levels and rates of bankruptcy. But rapidly developing areas of the economy, such as the Lancashire cotton industry, overseas trade, or the West Riding woollen trades, all experienced increases in the *level* of bankruptcy. But there was a less uniform relationship between prosperity and *rates* of bankruptcy. Although business mortality rose in Manchester and the West Riding, it may have fallen in Liverpool, or among the brewers in the 1740s and 1750s. Growth and prosperity were not uniformly associated with greater opportunities, competition, risk and uncertainty. A particularly critical factor was the level of thresholds of entry into any area of business. If the money, skills or connexions required were considerable then it was possible for opportunities to be seized more by existing firms than some flood of imitators; thresholds could do the work of market imperfections like patents or limited information. What seems clear is that as opportunities developed in various areas of the economy there was a fund of businessmen available who responded to those opportunities when they had the requisite resources. But abilities were limited. Though many saw opportunities, fewer were able to seize them. It is important therefore to distinguish the increase in the volume of risk-taking in Manchester from that in Liverpool, or that in distilling from that in brewing. Rising levels and rates of bankruptcy were only partly caused by more businessmen taking risks; they were also caused by their decisions becoming more risky.

Contemporaries somewhat foolishly distinguished between natural and unnatural risks. Among the former were storms, fires, war and riot; among the latter, speculation, over-extension and the use of credit. There is no reason to suppose that natural risks should have worsened after 1760, though warfare was indeed endemic in that period. If anything, the development of insurance facilities should have weakened such disabling forces. It is better to see the greater levels of risk attached to decision-making after the middle of the century as associated with novelty and lack of control. In the first place, decisions were increasingly being related to the unknown. For example, there had been no substantial domestic production of cotton goods before 1760, when technical developments created opportunities for prospective cotton lords. Businessmen could try to gauge the existence of latent demand for cotton goods – their advantages over woollens were obvious and the clamour for restrictions on Indian cotton imports early in the century provided evidence of a market available for domestic producers.[1] But they could not know how large domestic or overseas demand for English cotton goods might be, or how many businessmen were available to respond to the opportunities being carved out by the likes of Hargreaves and Arkwright. New methods of production or marketing are inevitably more risky than old ones. Therefore, if decision-making more frequently takes place in a novel environment, then riskiness is on the increase.

Novelty did not alone heighten risks. Equally important was the fact that businessmen had only limited control over their environment and firms and that control weakened as the distance or time attached to any decision increased. Merchants were peculiarly vulnerable here. Businesses trading over long distances always had a greater element of uncertainty to deal with. Of critical importance, the quality of information upon which decisions rested would be poorer or more variable and the ability to implement precisely those decisions less. Relying on price data that was months or years old and on agents who were

[1] Summarised in D. C. Coleman, *The economy of England 1450–1750* (Oxford, 1977), pp. 162–3.

sometimes dependable, but sometimes not, was a recipe for risk and uncertainty. And such factors were not exclusive to overseas trade; businessmen operating solely within the domestic sphere had to take account of distance. What is clear is that, firstly, the economy became more reliant on overseas trade and, secondly, that there was a steady progress of regional specialisation within the home economy, which increased the time and distance attached to decision-making by businesses operating at home. But these developments were probably not matched by improvements in the speed or quality of information or in the ability to implement decisions. Not until well into the nineteenth century, with heightened centralisation of production in the factory, the railway and the telegraph, could businessmen hope to tackle these problems in a meaningful way. All in all, in the eighteenth century, decision-making became more risky.

These factors were exacerbated by the fact that sectors like the West Riding wool trades or Lancashire cotton production grew via the formation of new firms, which came onto the scene in great numbers. But they were invariably young ones, and young firms are by definition inexperienced and immature. The decisions they take are more speculative and less certain than those of old-established firms which can draw on a fund of experience. Consequently, areas of the economy where the rush of imitators was especially strong were bound to be characterised by less control and more risk. These were certainly themes which preoccupied onlookers at the time.

None of this is surprising, for obviously the greater the degree of predictability attached to business decision-making then the less the risk. But it does draw attention to the fact that some parts of the business world were bound to be more precarious than others. Altogether, on the general level, businesses were more or less risky according to the size of the market they were trying to satisfy, the number and output of their competitors, the quality of information upon which decisions were based and, finally, the success with which decisions were implemented.

These explanations of bankruptcy have been uncovered by looking at long-term patterns of failure. But most businessmen did not fail simply because they were slow imitators who had poor information and control. Short-term factors were also crucial. Although wars, harvests and cycles all played a part, the central feature here was monetary conditions, more especially credit. Changing patterns of liquidity were crucial and businessmen were always preoccupied with what might be called the 'problem of credit'. For any businessman, the availability of funds depended not just on the profitability of the decisions he made, but on his utilisation of credit. Although businesses did contract formal loans, increasingly they called on trade credit to provide some of their financial resources. Indeed, credit was the key link between the long- and short-term determinants of bankruptcy. Money was needed to seize the opportunities which were being created. Yet friends, relations, fellow believers, partners and ploughed-back profits were limited sources and consequently many businessmen, especially young ones, turned to trade credit. Access to credit fundamentally determined the rates and patterns of new business formation and the expansion of existing firms providing, as it did, one of the main ways in which pools of savings satisfied the demand for funds from those well sited to exploit and occasionally create opportunities.

Credit might take the form of book debts, but it became increasingly linked to bills of exchange and accommodation notes. Yet whichever form was used, the loan was backed by nothing but personal security. Credit was given and taken on trust, in the *expectation* that it would be repaid. But essentially it was an unsecured loan and, consequently, vulnerable to the ebb and flow of confidence. The frequency of financial crises in the last thirty years of the century shows how fragile confidence might be on the general level. But on the local or particular level too the vulnerability of credit was a crucial determinant of success and failure. If creditors remained confident then the businessman had few worries, but as soon as seeds of doubt were sown in their minds he faced an uphill struggle. So, although credit was vital in allowing economic opportunities to be exploited and was intimately linked to growth and prosperity, it had its dark side. It stood, Janus-like, facing success and riches in one direction and decay and bankruptcy in the other. Particularly among the imitators, the success of some and the failure of others during early industrialisation can be properly understood only if due weight is given to the skill, fortune or stupidity with which credit was used.

Hierarchies of credit and debt existed in eighteenth-century England, with particular groups more likely to bestow or to receive credit. Merchants, wealthy wholesalers and those outside trade, like gentlemen and widows, provided a lot of the funds that allowed businesses to form, operate and grow. Small businessmen looked to them, especially to merchants and wholesalers, to support them, and those wealthy businessmen and individuals expected to satisfy them. Your position in the business world depended not only on what you did but whether, on balance, you took or gave credit. Young businessmen, standing at the bottom of the ladder, took more than they gave. But if they were successful they would step up the ladder, giving more and taking less as they went.

The instability of credit, growth and the business environment cannot be ignored. In the second half of the eighteenth century, as some sectors declined and others flourished, fluctuations in bankruptcies intensified. Growth not only helped create higher trend rates of bankruptcy; it also helped, like a sea shore battered by the waves, to pile up and at other times wash away bankruptcies. Even if most businesses managed to avoid bankruptcy and failure, it is worth remembering that all firms made their decisions within this more erratic and unpredictable environment. Businessmen, whose eyes rarely saw beyond horizons a few years hence, were preoccupied with the rough seas that immediately faced them. They knew that they had hard, as well as easy, waters to navigate. For them, trend economic growth was an El Dorado, always beyond reach, but spoken of expectantly. But reports of the fabled land of gold were never alike. Therefore it is hardly possible to believe that businessmen knew with much accuracy what was happening or what was going to happen. Instability heightened uncertainty and added to the speculative tendencies inherent in eighteenth-century enterprise. One moraliser rightly argued that 'Speculation... is only another term for high gambling.'[2] Of course, success depended on more than just luck. But the glorification of the great names of the Industrial Revolution tends to belittle the enormous problems they had to overcome and exaggerates the certainty with which those problems were overcome.

Most historians have given undue attention to the frontrunners among eighteenth-century businessmen. Inventors and innovators were a special minority among all firms. Yet although such great men rode their luck and took their chances, it would be ungracious not to admit that their skills must also have been great. To negotiate the perils took much more skill than Smiles was prepared to allow them. The skills needed to survive were considerable; the skills needed to excel were enormous. In that way, just as Schumpeter had hoped, a study of bankruptcy makes us appreciate the achievements of entrepreneurship. But it also makes us appreciate the wider range of business experience at every level during the eighteenth century. Wedgwood and Arkwright were exceptional, both in their skills and their luck. But the mass of imitators did their imitating job so well and in such numbers that not only was growth realised, but instability worsened and rates of bankruptcy increased. As the imitators flooded in to exploit opportunities being created, both wittingly and unwittingly, by the entrepreneurs, the economy was pushed to new heights – at the price, however, of a greater dependence on credit.

Studying bankruptcy stretches perceptions of eighteenth-century business in another way. It has not only taken us away from the inventor and innovator and towards the imitator, but it has moved the focus of attention away from its exclusive preoccupation with production towards distribution. Large parts of the business world were made up of men linking supply and demand, struggling with a lack of coinage, poor communications and fickle markets. Merchants and wholesalers were as representative of businessmen as the better-known industrialists and technologists. Indeed, if anything, the merchants' supremacy was not successfully contested until the nineteenth century. Until then, they remained dominant in wealth, status and importance among businessmen.

[2] C. Moore, *A full inquiry into the subject of suicide*, 2 vols. (London, 1790), Vol. II, p. 357.

Moreover, they and other wholesalers were central coordinators of production and exchange, linking the disparate parts of an erratically connected economy to one another. And we have seen how difficult this role was from their tiny but common gravestones in the *London Gazette*. If they are not the fallen heroes of enterprise, successful merchants and middlemen are the forgotten soldiers.

The success of the English economy in the eighteenth century was never guaranteed. Bankruptcy happened too frequently and forcefully for either contemporaries or historians to indulge in fanciful notions about the inevitability of progress. Opportunities were being created, wealth was being amassed. But this was caused by luck and market imperfections as well as skill and industry. The power of competition and the force of risk and uncertainty combined to rid businessmen of faith in the future at just the moment when, with hindsight, we can see that such faith would have been most justified. To them, experience, information, and caution – the combined skills of risk avoidance – were as important as adventurousness, expectations and risk-taking. The eighteenth-century English economy was formed and moulded by hopes and fears, by negative as well as positive factors. Success melded with failure to produce, by 1800, the unique experience of self-sustained economic growth. But the path was uncertain and tortuous, even if it did lead eventually to a better land.

APPENDICES

Year	Raw	Adjusted[a]	Year	Raw	Adjusted[a]
1688	28		1716	201	159
1689	18		1717	174	137
1690	22		1718	179	141
			1719	243	192
1691	21		1720	260	205
1692	28				
1693	20		1721	285	225
1694	35		1722	268	212
1695	42		1723[b]	[191]	[151]
			1724[b]	—	—
1696	18		1725	385	304
1697	54				
1698	68		1726	461	364
1699	67		1727	498	393
1700	96		1728	456	360
			1729	246	194
1701	72		1730	219	173
1702	70				
1703	93		1731	197	156
1704	81		1732	235	186
1705	159		1733	217	171
			1734	270	213
1706	567		1735	281	222
1707	298				
1708	210		1736	289	228
1709	273		1737	260	205
1710	248		1738	249	197
			1739	285	225
1711	277	218	1740	303	239
1712	255	201			
1713	229	181	1741	280	221
1714	193	152	1742	277	219
1715	197	156	1743	228	180

APPENDIX I (*cont.*)

Year	Raw	Adjusted[a]	Year	Raw	Adjusted[a]
1744	215	170	1771	426	
1745	213	168	1772	537	
			1773	514	
1746	185	146	1774	333	
1747	205	162	1775	357	
1748	239	189			
1749	216	171	1776	428	
1750	233	184	1777	537	
			1778	682	
1751	197	156	1779	531	
1752	189	149	1780	435	
1753	263	208			
1754	274	216	1781	451	
1755	248	196	1782	549	
			1783	521	
1756	306	242	1784	536	
1757	298	235	1785	496	
1758	360	284			
1759	285	225	1786	495	
1760	242	191	1787	500	
			1788	705	
1761	216	171	1789	563	
1762	262	207	1790	578	
1763	285	225			
1764	338	267	1791	597	
1765	240		1792	622	
			1793	1276	
1766	338		1794	817	
1767	358		1795	713	
1768	350				
1769	356		1796	747	
1770	408		1797	863	
			1798	725	
			1799	546	
			1800	721	

Source: *London Gazette* (1688–1710 and 1765–1800); P.R.O., B4/1–20 (1711–64).

[a] Column 3 is calculated by multiplying the values of column 2 by 0.79 for the years 1711 to 1764 inclusive.

[b] Figures for 1723 are for five months only; no data available for 1724.

APPENDIX 2 THE GEOGRAPHY OF BANKRUPTCY, 1688–1800
(AS PERCENTAGE OF TOTAL BANKRUPTS FOR GIVEN PERIODS)

County	1701–20	1721–40	1741–60	1761–80	1781–1800	1688–1800
Beds.	0.4	0.3	0.3	0.2	0.2	0.25
Berks.	1.3	1.5	0.9	0.8	0.8	1.06
Bucks.	0.2	0.6	0.6	0.6	0.4	0.47
Cambs.	0.9	0.6	0.5	0.5	0.5	0.63
Ches.	1.5	1.6	1.0	1.0	1.3	1.29
Corn.	0.7	0.5	0.7	0.7	0.7	0.58
Cumbld.	0.4	0.3	0.7	0.7	0.8	0.51
Derby.	0.4	0.2	0.3	0.5	0.7	0.37
Devon	4.1	1.9	2.0	1.9	1.8	2.35
Dorset	0.5	0.7	0.4	0.5	0.5	0.54
Durham	0.3	0.7	0.9	1.0	1.0	0.73
Essex	1.8	1.9	2.1	1.7	1.5	1.67
Glos.	3.0	3.9	5.7	4.6	4.4	4.08
Hants.	2.1	1.7	2.1	1.7	1.8	1.82
Heref.	0.4	0.4	0.3	0.4	0.7	0.38
Herts.	0.9	0.7	0.9	0.7	0.6	0.74
Hunts.	0.3	0.4	0.3	0.3	0.2	0.27
Kent	2.0	2.0	2.1	2.0	1.9	1.94
Lancs.	1.9	3.2	4.2	5.6	8.4	4.27
Leics.	0.7	0.4	0.4	0.7	0.9	0.59
Lincs.	0.9	1.2	1.2	0.8	1.2	1.10
London	52.5	46.8	42.0	44.6	37.2	45.95
Middx.	3.6	4.3	3.9	4.7	4.3	3.94
Monmouths.	0.2	0.1	0.2	0.1	0.3	0.14
Norfolk	3.8	5.0	4.6	2.1	1.3	3.35
Northants.	0.5	0.6	0.6	0.5	0.6	0.48
Northmb.	0.7	0.7	1.2	0.8	1.1	0.94
Notts.	0.5	0.5	0.5	0.6	0.6	0.51
Oxon.	1.0	0.8	0.5	0.6	0.9	0.85
Rutland	0.1	0.1	0.1	0.1	0.1	0.06
Salop.	0.6	0.6	0.6	0.6	0.9	0.63
Som.	1.3	1.8	2.0	1.6	2.4	1.66
Staffs.	0.5	1.1	0.7	1.5	1.7	1.06
Suffolk	1.7	2.3	1.8	1.2	1.1	1.44
Surrey	2.5	2.3	2.7	2.9	3.2	2.60

APPENDIX 2 *(cont.)*

County	1701–20	1721–40	1741–60	1761–80	1781–1800	1688–1800
Sussex	0.6	0.7	0.9	1.0	1.0	0.82
Warwicks.	0.6	1.3	1.4	2.4	3.5	1.72
Westmld.	0.1	0.2	0.2	0.1	0.3	0.10
Wilts.	1.8	1.6	1.8	1.4	1.2	1.52
Worcs.	1.0	1.4	1.2	1.7	2.0	1.34
Yorks.	2.8	3.5	5.8	4.7	5.8	4.43

Source: as for Appendix 1.

APPENDIX 3 SECTORAL AND OCCUPATIONAL CATEGORIES

Agriculture: Cattle dealer, Corn dealer, Cowkeeper, Dairyman, Drover, Farmer, Gardener, Goose dealer, Grazier, Hay dealer, Husbandman, Market gardener, Nurseryman, Pig dealer, Sheep dealer, Yeoman.

Fuel: Coal dealer, Lime dealer, Lime maker.

Food: Bacon dealer, Baker, Biscuit baker, Butcher, Butter dealer, Cheese dealer, Cheesemonger, Chocolate manufacturer, Confectioner, Egg dealer, Fish dealer, Flour dealer, Fruit dealer, Greengrocer, Grocer, Lemon dealer, Meal dealer, Milk dealer, Miller, Misc., Oatmeal maker, Pork butcher, Potato dealer, Poultry dealer, Salt dealer, Salt maker, Sugar dealer, Sugar maker, Victualler.

Drink: Ale dealer, Ale maker, Beer dealer, Beer maker, Brewer, Cider dealer, Cider maker, Coffee-house keeper, Coffeeman, Distiller, Hop dealer, Innkeeper, Malt dealer, Porter dealer, Porter maker, Spirit dealer, Tea dealer, Vinegar maker, Water dealer, Wine cooper, Wine dealer, Yeast dealer.

Construction: Architect, Brick dealer, Brick maker, Bricklayer, Builder, Carpenter, Carver, Glass dealer, Glass maker, Glass worker, Glazier, House dealer, Marble dealer, Mason, Painter, Paviour, Plasterer, Plumber, Sawyer, Slate dealer, Slater, Statuary, Stone dealer, Tile maker, Timber dealer, Wood dealer.

Textiles and clothes: Breeches maker, Clothier, Cotton dealer, Cotton maker, Dyestuffs, Haberdasher, Hat dealer, Hat maker, Hemp dealer, Hemp maker, Hosier, Lace, Leather dealer, Leather processor, Linen dealer, Linen maker, Mercer, Milliner, Misc., Shoe dealer, Shoe maker, Silk dealer, Silk maker, Stapler, Tailor, Wool processor, Woollen maker.

Finance: Attorney, Banker, Bill broker, Commission dealer, Gild worker, Goldsmith, Government finance, Money scrivener, Policy dealer, Precision metalsmith, Rare stone dealer, Refiner, Silver worker, Silversmith, Stock dealer.

Transport: Boat builder, Bridle and bit maker, Coach maker, Coach transport, Farrier, Horse dealer, Misc., Packer, River transport, Road transport, Rope and sail maker, Ship maker, Ship transport, Stablekeeper, Wheel maker.

Metal: Arms maker, Engraver, Gilder, Hardwareman, Iron dealer, Iron maker, Jeweller, Metal goods maker, Misc., Smith, Toys, Watchmaker.

Wood: Bed maker, Cooper, Furniture maker, Misc., Undertaker, Upholstery, Woodworker.

Retail: Chapman, Dealer, Hawker, Pawnbroker, Tallyman, Trader.

Wholesale: Auctioneer, Jobber, Merchant, Misc., Salesman, Warehouseman, Wharfinger, Wholesaler.

Miscellaneous: Accommodation, Books, Candlemaker, Card, Chemicals, Church, Civic, Clerk, Dentist, Drugs, Familial, Gentleman, Hair and wigs, Institution, Knight, Labourer, Misc., Paper maker, Parchment, Pocketbook, Pottery dealer, Pottery maker, Print dealer, Printer, Snuff, Soap, Spinster, Surgeon, Tallow chandler, Titled, Tobacco, Wax, Widow.

APPENDIX 4 QUARTERLY TOTALS OF BANKRUPTS, 1696–1800

Year	Quarter	Adjusted total[a]	Deseasonalised adjusted total[b]	Percentage deviation[c]
1696	I	2.00	1.80	−84
	II	3.00	2.83	−76
	III	5.00	6.46	−47
	IV	8.00	7.59	−39
1697	I	12.00	10.79	−15
	II	13.00	12.26	−6
	III	10.00	12.92	−7
	IV	19.00	18.03	27
1698	I	28.00	25.18	74
	II	11.00	10.38	−32
	III	12.00	15.50	−1
	IV	17.00	16.13	−2
1699	I	14.00	12.59	−26
	II	16.00	15.09	−15
	III	15.00	19.38	3
	IV	22.00	20.87	6
1700	I	30.00	27.88	38
	II	23.00	21.70	4
	III	23.00	29.72	38
	IV	19.00	18.03	−20
1701	I	15.00	13.49	−42
	II	24.00	22.64	−5
	III	18.00	23.26	−6
	IV	15.00	14.23	−44
1702	I	16.00	14.39	−46
	II	24.00	22.64	−19
	III	14.00	18.10	−38
	IV	16.00	15.18	−49
1703	I	16.00	14.39	−53
	II	25.00	23.59	−25
	III	22.00	28.42	−12
	IV	30.00	28.46	−14
1704	I	21.00	18.89	−44
	II	19.00	17.93	−48
	III	11.00	14.21	−60
	IV	30.00	28.46	−21
1705	I	64.00	57.55	58
	II	23.00	21.70	−42
	III	21.00	27.13	−28
	IV	51.00	48.39	27
1706	I	31.00	27.88	−28
	II	91.00	85.85	120

Year	Quarter	Adjusted total[a]	Deseasonalised adjusted total[b]	Percentage deviation[c]
	III	166.00	214.47	442
	IV	279.00	264.71	560
1707	I	149.00	132.99	234
	II	64.00	60.38	49
	III	36.00	46.51	14
	IV	49.00	46.49	14
1708	I	47.00	42.27	3
	II	55.00	58.19	25
	III	50.00	64.60	54
	IV	58.00	55.03	30
1709	I	55.00	49.46	17
	II	53.00	50.00	17
	III	66.00	85.27	98
	IV	99.00	93.93	116
1710	I	90.00	80.94	85
	II	43.00	40.57	−8
	III	55.00	70.16	61
	IV	60.00	56.93	28
1711	I	60.04	53.99	22
	II	49.77	46.95	4
	III	48.98	63.28	40
	IV	60.04	56.96	25
1712	I	63.99	57.55	25
	II	48.98	46.21	−1
	III	37.13	47.97	2
	IV	51.35	48.72	4
1713	I	55.30	49.73	6
	II	50.56	47.70	0
	III	37.13	47.97	0
	IV	37.92	35.98	−26
1714	I	48.98	44.05	−9
	II	46.61	43.97	−10
	III	18.96	24.50	−50
	IV	37.92	35.98	−26
1715	I	39.50	35.52	−26
	II	39.50	37.26	−23
	III	35.55	45.93	−6
	IV	41.08	38.98	−20
1716	I	42.66	38.36	−21
	II	47.40	44.72	−9
	III	20.54	26.54	−46
	IV	48.19	45.72	−8
1717	I	37.92	34.10	−31
	II	40.29	38.01	−24

APPENDIX 4 *(cont.)*

Year	Quarter	Adjusted total[a]	Deseasonalised adjusted total[b]	Percentage deviation[c]
	III	30.81	39.81	−20
	IV	29.23	27.73	−44
1718	I	32.39	29.13	−41
	II	29.23	27.58	−45
	III	26.07	33.68	−34
	IV	53.32	50.97	−1
1719	I	37.92	34.10	−34
	II	46.61	43.97	−17
	III	53.72	69.41	29
	IV	53.72	50.97	−6
1720	I	55.30	49.73	−9
	II	39.50	37.26	−33
	III	35.55	45.93	−19
	IV	75.05	71.20	24
1721	I	68.73	61.81	8
	II	49.77	46.95	−19
	III	45.82	59.20	0
	IV	60.83	57.71	−2
1722	I	66.36	59.68	2
	II	60.83	57.39	−3
	III	28.44	36.74	−38
	IV	56.09	53.22	−10
1723	I	63.20	56.83	−4
	II	39.50	37.26	−37
	III[d]	—		
	IV	—		
1724[d]	I	—		
	II	—		
	III	—		
	IV	—		
1725	I	74.26	66.78	12
	II	85.32	80.49	35
	III	56.09	72.47	21
	IV	88.48	83.95	39
1726	I	87.69	78.86	31
	II	101.12	95.40	57
	III	69.52	89.82	47
	IV	105.86	100.44	64
1727	I	123.24	110.83	82
	II	105.07	99.12	62
	III	63.99	82.67	35
	IV	98.75	93.69	53
1728	I	120.08	107.97	76
	II	94.80	89.43	45

APPENDIX 4 (*cont.*)

Year	Quarter	Adjusted total[a]	Deseasonalised adjusted total[b]	Percentage deviation[c]
	III	60.83	78.59	28
	IV	84.53	80.20	31
1729	I	77.42	69.62	14
	II	54.51	51.43	−16
	III	29.23	37.77	−38
	IV	33.18	31.48	−49
1730	I	36.34	32.68	−46
	II	50.56	47.70	−22
	III	29.23	37.77	−38
	IV	56.88	53.97	−12
1731	I	39.50	35.52	−41
	II	45.82	43.22	−29
	III	24.49	31.64	−48
	IV	45.82	43.47	−28
1732	I	45.82	41.21	−31
	II	54.51	51.43	−15
	III	31.60	40.83	−32
	IV	53.72	50.97	−15
1733	I	41.87	37.65	−36
	II	45.03	42.48	−28
	III	30.81	39.81	−32
	IV	53.72	50.97	−23
1734	I	64.78	58.26	2
	II	54.51	51.43	−10
	III	34.76	44.91	−21
	IV	59.25	56.21	1
1735	I	63.20	56.84	4
	II	55.30	52.17	−4
	III	56.88	73.49	37
	IV	46.61	44.22	−15
1736	I	60.04	53.99	5
	II	50.56	47.70	−7
	III	48.19	62.26	24
	IV	69.52	65.96	32
1737	I	50.56	45.47	−8
	II	56.88	53.66	8
	III	50.56	65.32	30
	IV	47.40	44.97	−10
1738	I	49.77	44.76	−11
	II	55.30	52.17	4
	III	30.81	39.81	−20
	IV	60.83	57.71	16
1739	I	61.62	55.41	12
	II	62.41	58.88	18

APPENDIX 4 (*cont.*)

Year	Quarter	Adjusted total[a]	Deseasonalised adjusted total[b]	Percentage deviation[c]
	III	39.50	51.03	3
	IV	61.62	58.46	18
1740	I	69.52	62.52	26
	II	67.15	63.35	28
	III	47.74	61.24	23
	IV	55.30	52.47	6
1741	I	64.78	58.26	18
	II	60.04	56.64	14
	III	33.18	42.87	−14
	IV	63.20	59.96	21
1742	I	66.36	59.68	21
	II	62.41	58.88	20
	III	36.34	46.95	−5
	IV	53.72	50.97	4
1743	I	61.62	55.41	14
	II	32.39	30.56	−37
	III	42.66	55.12	14
	IV	43.45	41.22	−14
1744	I	41.87	37.65	−21
	II	54.51	51.42	8
	III	28.44	36.74	−22
	IV	45.03	42.72	−9
1745	I	56.88	51.15	10
	II	36.34	34.28	−26
	III	45.03	58.18	25
	IV	30.02	28.48	−39
1746	I	48.19	43.34	−6
	II	36.34	34.28	−27
	III	20.54	26.54	−43
	IV	41.08	38.98	−17
1747	I	37.13	33.39	−28
	II	44.24	41.74	−10
	III	44.24	57.16	23
	IV	36.34	34.48	−26
1748	I	59.25	53.28	16
	II	41.87	39.50	−24
	III	39.50	51.03	10
	IV	48.19	45.72	−1
1749	I	45.82	41.21	−10
	II	52.93	49.93	8
	III	34.76	44.91	−3
	IV	37.13	35.23	−24
1750	I	70.31	63.23	38
	II	50.56	47.70	3

APPENDIX 4 (*cont.*)

Year	Quarter	Adjusted total[a]	Deseasonalised adjusted total[b]	Percentage deviation[c]
	III	25.28	32.66	−30
	IV	37.92	35.98	−23
1751	I	39.50	35.52	−24
	II	38.71	36.52	−24
	III	29.23	37.76	−22
	IV	48.19	45.72	−6
1752	I	45.82	41.21	−15
	II	37.92	35.77	−27
	III	19.75	25.52	−48
	IV	45.82	43.47	−11
1753	I	53.72	48.31	−2
	II	60.04	56.64	16
	III	39.50	51.03	4
	IV	54.51	51.72	5
1754	I	69.52	62.52	27
	II	60.04	56.64	14
	III	41.08	53.07	7
	IV	45.82	43.47	−13
1755	I	58.46	52.57	6
	II	60.04	56.64	13
	III	39.50	51.03	1
	IV	37.92	35.98	−28
1756	I	85.32	76.73	53
	II	55.30	52.17	2
	III	43.45	56.14	9
	IV	57.67	54.72	5
1757	I	56.09	50.44	−3
	II	68.73	64.84	24
	III	38.71	50.01	−5
	IV	71.89	68.21	29
1758	I	67.94	61.10	16
	II	63.20	59.62	12
	III	59.25	76.55	42
	IV	94.01	89.19	63
1759	I	68.73	61.81	12
	II	61.62	58.13	3
	III	33.97	43.89	−23
	IV	60.83	57.71	−1
1760	I	61.62	55.41	−6
	II	56.88	53.66	−10
	III	37.92	48.99	−19
	IV	34.76	32.98	−46
1761	I	45.03	40.49	−34
	II	52.93	49.93	−20

APPENDIX 4 (*cont.*)

Year	Quarter	Adjusted total[a]	Deseasonalised adjusted total[b]	Percentage deviation[c]
	III	28.44	36.74	−42
	IV	44.24	41.97	−34
1762	I	56.09	50.44	−20
	II	51.35	48.44	−25
	III	33.18	42.87	−35
	IV	66.36	62.96	−5
1763	I	51.35	46.18	−31
	II	44.24	41.74	−38
	III	45.82	59.20	−15
	IV	83.74	79.45	14
1764	I	93.22	83.83	20
	II	63.99	60.37	−15
	III	53.72	69.41	−4
	IV	56.09	53.22	−27
1765	I	63.00	56.65	−24
	II	64.00	60.38	−21
	III	37.00	47.80	−38
	IV	76.00	72.11	−9
1766	I	85.00	76.44	−4
	II	81.00	76.42	−5
	III	73.00	94.32	17
	IV	99.00	93.93	16
1767	I	99.00	89.03	10
	II	95.00	89.62	10
	III	73.00	94.32	15
	IV	91.00	86.34	5
1768	I	87.00	78.24	−6
	II	93.00	87.74	4
	III	74.00	95.61	12
	IV	96.00	91.08	5
1769	I	100.00	89.93	3
	II	92.00	86.79	−2
	III	57.00	73.64	−18
	IV	107.00	101.52	11
1770	I	119.00	107.01	16
	II	103.00	97.17	3
	III	88.00	113.70	19
	IV	98.00	92.98	−5
1771	I	127.00	114.21	14
	II	112.00	105.66	4
	III	80.00	103.36	0
	IV	107.00	101.52	−2
1772	I	110.00	98.92	−5
	II	118.00	111.32	5

APPENDIX 4 (*cont.*)

Year	Quarter	Adjusted total[a]	Deseasonalised adjusted total[b]	Percentage deviation[c]
	III	152.00	196.38	84
	IV	157.00	148.96	38
1773	I	154.00	138.49	28
	II	156.00	147.17	35
	III	95.00	122.74	12
	IV	109.00	103.42	−6
1774	I	102.00	91.73	−17
	II	85.00	80.19	−28
	III	66.00	85.27	−24
	IV	80.00	75.90	−33
1775	I	96.00	86.33	−24
	II	81.00	76.42	−33
	III	84.00	108.53	−6
	IV	96.00	91.08	−22
1776	I	117.00	105.22	−10
	II	128.00	120.76	3
	III	70.00	90.44	−24
	IV	113.00	107.21	−10
1777	I	148.00	133.09	12
	II	136.00	128.30	6
	III	105.00	135.66	12
	IV	148.00	140.42	16
1778	I	173.00	155.58	28
	II	193.00	182.08	49
	III	145.00	187.34	53
	IV	171.00	162.24	32
1779	I	151.00	135.79	11
	II	153.00	144.34	17
	III	91.00	117.57	−5
	IV	136.00	129.03	4
1780	I	121.00	108.81	−12
	II	117.00	110.38	−11
	III	74.00	95.61	−22
	IV	123.00	116.70	−6
1781	I	116.00	104.32	−16
	II	110.00	103.77	−17
	III	97.00	125.32	−1
	IV	128.00	121.44	−5
1782	I	151.00	135.79	7
	II	144.00	135.85	5
	III	110.00	142.12	9
	IV	144.00	136.62	4
1783	I	148.00	133.09	1
	II	144.00	135.85	2

APPENDIX 4 (*cont.*)

Year	Quarter	Adjusted total[a]	Deseasonalised adjusted total[b]	Percentage deviation[c]
	III	101.00	130.49	−3
	IV	128.00	121.44	−10
1784	I	148.00	133.09	−1
	II	145.00	136.79	1
	III	94.00	121.45	−11
	IV	150.00	142.32	4
1785	I	130.00	116.91	−14
	II	135.00	127.36	−8
	III	104.00	134.37	−4
	IV	127.00	120.49	−17
1786	I	123.00	110.61	−25
	II	164.00	154.72	5
	III	88.00	113.70	−24
	IV	120.00	113.85	−24
1787	I	128.00	115.11	−23
	II	131.00	123.59	−19
	III	104.00	134.37	−12
	IV	137.00	129.98	−16
1788	I	113.00	101.62	−34
	II	245.00	231.13	48
	III	189.00	244.19	56
	IV	158.00	149.91	−6
1789	I	158.00	142.09	−11
	II	157.00	148.11	−8
	III	86.00	111.11	−32
	IV	162.00	153.70	−7
1790	I	144.00	129.50	−22
	II	159.00	150.00	−10
	III	103.00	133.08	−21
	IV	172.00	163.19	−4
1791	I	162.00	145.68	−14
	II	141.00	133.02	−22
	III	130.00	167.96	−1
	IV	164.00	155.60	−8
1792	I	146.00	131.30	−22
	II	163.00	153.77	−10
	III	125.00	161.50	−6
	IV	189.00	179.32	4
1793	I	265.00	238.31	38
	II	532.00	501.89	189
	III	259.00	334.53	91
	IV	220.00	208.73	18
1794	I	225.00	202.34	14
	II	240.00	226.42	26

APPENDIX 4 (*cont.*)

Year	Quarter	Adjusted total[a]	Deseasonalised adjusted total[b]	Percentage deviation[c]
	III	155.00	200.26	10
	IV	197.00	186.91	2
1795	I	190.00	170.86	−7
	II	213.00	200.94	8
	III	130.00	167.96	−15
	IV	178.00	168.88	−10
1796	I	159.00	142.99	−24
	II	220.00	207.55	10
	III	154.00	198.97	4
	IV	215.00	203.99	6
1797	I	240.00	215.83	12
	II	289.00	272.64	40
	III	152.00	196.38	0
	IV	182.00	172.68	−12
1798	I	220.00	197.84	0
	II	217.00	204.72	3
	III	151.00	195.09	−3
	IV	137.00	129.98	−36
1799	I	125.00	112.41	−45
	II	145.00	136.79	−34
	III	98.00	126.62	−39
	IV	178.00	168.88	−20
1800	I	215.00	193.35	−8
	II	193.00	182.08	−15
	III	132.00	170.54	−21
	IV	181.00	171.73	−21

Source: 1696–1800, as for Appendix 1. 1801–8 (not shown here but necessary for moving average calculations), Silberling, 'British prices and business cycles', p. 251.

[a] Adjusted quarterly totals of bankrupts.

[b] Deseasonalised adjusted quarterly totals.

[c] Percentage deviations of deseasonalised quarterly totals from a sixty-one quarter moving average.

[d] No data available.

BIBLIOGRAPHY

MANUSCRIPT SOURCES

All the files listed under P.R.O., B3 and those others marked with an asterix (*) were used in the analysis of the 152 files for Chapter 9.

Public Record Office
B3: 1, 2, 3, 178–83, 184–8, 190, 191–2, 194–6, 198–9, 200, 202, 204, 205–6, 207, 811, 812–13, 814–15, 816, 818–20, 821–2, 824–6, 828, 1257, 1258–9, 1260, 1261, 1512, 1514, 1515, 1517, 1518, 1519, 1658, 1659, 1661–2, 1839–42, 1843, 1844, 1845–8, 1849, 1850, 1851, 2110, 2111–13, 2114, 2115, 2116, 2117–18, 2119, 2120, 2123, 2653, 2654, 2655, 2656, 2803, 2804, 2805, 2903, 2905, 2907–8, 2909, 2910, 3169, 3170, 3171, 3172, 3175, 3176, 3177, 3178, 3182–3, 3186, 3187–9, 3192–3, 3194, 3675–6, 3677–8, 3679–80, 3681–8, 3853, 3860, 3861–2, 3864–5, 3866–7, 4150, 4151–2, 4153, 4154, 4160, 4433–5, 4436, 4437, 4438–9, 4440–1, 4442–3, 4446–9, 4450, 4451–2, 4453–4, 4455, 4456–7, 4888–90, 4891, 4892–3, 4894, 4896, 4897, 4898, 5099–100, 5161, 5162, 5163, 5412, 5433, 5451, 5452, 5453, 5457, 5458, 5468, 5470, 5471, 5495, 5496, 5497, 5502, 5517, 5521, 5535, 5536, 5538, 5539, 5557, 5562, 5586, 5610, 5621, 5622, 5624, 5810.
B4/1–25, Docket Books 1711–1801.
B5/20, Register of certificates of conformity 1710–14.
B6/5–10, Register of certificates of conformity 1774–1801.

CHES 10/1 *.

Chancery Masters Exhibits
C103/155, C103/174, C103/175.
C104/77–80.
C105/31.
C107/1–15.
C108/30 *, C108/298 *.
C109/29 *, C109/242 *.
C110/151 *, C110/153, C110/157 *.
C217/79/2.

Bristol Record Office
17569 (2)g, Claimants on the estate of a bankrupt *.
AC/WH 18 (10), Case of a bankrupt *.

Cambridge University Library
Add. Mss. 2798, The Plumstead Letterbook 1756–8.

Essex Record Office
D/DRc B22, Case of a bankrupt *.
D/DRL F3, A composition.
T/P 146/10, List of Essex bankrupts.

Gloucester Record Office
D149/F161, Letters relating to debts.
D149/E88, Letters.
D149/T726–36, Case of a bankrupt *.

Guildhall Library, London
Ms. 7144, Case of a bankrupt *.
Ms. 8601, The account book of the assignees of Alexander Hog, grocer and bankrupt.
Ms. 8623, Correspondence concerning Hog's bankruptcy.
Add. Mss. 403, Correspondence relating to a bankruptcy.

Leeds Archive Office
Carr Mss. CA1 and 3, Papers of an attorney.

London Friends Meeting House Library
Horsleydown Monthly Meeting: Disorderly walking and certificates, given and received
 1728–1805.
James Jenkins, Records and recollections, 1761 to 1821.
Third to Fifteenth Minute book of the Horsleydown Monthly Meeting.

Sheffield City Library Archives
Tibbits Collection
TC 503-4, Papers of a bankruptcy.
TC 505-6, 11, 13, Papers of a bankruptcy.

Wheat Collection
WC 1173, Papers of a bankruptcy.
WC 1201, Papers of a bankruptcy.
WC 1734-5, A composition.
WC 1977, A composition.

Shropshire Record Office
1416 Box 90a, Bygott papers.

Suffolk Record Office (Bury St Edmunds branch)
HA 521, Diary of James Oakes, banker, Bury St Edmunds.

PRIMARY PRINTED SOURCES

This section of the bibliography lists material published before 1850. In this and the following section place of publication is London unless stated otherwise.

Advice to creditors, or a safe and sure way to secure bad debts (1687).

J. Aikin, *A description of the country from thirty to forty miles round Manchester* (1795; reprinted Newton Abbot, 1968).

An alphabetical list of the names, places of abode, and occupations of those persons who have appeared in the London Gazette to be discharged out of prison under the compulsive clause of the late insolvency act (1761).

An answer to a false and scandalous case, intituled, the case of the creditors of Joseph Long, late of London, Merchant (1719?).

Angliae tutamen: or the safety of England. By a person of honour (1695).

J. F. Archbold, *The law and practice of bankruptcy, as founded on the recent statute* (1827).

M. D'Archenholz, *A picture of England* (Dublin, 1790).

J. F. Armour, *Proposals for restoring credit* (1721).

W. Bailey, *List of bankrupts 1772–1793* (1794).

Baldwin's new complete guide to all persons (1768).

Bancks's Manchester and Salford directory (Manchester, 1800).

The bankrupt laws. Report to the Common Council, from the special committee appointed to take into consideration the present state of the bankrupt laws. Presented 15 March 1827, in *Reports of the Common Council* [of the City of London], 1827–8.

The bankrupts directory: or suitable rules and directions, both for bankrupt and creditor, how to manage their affairs to the best advantage (1708).

Sir F. Baring, Bart., *Further observations on the establishment of the Bank of England, and on the paper circulation of the country* (1797).

   Observations on the establishment of the Bank of England, and on the paper circulation of the country (1797).

J. Bentham, *An introductory view of the rationale of evidence*, in *The works of Jeremy Bentham*, Vol. VI, ed. J. Bowring (Edinburgh, 1843).

[Berkeley,] *The works of George Berkeley Bishop of Cloyne*, ed. T. E. Jessop, 9 vols. (1953).

A bill for a better discovery of the estate of Mr. John Aynsworth, late of London, merchant (1707?).

A bill to give leave for William Ellins to surrender himself to a Commission of Bankrupts for the benefit of his creditors (1713?).

A bill to impower the Lord High Treasurer of England, or Commissioners of the Treasury for the time being, to compound with Benjamin Nicholl, citizen and late merchant of London, and his securities, for the debt of him owing to Her Majesty (1706?).

A bill for vesting the estate and effects of Robert Peter, citizen and girdler of London, in trustees, for the speedier payment of his debts (1713?).

G. Billinghurst, *The judges resolutions upon the several statutes concerning bankrupts, with the like resolutions on the statutes of 13 Eliz. and 27 Eliz. touching fraudulent conveyances* (1676).

W. Blackstone, *Commentaries on the laws of England*, 4 vols. (Oxford, 1766–9).

Lord Bolinbroke, *Contributions to the Craftsman*, ed. S. Varey (Oxford, 1982).

J. Boswell, *Reflections on the late alarming bankruptcies in Scotland* (Edinburgh, 1772).

S. Bradford, *The honest and dishonest ways of getting wealth* (1720).

T. Brewman, *An authentic list of persons who have surrendered themselves, in consequence of the late act, into the custody of the marshal of the King's Bench prison, between the seventh of June, 1780, and the thirty first of January, 1781* (1781).

J. Britton, J. N. Brewer, J. Hodgson and F. C. Laird, eds., *The beauties of England*, Vol. xv (1814).

J. Brown, *An estimate of the manners and principles of the times* (Dublin, 1757).

J. B. Burgess, *Considerations on the law of insolvency, with a proposal for reform* (1783).

J. Burgh, *The dignity of human nature* (1754).

E. Calamy, *A sermon at the merchants lecture in Salters Hall on Decemb. the 7th upon occasion of the many late bankrupts* (1708).

Calendar of State Papers Domestic.

Calendar of Treasury Books.

R. Campbell, *The London tradesman* (1747; reprinted Newton Abbot, 1969).

T. Carlyle, *Past and present* (1978).

Selected writings (Harmondsworth, 1980).

J. Cary, *An essay on the coyn and credit of England: as they stand with respect to its trade* (1696).

An essay on the state of England, in relation to its trade, its poor, and its taxes, for carrying on the present war against France (Bristol, 1695).

The case of bankrupts and insolvents considered (1734).

The case of the borrowers of the Charitable Corporation (1731?).

The case of the Charitable Corporation (1730?).

The case of the Charitable Corporation (1730?). (Different from the previous pamphlet.)

Case of the creditors of Alexander Urquhart, esq. (1724?).

The case of the creditors of John Coggs, and John Dann, goldsmiths (1710?).

The case of the creditors of Thomas Pitkin; discovering the fraudulent contrivance and practices of Thomas Brerewood, the said Pitkin's principal accomplice (1706?).

The case of the debtors now confined in the several gaols of this kingdom (1750?).

The case of divers poor distressed persons, who are under restraint, although not actually in prison (1725?).

The case of Mr George Wilcocks, attorney at law (1706?).

The case of great number of poor confined debtors, within the several prisons of Ludgate, the two compters, and other prisons in and about the City of London, as well as on behalf of themselves, as also of other insolvent debtors (1714?).

The case of insolvent debtors confined in the several gaols in this kingdom (1737?).

The case of the insolvent debtors, now in prison (1725?).

The case of Mr John Aynsworth's creditors (1707?).

The case of John Praed, esq.; most humbly submitted to the High Court of Parliament (1717?).

The case of the merchants and traders in and about the City of London, on behalf of themselves and the traders of this kingdom (1707?).

The case of persons in prison who are under commissions of bankruptcy (1737?).

The case of the poor confined debtors within the several prisons of this kingdom (1719/20?).

The case of the poor insolvent prisoners for debt, in the several gaols of this kingdom (1721?).

The case of the poor prisoners for debt and damages (1711?).

The case of Robert Martin, Thomas Glanfield, and Richard Chandler, creditors and assignees of the estate and effects of Thomas Kerridge, esq; under an act of parliament passed in the tenth year of His present Majesty's reign, entitled, an act for the relief of the insolvent debtors; on behalf of themselves, and other the creditors of the said Thomas Kerridge (1737?).

The case of the shelterers in the Mint (1722?).

The case of Mr Thomas Brerewood (1707?).

The case of Thomas Tomkins, citizen, and late merchant in London (1705?).

Cato's letters (2nd edn, 1721).

The cause of bankrupts and insolvents considered (1734).

G. Chalmers, *An estimate of the comparative strength of Great Britain* (1794).

Lord Chesterfield, *Letters written to his natural son on manners and morals* (reprinted New York, n.d.).

E. Chitty and F. Forster, *A digested index to the common law reports relating to conveyancing and bankruptcy commencing with the reign of Elizabeth, in 1558, to the present time* (1841).

J. Chitty, *A treatise on the laws of commerce and manufactures, and the contracts relating thereto*, 4 vols. (1820–4).

E. Christian, *The origins, progress, and present practice of the bankrupt laws*, 2 vols. (1812 and 1814).

   Practical instructions for suing out and prosecuting a commission of bankrupt; with the best modern precedents, and a digest of supplemental cases (1816).

James Claypoole's letterbook. London and Philadelphia 1681–1684, ed. M. Balderstone (San Marino, Calif., 1967).

W. Cobbett, ed., *The parliamentary history of England*, 36 vols. (1806–20).

E. Coke, *Institutes of laws of England* (1648), Part iv.

S. T. Coleridge, *Lay sermons*, in *The collected works of Samuel Taylor Coleridge*, Vol. vi, ed. R. J. White (1972).

Collection of ballads, broadsides etc. (Scrapbook of cuttings at the British Library).

P. Colquhoun, *An important crisis in the calico and muslin manufactory in Great Britain explained* (1788).

M. Combrune, *An enquiry into the prices of wheat, malt and occasionally other provisions* (1768).

The Common Council of the Corporation of London, *The consideration by the court of the report from the committee appointed to enquire into the practice and fees of the Court of Requests. Held 29 July 1774* (1774?).

The compleat compting-house companion: or young merchant and tradesman's sure guide. By a society of merchants and tradesmen (1763).

The compleat tradesman: or the exact dealers daily companion. By N. H. (merchant in the City of London) (1684).

M. Concanen, *A plan for the effectual distribution of bankrupt estates; with remarks on the losses to which the public are subject* (1800).

Considerations upon commissions of bankrupts (1727).

Considerations on imprisonment for debt, with intent to benefit prisoners for such, consistent with all the justice that can be done to their creditors, and with certain advantage to the public. By an honest debtor, King's-Bench prison (1807).

Considerations on money, bullions, and foreign exchanges; being an enquiry into the present state of the British coinage; particularly with regard to the scarcity of silver money (1772).

Considerations on the present state of the nation, as to publick credit, stocks, the landed and trading interests (1720).

Considerations shewing the reasonableness of having an act for the discharge of insolvent debtors without limitation of sum (1724/5?).

E. Cooke, *An enquiry into the state of law of debtor and creditor in England* (1829).

W. Cooke, *A compendious system of the bankrupt laws* (1785).

R. Courteville, *Arguments respecting insolvency* (n.d.).

[Cruttenden,] *Atlantic merchant-apothecary. Letters of Joseph Cruttenden 1710–1717*, ed. I. K. Steele (Toronto, 1977).

S. Cullen, *Reform of the bankrupt court. By a commissioner of bankrupt* (1829).

J. Currie, *A letter commercial and political, addressed to the Rt. Honble. William Pitt, in which the real interests of Britain in the present crisis are considered...* (1793).

H. Dance, *Remarks on the practical effect of imprisonment for debt* (1829).

C. Davenant, *Discourses on the public revenues and on the trade of England*, in C. Whitworth, ed., *The political and commercial works of Charles D'Avenant*, 5 vols. (1771), Vol. I, pp. 125–459.

T. Davies, *The laws relating to bankrupts, brought home to the present time* (1744).

The debtor and creditor's assistant; or a key to the King's Bench and Fleet prisons (1793).

D. Defoe, *The complete English tradesman* (1726).

Defoe's review, Facsimile Text Society, 22 vols. (New York, 1939).

An essay upon projects (1697).

An essay upon publick credit (1710).

The letters of Daniel Defoe, ed. G. H. Healey (Oxford, 1955).

Remarks on the bill to prevent frauds committed by bankrupts, with observations on the effect it may have upon trade, in *The works of Daniel Defoe*, Vol. III, ed. W. Hazlitt (1843).

A tour through the whole island of Great Britain, ed. P. Rogers (Harmondsworth, 1978).

T. Dekker, *The seven deadly sinnes of Londen* (1606), in A. G. Gosart, ed., *The non-dramatic works of Thomas Dekker*, 4 vols. (1885), Vol. II, pp. 1–81.

The deplorable case of the poor people in the Mint (1722?).

The deplorable case of such unfortunate debtors as have been declared bankrupts (1720?).

A dissertation upon credit (n.d.).

J. Dornford. *Seven letters to the Lords and Commons of Great Britain upon the impolicy, inhumanity, and injustice, of our present mode of arresting the bodies of debtors* (1786).

Seven letters to the Lords of the Privy Council on the police (1785).

M. Draper, *The spendthrift* (1731).

An essay on credit and the bankrupt act (1707).

Essays on the spirit of legislation, in encouragement of agriculture, population, manufactures, and commerce (1772).

The exact dealer refined (1702).

Extracts from the minutes and advices of the yearly meeting of Friends held in London (1783).

E. Farley, *Imprisonment for debt unconstitutional and oppressive, proved from the fundamental principles of the British constitution* (1788).

H. Fielding, *An enquiry into the causes of the late increase of robbers* (1751), in *The collected works of Henry Fielding*, 16 vols. (New York, 1967), Vol. XIII.

W. Fleetwood, *The justice of paying debts. A sermon preach'd in the City* (1718).

S. Foote, *The bankrupt* (1776).

W. Forsyth, *A treatise on the law relating to compositions and arrangements with creditors* (3rd edn, 1854).

The gentleman accomptant: or, an essay to unfold the mystery of accompts, by way of debitor and creditor, commonly called merchants accompts (1721).

Gentleman's Magazine.

I. Gervaise, *The system or theory of the trade of the world* (1720).

E. Gibbon, *Memoirs of my life*, ed. B. Radice (Harmondsworth, 1984).

T. Gisborne, *An enquiry into the duties of man in the higher and middle classes of society of Great Britain, resulting from their respective stations, professions, & employments* (1794).

O. Goldsmith, *The Bee*, in *The collected works of Oliver Goldsmith*, ed. A. Friedman, 4 vols. (Oxford, 1966), Vol. I.

T. Goodinge, *The law against bankrupts: or, a treatise wherein the statutes against bankrupts are explain'd* (3rd edn, 1713).

Gore's Liverpool directory (various edns), ed. G. T. and I. Shaw (Liverpool, 1907–32).

R. Gough, *The history of Myddle*, ed. D. Hey (Harmondsworth, 1981).

A. Grant, *The public monitor; or a plan for the more speedy recovery of small debts* (1789).

E. Green, *The spirit of the bankrupt laws* (3rd edn, 1776).

The Grenville papers, ed. W. J. Smith, 4 vols. (1853), Vol. IV.

Hansard's parliamentary debates.

J. Harris, *An essay upon money and coins. Pt. I* (1757; reprinted in J. R. McCulloch, ed., *A select collection of scarce and valuable tracts on money* (1856), pp. 339–429.).

Historical Manuscripts Commission, *Calendar of the correspondence of Philip Doddridge D.D. (1702–1751)*, ed. G. F. Nuttall, JP 26 (1979).

The manuscripts of the House of Lords, 1690–1714 (1892–1962).

The manuscripts of his grace the Duke of Portland, 10 vols. (1891–1931), Vol. IV.

Holden's triennial directory (4th edn, 1808).

E. Holme, *The Manchester and Salford directory* (Manchester, 1788).

An honest scheme, for improving the trade and credit of the nation (1727).

J. Howard, *The state of the prisons* (reprinted 1929).

An humble address to a member of parliament, from the confined debtors in the King's Bench; in behalf of themselves and the rest of their fellow sufferers throughout His Majesty's dominion (1740?).

The humble petition of the confined prisoners in the Fleet prison (1729?).

...*The humble petition of the debtors confined in His Majesty's prison of the Fleet* (1789).

...*The humble petition of above two hundred freemen of the honourable City of London, which are imprisoned in Ludgate under the rigour of the law, by the oppression of their creditors and obdurate adversaries* (1800?).

...*The humble petition of the prisoners of the King's-Bench prison* (1725?).

An humble proposal to cause bancrupts make better and more speedier payment of their debts to their creditors, than, by long experience hath been found, the statutes against bancrupts do effect (1679).

...*The humble representation of several prisoners in the Fleet, in reference to the present regulating bill* (1729?).

Humbly offered, by the petitioners of the King's Bench, in behalf of themselves, and many thousands, for passing the bill for the insolvent debtors (1725?).

W. Hutton, *An history of Birmingham* (Birmingham, 1781; reprinted East Ardsley, 1976). *Imprisonment of mens bodyes for debt, as the practice of England now stands* (1641).

Instructions for masters, traders, labourers, &c. also for servants, apprentices, and youth (1718).

Joshua Johnson's letterbook, 1771–1774, ed. J. M. Price, London Record Society Publications, Vol. XV (1979).

S. Johnson, *A dictionary of the English language* (1755; reprinted 1979).

Journals of the House of Commons.

Journals of the House of Lords.

Kent's directory (1771, 1782 and 1799 edns).

J. Lacy, *Letter* (1730?).

A letter to a member of parliament, concerning a bankrupt bill (Dublin, 1745).

A letter to a member of parliament by a merchant, (1717?).

Lex Londinerisis; or, the City law (1680).

London Chronicle.

London Gazette.

London Journal.

D. Macpherson, *Annals of commerce,* 4 vols. (1805).

G. Malynes, *Lex mercatoria, or the ancient law-merchant* (1622).

The management and oeconomy of trade, or the young trader's guide. By a Citizen of London (1783).

Manchester Mercury.

B. Mandeville, *The fable of the bees,* ed. P. Harth (Harmondsworth, 1970).

J. Marshall, *A digest of all accounts* (1832).

The merchant's companion. By J.P. (1684).

B. Montagu, *Enquiries respecting the insolvent debtor's bill, with the opinions of Dr Paley, Mr Burke, and Dr Johnson, upon imprisonment for debt* (1815).

Inquiries respecting the courts of commissioners of bankrupts, and Lord Chancellor's courts (1825).

A summary of the law of composition with creditors (1823).

B. Montagu and S. Ayrton, *The law and practice of bankruptcy, as altered by the new statutes, orders and decisions,* 2 vols. (1837).

J. Montefiore, *A commercial dictionary: containing the present state of mercantile law, practice and custom* (1803).

C. Moore, *A full inquiry into the subject of suicide,* 2 vols. (1790).

...The most humble petition of the poor distressed, insolvent debtors, now under confinement in the several prisons in this kingdom (1725?).

The most indigent poor prisoners letter to a worthy member of parliament; with reasons humbly offer'd for a bill to free the subjects from taxes for their maintenance, by making every creditor maintain his own debtor (1697?).

R. D. Neale, *The prisoner's guide; or every debtor his own lawyer* (3rd edn, 1813).

J. Neild, *An account of the rise, progress, and present state, of the society for the discharge and relief of persons imprisoned for small debts throughout England* (1796).

The new annual directory (1800).

John Norton & Sons merchants of London and Virginia. Being the papers of their counting house for the years 1750 to 1795, ed. F. N. Mason (Richmond, Va., 1937; reprinted in Newton Abbot, 1968).

Observations on the bankrupts bill: occasion'd by the many misrepresentations, and unjust reflections, of Mr. Daniel De Foe, in his several discourses on that head, humbly offered to the consideration of all fair traders. By a well-wisher to trade and credit (1706).

Observations on the bill now depending in parliament for the more easy and speedy recovery of small debts within the City of London and liberties thereof (1736?).

Observations and proposals most humbly offered to the parliament by several creditors, merchants and traders of London, relating to the bill now depending concerning bankrupts (1719?).

Observations on the state of bankrupts, under the present laws in a letter to a member of parliament (1760).

J. Oglethorpe, *A new and accurate account of the provinces of South-Carolina and Georgia* (1732), reprinted in T. R. Reese, ed., *The most delightful country of the universe. Promotional literature of the colony of Georgia 1717–1734* (Savannah, Ga., 1972), pp. 130–43.

J. Osborn, *A compleat guide to all persons who have any trade or concern with the City of London and parts adjacent* (1740 and various edns).

R. Owen, *The life of Robert Owen by himself* (1857; reprinted with an introduction by J. Butt, 1971).

W. Paget, *The humours of the Fleet: an humorous, descriptive poem* (1749).

Parliamentary papers.

W. Petty, *The Petty papers, some unpublished writings of Sir William Petty*, ed. from the Bowood Papers by the Marquis of Lansdowne, 2 vols. (1927).

The Petty–Southwell correspondence, 1676–1687, ed. from the Bowood Papers by the Marquis of Lansdowne (1928).

M. Pitt, *The cry of the oppressed. Being a true and tragical account of the unparallel'd sufferings of multitudes of poor imprisoned debtors, in most of the gaols in England* (1691).

W. Playfair, *Better prospects to the merchants and manufacturers of Great Britain* (1793).

M. Postlethwayt, *The universal dictionary of trade and commerce*, 2 vols. (1757).

C. Povey, *The unhappiness of England, as to its trade by sea and land* (1701).

The precipitation and fall of Mess. Douglas, Heron, and Company. By a committee of inquiry appointed by the proprietors (Edinburgh, 1778).

A present for an apprentice: or a sure guide to gain both esteem and an estate. By a late Lord Mayor of London (1740).

P. Price, *Gravainu mercatoris: or, the tradesman's complaint of the abuses in the execution of the statutes against bankrupts. Humbly offered to the consideration of both houses of parliament* (1694?).

A proposal for rendering bankruptcies less frequent in and about London (1732).

Proposals for promoting industry and advancing proper credit; advantageous to creditors in particular and the nation in general (1732).

Proposals for restraining the abuse of paper credit in Scotland (Edinburgh, 1765).

J. Prujean, *A treatise upon the laws of England now in force for the recovery of debt, pointing out the many abuses of them; together with a plan for administering more speedy and equitable justice to creditors and to debtors* (1791).

Queries humbly submitted in behalf of the bill for explaining and amending the act for recovery of small debts within the Tower-Hamlets (1752?).

E. Raffald, *The Manchester directory* (Manchester, 1772 and 1773).

The Manchester and Salford directory (Manchester, 1781).

Reasons for an act for the discharge of insolvent debtors. By the debtors in His Majesty's prison, the Fleet (1725?).

Reasons against confining persons in prison for debt, humbly offer'd to the consideration of parliament (1729?).

Reasons humbly offered for an act for relief of insolvent debtors, and fugitives for debt (1753?).

Reasons humbly offer'd for altering and amending the laws concerning bankrupts, and for preventing great losses that are daily sustained by their creditors, since the expiration of the late acts, of the fourth and fifth years of the reign of Her late Majesty Queen Anne (1720?).

Reasons humbly offered to the consideration of the parliament of Great Britain for lessening the present heavy national debt and taxes, inlarging the sinking fund, remedying the ill state of the coin, and thereby reviving trade and credit (1730).

Reasons humbly offered in favour of the bill (now depending in parliament) for the more easy and speedy recovery of small debts, within the City of London, and the liberties thereof (1689?).

Reasons humbly offer'd for making more certain the liberty of such bankrupts who shall fairly and justly surrender themselves, and effects, pursuant to the act now in being to prevent frauds committed by bankrupts (1719?).

Reasons humbly offered for passing the bill, now depending in parliament, relating to bankrupts (1706?).

Reasons humbly offered, to shew, that an act for relief of insolvent prisoners and fugitives for debt is, at this juncture, expedient, upon further motives than have induced the legislator to pass former acts of that kind (1746?).

Reasons for passing an extensive act of insolvency, and making some law to redress the great grievance, of confining so many thousand useful subjects in our gaols for debt. From the debtors of the King's Bench (1729?).

Reflections on the causes which have produced the present distress in commercial credit (1793).

The relative duty of creditors and debtors considered (1743).

Remarks on the late act of parliament to prevent frauds frequently committed by bankrupts, with proposals for the amendment thereof (1707).

The remembrancer: addressed to young men in business. Showing how they may attain the way to be rich and respectable (1794).

W. Roscoe, *Thoughts on the causes of the present failures* (1793).

G. Rose, *A brief examination into the increase of the revenue, commerce and manufactures of Great Britain, from 1772 to 1799* (1799).

Scholer's Manchester and Salford directory (Manchester, 1794 and 1797).

Scot's Magazine.

W. Scott, *An essay of drapery* (1635; reprinted with an introduction by S. L. Thrapp, Boston, Mass., 1953).

Rev. W. Scott, *A sermon on bankruptcy, stopping payment, and the justice of paying our debts, preached at various churches in the City* (1773).

W. Sherlock, *The charity of lending without usury* (1692).

A short case of the charitable corporation (1730?).

J. Sinclair, *The history of the public revenue of the British empire*, 3 vols. (1803).

[A. Smith,] *The correspondence of Adam Smith*, The Glasgow Edition, ed. E. C. Mossner and I. S. Ross (Oxford, 1977).

An enquiry into the nature and causes of the wealth of nations, ed. E. Cannan (Chicago, 1976).
Lectures on jurisprudence, The Glasgow Edition, ed. R. L. Meek, D. D. Raphael and P. G. Stein (Oxford, 1978).
C. Smith, *Three tracts on the corn trade and corn laws* (1766).
W. Smith & Co., *A list of bankrupts, with their dividends, certificates, &c. &c. for the last twenty years and six months, viz from Jan.1, 1786, to June 24, 1806, inclusive* (1806).
Some considerations humbly offered to the High Court of Parliament, for the benefit of creditors, and relief of honest insolvents (1719?).
Some considerations humbly offered, relating to the relief of such unhappy gentlemen, who could not receive any benefit from the last insolvent act (1725?).
Some rules for the conduct of life: to which are added a few cautions for the use of such freemen of London as take apprentices (1795).
The Spectator, ed. D. F. Bond, 5 vols. (Oxford, 1965).
A speech without doors, in behalf of an insolvent debtor in the Fleet prison (1731?).
The statutes at large from Magna Carta to 41 Geo. III, ed. O. Ruffhead, 18 vols. (1769–1800).
R. Steele, *The tradesman's calling* (1684).
J. Steuart, *An enquiry into the principles of political oeconomy*, ed. A. S. Skinner, 2 vols. (Edinburgh, 1966).
J. Stone, *The reading upon the statute of the thirteenth of Elizabeth, chapter 7. Touching bankrupts* (1656).
[Stout,] *The autobiography of William Stout of Lancaster 1665–1752*, ed. J. D. Marshall (Manchester, 1967).
A succinct digest of the laws relating to bankrupts... (1791).
J. Swift, *The conduct of the allies*, ed. H. Davis (Oxford, 1951).
The history of the last four years of the Queen, ed. H. Davis (Oxford, 1951).
Poetical works, ed. H. Davis (Oxford, 1967).
H. Thornton, *An enquiry into the nature and effects of the paper credit of Great Britain*, ed. F. A. von Hayek (1939).
The Times.
The trial of John Folkard...William Folkard...Thomas Nugent...and others; for a conspiracy to defraud the creditors of John Folkard, a bankrupt (1812).
[Turner,] *The diary of Thomas Turner*, ed. D. Vaisey (Oxford, 1985).
The universal pocket companion (1741).
J. Vanderlint, *Money answers all things: or, an essay to make money sufficiently plentiful amongst all ranks of people* (1734).
Voltaire, *Letters on England* (1733; reprinted Harmondsworth, 1980).
[Walpole,] *The Yale edition of Horace Walpole's correspondence*, Vol. XXIII, ed. W. S. Lewis, W. H. Smith and G. L. Lam (1963).
T. Watts, *An essay on the proper method for forming the man of business* (1716), ed. A. H. Cole (Cambridge, Mass., 1946).
E. West, *A treatise of the law and practice of extents in chief and in aid* (1817).
T. Wilson, *A discourse upon usury*, ed. R. H. Tawney (1925).
W. Woolgar, *Youth's familiar monitor; or the young man's best companion* (1770).
A. Young, *A six months tour through the north of England* (1770).

SECONDARY MATERIAL

H. J. Aitken, 'The analysis of decisions', *Explorations in Entrepreneurial History*, I (1949), pp. 17–23.

W. Albert, *The turnpike road system in England 1663–1840* (Cambridge, 1972).

D. H. Aldcroft and P. Fearon, eds., *British economic fluctuations 1790–1913* (1972).

D. Alexander, *Retailing in England during the industrial revolution* (1970).

B. W. E. Alford, 'Entrepreneurship, business performance and industrial development', *Business History*, XIX (1977), pp. 116–33.

B. L. Anderson, 'Aspects of capital and credit in Lancashire during the eighteenth century' (University of Liverpool M.A. thesis, 1966).

'The Lancashire bill system and its Liverpool practitioners', in W. H. Chaloner and B. M. Ratcliffe, eds., *Trade and transport* (Manchester, 1977), pp. 59–97.

'Money and the structure of credit in the eighteenth century', *Business History*, XII (1970), pp. 85–101.

'Provincial aspects of the financial revolution of the eighteenth century', *Business History*, XI (1969), pp. 11–22.

T. S. Ashton, 'The bill of exchange and private banks in Lancashire, 1790–1830', *Economic History Review*, XV (1945), pp. 25–35.

Economic fluctuations in England 1700–1800 (Oxford, 1959).

An economic history of England: the eighteenth century (1955).

An eighteenth century industrialist. Peter Stubs of Warrington 1756–1806 (Manchester, 1939).

The industrial revolution 1760–1830 (Oxford, 1977).

Iron and steel in the industrial revolution (2nd edn, Manchester, 1951).

A. Bailey, 'The impact of the Napoleonic Wars on the development of the cotton industry in Lancashire: a study in the structure and behaviour of firms during the industrial revolution' (University of Cambridge Ph.D. thesis, 1985).

V. Barbour, 'Marine risks and insurance in the seventeenth century', *Journal of Economic and Business History*, I (1928–9), pp. 561–96.

D. G. Barnes, *A history of the English corn laws from 1660–1846* (1930).

E. D. Bebb, *Nonconformity and social and economic life 1660–1800* (1935).

J. V. Beckett, *Coal and tobacco. The Lowthers and the economic development of West Cumberland, 1660–1760* (Cambridge, 1981).

'Cumbrians and the South Sea Bubble, 1720', *Transactions of the Cumberland and Westmorland Antiquarian and Archaeological Society*, LXXXII (1982), pp. 141–50.

W. Beveridge, *Prices and wages in England* (1939).

'The trade cycle in Britain before 1850', *Oxford Economic Papers*, III (1940), pp. 74–109.

B. M. Biucchi, 'The industrial revolution in Switzerland', in C. M. Cippola, ed., *The Fontana economic history of Europe*, Vol. IV, Part ii (Brighton, 1976), pp. 627–55.

R. Bloom, 'Reflections on uncertainty in accounting from historical and current literature', *Accounting History*, IV (1980), pp. 6–14.

R. Bourne, *Queen Anne's navy in the West Indies* (New Haven, Conn., 1939).

P. J. Bowden, 'Agricultural prices, farm profits, and rents', in J. Thirsk, ed., *The Agrarian history of England and Wales*, Vol. IV, *1500–1640* (Cambridge, 1967), pp. 593–695.

'Agricultural prices, wages, farm profits, and rents', in J. Thirsk, ed., *The Agrarian history of England and Wales*, Vol. V, Part ii, *1640–1750* (Cambridge, 1985), pp. 1–118, 830–1.

F. Brady, 'So fast to ruin. The Ayr Bank crash', *Ayrshire Archaeological and Natural History Society Collection*, XI (1973), pp. 25–44.

J. S. Bromley, 'The French privateering war, 1702–13', in H. E. Bell and R. L. Ollard, eds., *Historical essays 1600–1750* (1963), pp. 203–31.

R. Brooke, *Liverpool as it was during the last quarter of the eighteenth century* (Liverpool, 1853).

R. Browning, 'The Duke of Newcastle and the financing of the Seven Years' War', *Journal of Economic History*, XXXI (1971), pp. 344–77.

B. J. Buchanan, 'The evolution of the English turnpike trusts: lessons from a case study', *Economic History Review*, XXXIX (1986), pp. 223–43.

K. H. Burley, 'An Essex clothier of the eighteenth century', *Economic History Review*, XI (1958–9), pp. 289–301.

'Some accounting records of an eighteenth century clothier', *Accounting Research*, IX (1958), pp. 50–60.

H. Butterfield, *The whig interpretation of history* (1931).

F. J. J. Cadwallader, 'In pursuit of the merchant debtor and bankrupt: 1066–1732' (University of London Ph.D. thesis, 1965).

R. H. Campbell and R. G. Wilson, eds., *Entrepreneurship in Britain 1750–1939* (1975).

D. Cannadine, 'The present and past in the English industrial revolution 1880–1980', *Past and Present*, CIII (1984), pp. 131–72.

J. Carswell, *The South Sea Bubble* (1960).

A. C. Carter, *Getting, spending and investing in early modern times* (Assen, 1975).

C. W. Chalklin, *The provincial towns of Georgian England* (1974).

J. D. Chambers, *Nottinghamshire in the eighteenth century* (1932).

S. D. Chapman, 'British marketing enterprise: the changing roles of merchants, manufacturers, and financiers, 1700–1860', *Business History Review*, LIII (1979), pp. 205–34.

The cotton industry in the industrial revolution (1972).

The early factory masters (Newton Abbot, 1967).

'Financial restrictions on the growth of firms in the cotton industry, 1790–1850', *Economic History Review*, XXXII (1979), pp. 50–69.

J. A. Chartres, 'The capital's provincial eyes: London's inns in the early eighteenth century', *London Journal*, III (1977), pp. 24–39.

'The marketing of agricultural produce', in J. Thirsk, ed., *The agrarian history of England and Wales*, Vol. v, Part ii, *1640–1750* (Cambridge, 1985), pp. 406–502.

'The place of inns in the commercial life of London and western England 1660–1760' (University of Oxford, D. Phil. thesis, 1973).

K. N. Chaudhuri, *The trading world of Asia and the English East India Company 1660–1760* (Cambridge, 1978).

S. G. Checkland, 'Economic attitudes in Liverpool, 1793–1807', *Economic History Review*, V (1952–3), pp. 58–75.

I. R. Christie, *Wars and revolutions. Britain 1760–1815* (1982).

J. H. Clapham, *The Bank of England. A history*, 2 vols. (Cambridge, 1944).

An economic history of modern Britain, 3 vols. (Cambridge, 1926–38).

'Industrial organization in the woollen and worsted industries of Yorkshire', *Economic Journal*, XVI (1906), pp. 515–22.

'The transference of the worsted industry from Norfolk to the West Riding', *Economic Journal*, XX (1910), pp. 195–210.

G. N. Clark, *The Dutch alliance and the war against French trade 1688–1697* (Manchester, 1923).

'War trade and trade war, 1701–1713', *Economic History Review*, I (1927–8), pp. 262–80.

P. Clark, *The English alehouse: a social history 1200–1830* (1983).

P. G. E. Clemens, 'The rise of Liverpool, 1665–1750', *Economic History Review*, XXIX (1976), pp. 211–25.

R. H. Coase, 'The nature of the firm', *Economica*, IV (1937), pp. 386–405.

R. Cobb, *Death in Paris* (Oxford, 1978).

A. H. Cole, *Business enterprise in its social setting* (Cambridge, Mass., 1959).

D. C. Coleman, *Courtaulds. An economic and social history*, 3 vols. (Oxford, 1969–80), Vol. I.

The domestic system in industry (1960).

The economy of England 1450–1750 (Oxford, 1977).

'Gentlemen and players', *Economic History Review*, XXVI (1973), pp. 92–116.

'Growth and decay during the industrial revolution: the case of East Anglia', *Scandinavian Economic History Review*, X (1962), pp. 115–27.

'Historians and businessmen', in D. C. Coleman and P. Mathias, eds., *Enterprise and history* (Cambridge, 1984), pp. 27–41.

P. J. Coleman, *Debtors and creditors in America. Insolvency, imprisonment for debt, and bankruptcy, 1607–1900* (Madison, Wisc., 1974).

S. R. Cope, *Walter Boyd. A merchant banker in the age of Napoleon* (1983).

P. J. Corfield, *The impact of English towns 1700–1800* (Oxford, 1982).

'The social and economic history of Norwich, 1650–1850: a study in urban growth' (University of London Ph.D. thesis, 1976).

P. J. Corfield and S. M. Kelly, '"Giving directions to the town": the early town directories', *Urban History Yearbook* (1984), pp. 22–35.

E. M. Coulter, *Georgia: a short history* (Chapel Hill, N.C., 1947).

N. F. R. Crafts, 'British economic growth 1700–1831: a review of the evidence', *Economic History Review*, XXXVI (1983), pp. 177–99.

British economic growth during the industrial revolution (Oxford, 1985).

F. Crouzet, 'Editor's introduction', in Crouzet, ed., *Capital formation in the industrial revolution* (1972), pp. 1–69.

The first industrialists (Cambridge, 1985).

P. Crowhurst, *The defence of British trade 1689–1815* (Folkestone, 1977).

J. E. Cule, 'Finance and industry in the eighteenth century. The firm of Boulton and Watt', *Economic History*, IV (1938–40), pp. 319–25.

L. M. Cullen, *Anglo-Irish trade 1660–1800* (Manchester, 1968).

J. H. Dales, 'Approaches to entrepreneurial history', *Explorations in Entrepreneurial History*, I (1949), pp. 10–14.

G. W. Daniels, 'The trading account of a London merchant in 1794', *Economic Journal*, XXXIII (1923), pp. 516–22.

H. C. Darby, ed., *A new historical geography of England after 1600* (Cambridge, 1976).

M. J. Daunton, 'Towns and economic growth in eighteenth century England', in P. Abrams and E. A. Wrigley, eds., *Towns in societies* (Cambridge, 1978), pp. 245–77.

R. Davis, *Allepo and Devonshire Square. English traders in the Levant in the eighteenth century* (1967).

'English foreign trade, 1660–1700', reprinted in W. E. Minchinton, ed., *The growth of English overseas trade in the seventeenth and eighteenth centuries* (1969), pp. 78–98.

'English foreign trade, 1700–1774', reprinted in W. E. Minchinton, ed., *The growth of English overseas trade in the seventeenth and eighteenth centuries* (1969), pp. 99–120.

'The English wine trade in the eighteenth and nineteenth centuries', *Annales Cisalpines d'Histoire Sociale*, III (1972), pp. 87–106.

The industrial revolution and British overseas trade (Leicester, 1979).

The rise of the English shipping industry (Newton Abbot, 1962).

'The rise of protection in England 1688–1786', *Economic History Review*, XIX (1966), pp. 306–17.

P. Deane, 'The output of the British woollen industry in the eighteenth century', *Journal of Economic History*, XVII (1957), pp. 207–23.

'War and industrialisation', in J. M. Winter, ed., *War and economic development* (Cambridge, 1975), pp. 91–102.

P. Deane and W. A. Cole, *British economic growth 1688–1959* (2nd edn, Cambridge, 1969).

P. G. M. Dickson, *The financial revolution in England* (1967).

K. F. Dixon, 'The development of the London money market 1780–1830' (University of London Ph.D. thesis, 1962).

I. Donnachie and J. Butt, 'The Wilsons of Wilsontown ironworks (1799–1813): a study in entrepreneurial failure', *Explorations in Entrepreneurial History*, 2nd series, IV (1967), pp. 150–68.

A. B. DuBois, *The English business company after the Bubble Act 1720–1800* (New York, 1938).

I. P. H. Duffy, 'Bankruptcy and insolvency in London in the late eighteenth and early nineteenth centuries' (University of Oxford D. Phil. thesis, 1973).

'English bankrupts, 1571–1861', *American Journal of Legal History*, XXIV (1980), pp. 283–305.

E. P. Duggan, 'Industrialization and the development of urban business communities: research problems, sources and techniques', *Local Historian*, XI (1975), pp. 457–65.

S. Dumbell, 'Early Liverpool cotton imports and the organisation of the cotton market in the eighteenth century', *Economic Journal*, XXXIII (1923), pp. 362–73.

R. V. Eagly and V. K. Smith, 'Domestic and international integration of the London money market, 1731–1789', *Journal of Economic History*, XXXVI (1976), pp. 198–212.

J. K. Edwards, 'The decline of the Norwich textiles industry', *Yorkshire Bulletin of Economic and Social Research*, XVI (1964), pp. 31–41.

'The economic development of Norwich, 1750–1850, with special reference to the worsted industry' (University of Leeds Ph.D. thesis, 1963).

M. M. Edwards, *The growth of the British cotton trade 1780–1815* (Manchester, 1967).

J. Ehrman, *The younger Pitt. The reluctant transition* (1983).

E. G. Evans, 'Planter indebtedness and the coming of the revolution in Virginia', *William and Mary Quarterly*, 3rd series, XIX (1962), pp. 510–33.

G. H. Evans, 'Business entrepreneurs, their major functions and related tenets', *Journal of Economic History*, XIX (1959), pp. 250–70.

'A theory of entrepreneurship', *Journal of Economic History*, II Supplement 2 (1942), pp. 142–6.
A. Everitt, 'The English urban inn, 1560–1760', in Everitt, ed., *Perspectives in English urban history* (1973), pp. 91–137.
C. R. Fay, *The corn laws and social England* (Cambridge, 1932).
J. Feather, *The provincial book trade in eighteenth-century England* (Cambridge, 1985).
C. H. Feinstein, 'Capital formation in Great Britain', in P. Mathias and M. M. Postan, eds., *The Cambridge economic history of Europe*, Vol. VII, Part i (Cambridge, 1978), pp. 28–96.
H. E. S. Fisher, *The Portugal trade. A study of Anglo-Portuguese commerce 1700–1770* (1971).
R. S. Fitton, 'Samuel and William Salte, an eighteenth century linen house', *Explorations in Entrepreneurial History*, 2nd series, VI (1969), pp. 286–96.
R. S. Fitton and A. P. Wadsworth, *The Strutts and the Arkwrights 1758–1830* (Manchester, 1958).
M. W. Flinn, 'Agricultural productivity and economic growth in England, 1700–1760: a comment', *Journal of Economic History*, XXVI (1966), pp. 93–8.
Origins of the industrial revolution (1966).
'Social theory and the industrial revolution', in T. Burns and S. B. Saul, eds., *Social theory and economic change* (1967), pp. 9–34.
R. Ford, 'Imprisonment for debt', *Michigan Law Review*, XXV (1926), pp. 24–49.
E. J. Foulkes, 'The cotton-spinning factories of Flintshire, 1777–1866', *Journal of the Flintshire Historical Society Publications*, XXI (1964), pp. 91–7.
A. D. Francis, *The wine trade* (1972).
C. J. French, 'The trade and shipping of London, 1700–1776' (University of Exeter Ph.D. thesis, 1980).
V. A. C. Gatrell, 'Labour, power, and the size of firms in Lancashire cotton in the second quarter of the nineteenth century', *Economic History Review*, XXX (1977), pp. 95–139.
A. D. Gayer, W. W. Rostow and A. J. Schwartz, *The growth and fluctuation of the British economy 1790–1850*, 2 vols. (Oxford, 1953).
M. D. George, *London life in the eighteenth century* (1925; reprinted Harmondsworth, 1979).
E. W. Gilboy, 'Demand as a factor in the industrial revolution', in R. M. Hartwell, ed., *The causes of the industrial revolution* (1967), pp. 121–38.
C. Gill, 'Blackwell Hall factors, 1795–1799', *Economic History Review*, VI (1953–4), pp. 268–81.
A. Gooder, 'The population crisis of 1727–30 in Warwickshire', *Midland History*, I, No. 4 (1972), pp. 1–22.
N. Goodison, *Ormolu, the work of Matthew Boulton* (1974).
C. W. F. Goss, *The London directories 1677–1855* (1932).
J. D. Gould, 'Agricultural fluctuations and the English economy in the eighteenth century', *Journal of Economic History*, XXII (1962), pp. 313–33.
R. Grassby, 'English merchant capitalism in the late seventeenth century', *Past and Present*, XLVI (1970), pp. 87–107.
'The rate of profit in seventeenth century England', *English Historical Review*, LXXXIV (1969), pp. 721–51.
'Social mobility and business enterprise in seventeenth-century England', in

D. Pennington and K. Thomas, eds., *Puritans and revolutionaries* (Oxford, 1978), pp. 355–81.
D. Gregory, *Regional transformation and industrial revolution. A geography of the Yorkshire woollen industry* (1982).
I. Grubb, *Quakerism and industry before 1800* (1930).
P. H. Haagen, 'Eighteenth-century English society and the debt law', in S. Cohen and A. Scull, eds., *Social control and the state* (Oxford, 1983), pp. 222–47.
H. J. Habakkuk, 'The rise and fall of English landed families, 1600–1800. II', *Transactions of the Royal Historical Society*, 5th series, XXX (1980), pp. 199–221.
E. E. Hagen, *On the theory of social change* (Cambridge, Mass., 1964).
H. Hamilton, 'The failure of the Ayr Bank, 1772', *Economic History Review*, VIII (1955–6), pp. 405–17.
The industrial revolution in Scotland (Oxford, 1932).
L. Hannah, *The rise of the corporate economy* (1976).
A. Harding, *A social history of English Law* (Harmondsworth, 1966).
C. K. Harley, 'British industrialization before 1841: evidence of slower growth during the industrial revolution', *Journal of Economic History*, XLII (1982), pp. 267–89.
C. J. Harrison, 'Grain price analysis and harvest qualities, 1465–1634', *Agricultural History Review*, XIX (1971), pp. 135–55.
N. B. Harte, 'The rise of protection and the English linen trade, 1690–1790', in Harte and K. G. Ponting, eds., *Textile history and economic history* (Manchester, 1973), pp. 74–112.
R. M. Hartwell, 'Business management in England during the period of early industrialisation: inducements and obstacles', in Hartwell, ed., *The industrial revolution* (Oxford, 1970), pp. 28–41.
The industrial revolution and economic growth (1971).
R. G. Hawtrey, *Currency and credit* (4th edn, 1950).
D. Hay, 'War, dearth and theft in the eighteenth century: the record of the English courts', *Past and Present*, XCV (1982), pp. 117–60.
B. Hilton, *Corn, cash, commerce. The economic policies of the Tory governments 1815–1830* (Oxford, 1977).
W. G. Hoffman, *British industry 1700–1950* (Oxford, 1955).
J. M. Holden, *The history of negotiable instruments in English law* (1955).
B. A. Holderness, 'The clergy as money-lenders in England, 1550–1700', in R. O'Day and F. Heal, eds., *Princes and paupers in the English church 1500–1800* (Leicester, 1981), pp. 195–209.
'Credit in English rural society before the nineteenth century, with special reference to the period 1650–1720', *Agricultural History Review*, XXIV (1976), pp. 97–109.
'Credit in a rural community, 1660–1800', *Midland History*, III (1975), pp. 94–115.
'Elizabeth Parkin and her investments, 1733–66. Aspects of the Sheffield money market in the eighteenth century', *Transactions of the Hunter Archaeological Society*, X (1973), pp. 81–7.
W. S. Holdsworth, *A history of English law*, 17 vols. (1922–72).
K. Honeyman, *Origins of enterprise* (Manchester, 1982).
E. Hopkins, 'Boulton before Watt: the earlier career reconsidered', *Midland History*, IX (1984), pp. 43–58.
J. Hoppit, 'Financial crises in eighteenth-century England', *Economic History Review*, XXXIX (1986), pp. 39–58.

'Risk and failure in English industry, *c.* 1700–1800' (University of Cambridge Ph.D. thesis, 1984).

'The use and abuse of credit in eighteenth-century England', in R. B. Outhwaite and N. McKendrick, eds., *Business life and public policy* (Cambridge, 1986), pp. 64–78.

J. K. Horsefield, 'The beginnings of paper money in England', *Journal of European Economic History*, VI (1977), pp. 117–32.

British monetary experiments 1650–1710 (1960).

'The duties of a banker', *Economica*, VIII (1941), pp. 37–51.

'Gibson and Johnson: a forgotten *cause celebre*', *Economica*, X (1943), pp. 233–7.

W. G. Hoskins, 'Harvest fluctuations and English economic history, 1480–1619', *Agricultural History Review*, XII (1964), pp. 28–46.

'Harvest fluctuations and English economic history, 1620–1759', *Agricultural History Review*, XVI (1968), pp. 15–31.

Industry, trade and people in Exeter 1688–1800 (Manchester, 1935).

A. Howe, *The cotton masters, 1830–1860* (Oxford, 1984).

P. Hudson, 'The role of banks in the finance of the West Yorkshire wool textile industry, *c.* 1780–1850', *Business History Review*, LV (1981), pp. 379–402.

F. E. Hyde, 'Economic theory and business history', *Business History*, V (1962), pp. 1–10.

F. E. Hyde, B. B. Parkinson and S. Marriner, 'The port of Liverpool and the crisis of 1793', *Economica*, XVIII (1951), pp. 363–78.

J. E. Inikori, 'English trade to Guinea: a study in the impact of foreign trade on the English economy 1750–1807' (University of Ibadan Ph.D. thesis, 1973).

'Market structure and the profits of the British African trade in the late eighteenth century', *Journal of Economic History*, XLI (1981), pp. 745–76.

J. Innes, 'The King's Bench prison in the later eighteenth century: law, authority and order in a London debtors' prison', in J. Brewer and J. Styles, eds., *An ungovernable people* (1980), pp. 250–98.

R. Ippolito, 'The effect of the "agricultural depression" on industrial demand in England, 1730–1750', *Economica*, XLII (1975), pp. 298–312.

R. V. Jackson, 'Growth and deceleration in English agriculture, 1660–1790', *Economic History Review*, XXXVIII (1985), pp. 333–51.

F. G. James, 'Charity endowments as sources of local credit in seventeenth- and eighteenth-century England', *Journal of Economic History*, VIII (1948), pp. 153–70.

D. T. Jenkins and K. G. Ponting, *The British wool textile industry 1770–1914* (1982).

W. S. Jevons, *Investigations in currency and finance* (1884).

A. H. John, 'Agricultural productivity and economic growth in England, 1700–60', *Journal of Economic History*, XXV (1965), pp. 19–34.

'English agricultural improvement and grain exports, 1660–1765', in D. C. Coleman and A. H. John, eds., *Trade, government and economy in pre-industrial England* (1976), pp. 45–67.

'Insurance investment and the London money market of the eighteenth century', *Economica*, XX (1953), pp. 137–58.

'War and the English economy, 1700–1763', *Economic History Review*, VII (1954–5), pp. 329–44.

D. W. Jones, 'London merchants and the crisis of the 1690s', in P. Clark and P. Slack, eds., *Crisis and order in English towns 1500–1700* (1972), pp. 311–55.

'London overseas-merchant groups at the end of the seventeenth century and the moves against the East India Company' (University of Oxford D.Phil. thesis, 1970).

E. L. Jones, *Seasons and prices* (1964).

S. Jones, 'The first currency revolution', *Journal of European Economic History*, X (1981), pp. 583–618.

'Government, currency and country banks in England, 1770–1797', *South African Journal of Economics*, XLIV (1976), pp. 252–73.

W. J. Jones, 'The foundations of English bankruptcy: statutes and commissions in the early modern period', *Transactions of the American Philosophical Society*, LXIX (1979), Part iii.

D. M. Joslin, 'London bankers in wartime, 1739–84', in L. S. Pressnell, ed., *Studies in the industrial revolution* (1960), pp. 156–77.

K. A. Kellock, 'London merchants and the pre-1776 American debts', *Guildhall Studies in London History*, I (1974), pp. 109–49.

H. S. K. Kent, *War and trade in northern seas* (Cambridge, 1973).

C. P. Kindleberger, 'Commercial expansion and the industrial revolution', *Journal of European Economic History*, IV (1975), pp. 613–54.

Manias, panics, and crashes (1978).

C. P. Kindleberger and J. P. Laffargue, eds., *Financial crises: theory, history and policy* (Cambridge and Paris, 1982).

I. M. Kirzner, *Perception, opportunity and profit: studies in the theory of entrepreneurship* (Chicago, 1979).

F. H. Knight, 'Profit and entrepreneurial functions', *Journal of Economic History*, II Supplement 2 (1942), pp. 126–32.

Risk, uncertainty and profit (Cambridge, Mass., 1921).

A. S. Kussmaul, *Servants in husbandry in early modern England* (Cambridge, 1981).

D. S. Landes, *The unbound Prometheus* (Cambridge, 1962).

J. Langton, 'Liverpool and its hinterland in the late eighteenth century', in B. L. Anderson and P. J. M. Storey, eds., *Commerce, industry and transport. Studies in economic change on Merseyside* (Liverpool, 1983), pp. 1–25.

C. H. Lee, *A cotton enterprise 1795–1840. A history of M'Connel and Kennedy fine cotton spinners* (Manchester, 1972).

G. A. Lee, 'The concept of profit in British accounting, 1760–1900', *Business History Review*, XLIX (1975), pp. 6–36.

J. A. S. L. Leighton-Boyce, *Smiths the bankers 1658–1958* (1958).

D. Levine, *Family formation in an age of nascent capitalism* (1977).

L. E. Levinthal, 'The early history of bankruptcy law', *University of Pennsylvania Law Review*, LXVI (1918), pp. 223–50.

J. P. Lewis, *Building cycles and Britain's growth* (1965).

P. H. Lindert, 'English occupations, 1670–1811', *Journal of Economic History*, XL (1980), pp. 685–712.

P. H. Lindert and J. G. Williamson, 'Revising England's social tables 1688–1812', *Explorations in Economic History*, XIX (1982), pp. 385–408; 'Errata', *Explorations in Economic History*, XX (1983), pp. 329–30.

P. J. Lineham, 'The campaign to abolish imprisonment for debt in England 1750–1840' (University of Canterbury, New Zealand, M.A. thesis, 1974).

E. Lipson, *The economic history of England*, 3 vols. (3rd edn., 1943).

A. J. Little, *Deceleration in the eighteenth-century British economy* (1976).

R. Lloyd-Jones and A. A. Le Roux, 'Marshall and the birth and death of firms: the growth and size distribution of firms in the early nineteenth-century cotton industry', *Business History*, XXIV (1982), pp. 141–55.

'The size of firms in the cotton industry: Manchester 1815–41', *Economic History Review*, XXXIII (1980), pp. 72–82.

M. F. Lloyd-Pritchard, 'The decline of Norwich', *Economic History Review*, III (1950–1), pp. 371–7.

M. C. Lovell, 'The role of the Bank of England as lender of last resort in the crises of the eighteenth century', *Explorations in Entrepreneurial History*, X (1957), pp. 8–21.

D. C. McClelland, *The achieving society* (Princeton, N. J., 1961).

J. J. McCusker, 'The current value of English exports, 1697 to 1800', *William and Mary Quarterly*, 3rd series, XXVIII (1971), pp. 607–28.

N. McKendrick, 'General introduction', in R. J. Overy, *William Morris, Viscount Nuffield* (1976), pp. vii–xliv.

'Josiah Wedgwood and cost accounting in the industrial revolution', *Economic History Review*, XXIII (1970), pp. 45–67.

N. McKendrick, J. Brewer and J. H. Plumb, *The birth of a consumer society* (1982).

J. de L. Mann, *The cloth industry in the west of England from 1640–1880* (Oxford, 1971).

'Clothiers and weavers in Wiltshire during the eighteenth century', in L. S. Pressnell, ed., *Studies in the industrial revolution* (1960), pp. 66–96.

'A Wiltshire family of clothiers: George and Hester Wansey, 1683–1714', *Economic History Review*, IX (1956–7), pp. 241–53.

J. de L. Mann, ed., *Documents illustrating the Wiltshire textile trades in the eighteenth century*, Wiltshire Archaeological and Natural History Society, Vol. XIX (Devizes, 1964).

S. Marriner, 'Accounting records in English bankruptcy proceedings to 1850', *Accounting History*, III (1978), pp. 4–21.

'English bankruptcy records and statistics before 1850', *Economic History Review*, XXXIII (1980), pp. 351–66.

D. Marshall, *Eighteenth century England* (1962).

P. Mathias, *The brewing industry in England, 1700–1830* (Cambridge, 1959).

The first industrial nation (1969).

The transformation of England (1979).

P. Mathias and P. K. O'Brien, 'Taxation in Britain and France, 1715–1810. A comparison of the social and economic incidence of taxes collected for the central governments', *Journal of European Economic History*, V (1976), pp. 601–50.

R. C. O. Matthews, *The trade cycle* (Welwyn and Cambridge, 1959).

'The trade cycle in Great Britain, 1790–1850', *Oxford Economic Papers*, VI (1954), pp. 1–32.

M. Miles, '"Eminent attorneys": some aspects of West Riding attorneyship *c*. 1750–1830' (University of Birmingham Ph.D. thesis, 1982).

'The money market in the early industrial revolution: the evidence from West Riding attorneys *c*. 1750–1800', *Business History*, XXIII (1981), pp. 127–46.

J. Mills, 'On credit cycles, and the origin of commercial panics', *Transactions of the Manchester Statistical Society* (1867–8), pp. 5–40.

W. E. Minchinton, 'Bristol – metropolis of the west in the eighteenth century', *Transactions of the Royal Historical Society*, 5th series, IV (1954), pp. 69–85.

'The merchants of England in the eighteenth century', *Explorations in Entrepreneurial History*, X (1957), pp. 62–71.

W. E. Minchinton, ed., *The trade of Bristol in the eighteenth century*, Bristol Record Society Publications, Vol. XX (Bristol, 1957).

G. E. Mingay, 'The agricultural depression 1730–50', *Economic History Review*, VIII (1955–6), pp. 323–38.

English landed society in the eighteenth century (1963).

H. P. Minsky, 'The financial instability hypothesis: captalist processes and the behaviour of the economy', in C. P. Kindleberger and J. P. Laffargue, eds., *Financial crises: theory, history and policy* (Cambridge and Paris, 1982), pp. 13–39.

I. Mintz, *Cyclical fluctuations in the exports of the United States since 1879* (New York, 1967).

P. E. Mirowski, 'Adam Smith, empiricism, and the rate of profit in eighteenth-century England', *History of Political Economy*, XIV (1982), pp. 178–98.

'The birth of the business cycle' (University of Michigan Ph.D. thesis, 1979).

'Macroeconomic instability and the "natural" processes in early neoclassical economics', *Journal of Economic History*, XLIV (1984), pp. 345–54.

'The rise (and retreat) of a market: English joint stock shares in the eighteenth century', *Journal of Economic History*, XLI (1981), pp. 559–77.

B. R. Mitchell and P. Deane, *Abstract of British historical statistics* (Cambridge, 1962).

I. Mitchell, 'The development of urban retailing 1700–1815', in P. Clark, ed., *The transformation of English provincial towns 1600–1800* (1984), pp. 259–83.

'Urban markets and retail distribution 1730–1815 with particular reference to Macclesfield, Stockport and Chester' (University of Oxford D. Phil. thesis, 1974).

E. A. L. Moir, 'The gentlemen clothiers: a study of the organisation of the Gloucestershire cloth industry, 1750–1835', in H. P. R. Finberg, ed., *Gloucestershire studies* (Leicester, 1957), pp. 225–66.

J. Mokyr, 'Demand vs. supply in the industrial revolution', *Journal of Economic History*, XXXVII (1977), pp. 987–1008.

M. S. Moss and J. R. Hume, 'Business failure in Scotland 1839–1913: a research note', *Business History*, XXV (1983), pp. 3–10.

R. C. Nash, 'English transatlantic trade, 1660–1730: a quantitative study' (University of Cambridge Ph.D. thesis, 1982).

L. D. Neal, 'Interpreting power and profit in economic history: a case study of the Seven Years War', *Journal of Economic History*, XXXVII (1977), pp. 20–35.

J. E. Norton, *Guide to the national and provincial directories of England and Wales, excluding London, published before 1856* (1950).

P. K. O'Brien, 'Government revenue, 1793–1815 – a study in fiscal and financial policy in the wars against France' (University of Oxford D.Phil. thesis, 1967).

D. J. Ormrod, 'Anglo-Dutch commerce 1700–1760' (University of Cambridge Ph.D. thesis, 1973).

English grain exports and the structure of agrarian capitalism 1700–1760 (Hull, 1985).

R. Pares, *War and trade in the West Indies 1739–1763* (Oxford, 1936).

A West-India fortune (1950).

B. T. Parsons, 'The behaviour of prices on the London stock market in the early eighteenth century' (University of Chicago Ph.D. thesis, 1974).

E. Pawson, *Transport and economy: the turnpike roads of eighteenth century Britain* (1977).

P. L. Payne, *British entrepreneurship in the nineteenth century* (1974).

The early Scottish limited companies 1856–1895 (Edinburgh, 1980).

E. T. Penrose, *The theory of the growth of the firm* (Oxford, 1959).

H. J. Perkin, *The origins of modern English society 1780–1880* (1969).

J. H. Plumb, *Sir Robert Walpole, the making of a statesman* (1956).

S. Pollard, *The genesis of modern management* (1965).

Peaceful conquest. The industrialization of Europe 1760–1970 (Oxford, 1981).

K. G. Ponting, *The west of England cloth industry* (1957).

L. S. Pressnell, *Country banking in the industrial revolution* (Oxford, 1956).

  'The rate of interest in the eighteenth century', in Pressnell, ed., *Studies in the industrial revolution* (1960), pp. 178–214.

J. M. Price, *Capital and credit in British overseas trade: the view from the Chesapeake, 1700–1776* (Cambridge, Mass., 1980).

France and the Chesapeake, 2 vols. (Ann Arbor, Mich., 1973).

  'The last phase of the Virginia–London consignment trade: James Buchanan & Co., 1758–1768', *William and Mary Quarterly*, 3rd series, XLIII (1986), pp. 64–98.

  'Multilateralism and/or bilateralism: the settlement of British trade balances with "The North", c. 1700', *Economic History Review*, XIV (1961–2), pp. 254–74.

  'New time series for Scotland's and Britain's trade with the thirteen colonies and states, 1740–1791', *William and Mary Quarterly*, 3rd series, XXXII (1975), pp. 307–25.

A. Redford, *Manchester merchants and foreign trade 1794–1858* (Manchester, 1934).

F. Redlich, 'A new concept of entrepreneurship', *Explorations in Entrepreneurial History*, V (1952), pp. 75–7.

  'The origin of the concept of "entrepreneur" and "creative entrepreneur"', *Explorations in Entrepreneurial History*, I (1949), pp. 1–7.

W. G. Rimmer, 'The industrial profile of Leeds 1740–1840', *Publications of the Thoresby Society*, L (1967), pp. 130–57.

  Marshalls of Leeds: flax spinners 1788–1886 (Cambridge, 1960).

W. I. Roberts, 'Samuel Storke: an eighteenth-century London merchant trading to the American colonies', *Business History Review*, XXXIX (1965), pp. 147–70.

E. Robinson, 'Eighteenth-century commerce and fashion: Matthew Boulton's marketing techniques', *Economic History Review*, XVI (1963–4), pp. 39–60.

E. A. G. Robinson, *The structure of competitive industry* (Welwyn and Cambridge, 1958).

R. G. Rodger, 'Business failure in Scotland 1839–1913', *Business History*, XXVII (1985), pp. 75–99.

J. E. T. Rogers, *A history of agriculture and prices in England*, 7 vols. (Oxford, 1866–1902).

S. M. Rosenblatt, 'The significance of credit in the tobacco consignment trade: a study of John Norton & Sons, 1768–1775', *William and Mary Quarterly*, 3rd series, XIX (1962), pp. 383–99.

W. W. Rostow, *British economy of the nineteenth century* (Oxford, 1948).

The stages of economic growth (Cambridge, 1960).

K. W. Rothschild, 'Price theory and oligopoly', *Economic Journal*, LVII (1947), pp. 290–320.

M. B. Rowlands, *Masters and men in the West Midlands metalware trades before the industrial revolution* (Manchester, 1975).

W. D. Rubinstein, *Men of property* (1981).

E. B. Schumpeter, *English overseas trade statistics 1697–1808* (Oxford, 1960).
'English prices and public finance, 1660–1822', *Review of Economic Statistics*, XX (1938), pp. 21–37.
J. A. Schumpeter, 'The creative response in economic history', *Journal of Economic History*, VII (1947), pp. 149–59.
'Economic theory and entrepreneurial history', in H. G. J. Aitken, ed., *Explorations in enterprise* (Cambridge, Mass., 1965), pp. 45–64.
The theory of economic development (Cambridge, Mass., 1934).
L. D. Schwarz, 'Social class and social geography, the middle classes in London at the end of the eighteenth century', *Social History*, VII (1982), pp. 167–85.
L. D. Schwarz and L. J. Jones, 'Wealth, occupations, and insurance in the late eighteenth century: the policy registers of the Sun Fire Office', *Economic History Review*, XXXVI (1983), pp. 365–73.
W. R. Scott, *The constitution and finance of English, Scottish and Irish joint-stock companies to 1720*, 3 vols. (Cambridge, 1910–12).
P. Seaver, 'The Puritan work ethic revisited', *Journal of British Studies*, XIX (1980), pp. 35–53.
J. Sekora, *Luxury. The concept in western thought, Eden to Smollett* (Baltimore, Md., 1977).
G. Shaw, 'The content and reliability of nineteenth-century trade directories', *Local Historian*, XIII (1978), pp. 205–9.
W. A. Shaw, *Select tracts and documents illustrative of English monetary history 1626–1730* (1896).
J. F. Shepherd and G. M. Walton, *Shipping, maritime trade, and the economic development of colonial North America* (Cambridge, 1972).
R. B. Sheridan, 'The British credit crisis of 1772 and the American colonies', *Journal of Economic History*, XX (1960), pp. 161–86.
N. J. Silberling, 'British prices and business cycles, 1779–1850', *Review of Economic Statistics*, V, Supplement 2 (1923).
H. A. Simon, 'Theories of decision-making in economics and behavioural science', in G. P. E. Clarkson, ed., *Managerial economics: selected readings* (Harmondsworth, 1968), pp. 13–49.
A. Smiles, *Samuel Smiles and his surroundings* (1956).
S. Smiles, *Business biography* (1863).
Self-help (1859; reprinted 1910).
K. D. M. Snell, *Annals of the labouring poor* (Cambridge, 1985).
D. Solomons, 'The historical development of costing', in Solomons, ed., *Studies in costing* (1952), pp. 1–52.
W. Sombart, *Luxury and capitalism* (Ann Arbor, Mich., 1967).
W. A. Speck, *Stability and strife* (1977).
F. C. Spooner, *Risks at sea. Amsterdam insurance and maritime Europe, 1766–1780* (Cambridge, 1983).
R. Stewart-Brown, *Liverpool ships in the eighteenth century* (Liverpool, 1932).
L. and J. C. F. Stone, *An open elite?* (Oxford, 1984).
B. E. Supple, *Commercial crises and change in England 1600–1642* (Cambridge, 1959).
L. S. Sutherland, 'Sir George Colebrooke's world corner in alum, 1771–73', *Economic History*, III (1936), pp. 237–58.
'The law merchant in England in the seventeenth and eighteenth centuries', *Transactions of the Royal Historical Society*, 4th series, XVII (1934), pp. 149–76.
A London merchant 1695–1774 (Oxford, 1933).

J. Thirsk, 'Agricultural innovations and their diffusion', in Thirsk, ed., *The agrarian history of England and Wales*, Vol. v, Part ii, *1640–1750* (Cambridge, 1985), pp. 533–89.
Economic policy and projects (Oxford, 1978).
B. Thomas, 'The rhythm of growth in the Atlantic economy of the eighteenth century', *Research in Economic History*, iii (1978), pp. 1–46.
D. W. Thomas, 'The Mills family: London sugar merchants of the eighteenth century', *Business History*, xi (1969), pp. 3–10.
A. Thompson, *The dynamics of the industrial revolution* (1973).
E. P. Thompson, 'The crime of anonymity', in D. Hay, P. Linebaugh and Thompson, eds., *Albion's fatal tree* (1975), pp. 255–344.
Whigs and hunters (1975).
G. Timmins, 'Measuring industrial growth from trade directories', *Local Historian*, xiii (1979), pp. 349–52.
B. Trinder, *The industrial revolution in Shropshire* (Chichester, 1973).
G. S. L. Tucker, *Progress and profit in British economic thought 1650–1850* (Cambridge, 1960).
G. H. Tupling, *Lancashire directories 1684–1957* (1968).
G. Turnbull, 'Scotch linen, storms, wars and privateers. John Wilson & Son, Leeds linen merchants, 1754–1800', *Journal of Transport History*, 3rd series, iii (1982), pp. 47–69.
M. Turner, *Enclosures in Britain 1750–1830* (1984).
G. Unwin, *Samuel Oldknow and the Arkwrights* (Manchester, 1924).
D. Veall, *The popular movement for law reform 1640–1660* (Oxford, 1970).
The Victoria county histories.
S. M. Wade, 'The idea of luxury in eighteenth-century England' (University of Harvard Ph.D. thesis, 1968).
A. P. Wadsworth and J. de L. Mann, *The cotton trade and industrial Lancashire 1600–1780* (Manchester, 1931).
J. R. Ward, *The finance of canal building in eighteenth century England* (Oxford, 1974).
'Speculative building at Bristol and Clifton, 1783–1793', *Business History*, xx (1978), pp. 3–18.
W. R. Ward, *The English land tax in the eighteenth century* (Oxford, 1953).
M. R. Watts, *The dissenters* (Oxford, 1978).
L. Weatherill, 'Capital and credit in the pottery industry before 1770', *Business History*, xxiv (1982), pp. 243–58.
E. Welbourne, 'Bankruptcy before the era of Victorian reform', *Cambridge Historical Journal*, iv (1932), pp. 51–62.
R. B. Westerfield, *Middlemen in English business particularly between 1660 and 1760* (New Haven, Conn., 1915; reprinted Newton Abbot, 1968).
P. Wilde, 'The use of business directories in comparing the industrial structure of towns. An example from the south-west Pennines', *Local Historian*, xii (1976), pp. 152–6.
T. S. Willan, *An eighteenth century shopkeeper. Abraham Dent of Kirkby Stephen* (Manchester, 1970).
The English coasting trade 1600–1750 (Manchester, 1938).
C. H. Wilson, *England's apprenticeship, 1603–1760* (1965).
'The entrepreneur in the industrial revolution in Britain', *Explorations in Entrepreneurial History*, vii (1955), pp. 129–45.

J. H. Wilson, 'Industrial activity in the eighteenth century', *Economica*, VII (1940), pp. 150–60.

R. G. Wilson, *Gentlemen merchants. The merchant community in Leeds 1700–1830* (Manchester, 1971).

'The supremacy of the Yorkshire cloth industry in the eighteenth century', in N. B. Harte and K. G. Ponting, eds., *Textile history and economic history* (Manchester, 1973), pp. 225–46.

W. H. D. Winder, 'The Courts of Requests', *Law Quarterly Review*, LII (1936), pp. 369–94.

S. G. Winter, 'Economic "natural selection" and the theory of the firm', *Yale Economic Essays*, IV (1964), pp. 225–72.

'Satisficing, selection, and the innovating remnant', *Quarterly Journal of Economics*, LXXXV (1971), pp. 237–61.

E. A. Wrigley, 'A simple model of London's importance in changing English society and economy 1650–1750', *Past and Present*, XXXVII (1967), pp. 44–70.

E. A. Wrigley and R. S. Schofield, *The population history of England 1541–1871* (1981).

B. S. Yamey, 'Accounting and the rise of capitalism: further notes on a theme by Sombart', *Journal of Accounting Research*, II (1964), pp. 117–36.

'Scientific bookkeeping and the rise of capitalism', *Economic History Review*, I (1949), pp. 99–113.

'Some reflections in the history of financial accounting in England 1500–1900', in W. T. Baxter and S. Davidson, eds., *Studies in accounting theory* (1962), pp. 14–43.

K. A. Yeoman, *Statistics for the social scientist: 1 Introducing statistics* (Harmondsworth, 1980).

INDEX

Printed in the United States
By Bookmasters